NOTHING HAPPENS FOR A REASON

BY JAMES HAWTHORNE

Prologue: Goodbye Blue Sky

I wanted to cry.

Why couldn't I cry? Crying had never been a problem for me. Well, I take that back… it had been a problem in the sense that when I was younger I often cried too easily.

But here I was at my mother's funeral and she was lying in a casket less than ten feet away and nobody in the world would think badly of me if my eyes filled with tears and I collapsed under the pain of losing her. I wasn't even quite fourteen yet.

My dad was crying. Her death was pounding the shit out of him like a shadow boxer that never quit, never gave him a day off. My sister Janet was crying, my half-brother Roger was crying, my grandma Anna was crying, my aunt Ruth and all the other siblings were crying.

I sat there wishing somebody would come up and slap me or yell at me. Help me get the tears flowing. Help my subconscious recognize there was a real body in that casket, not a remarkably lifelike mannequin.

The pain existed and had to go someplace. It didn't come out of me in the form of expressed grief so it crawled back inside of me and colored the way I looked at the world from then on.

Chapter 1: Ooh Child

I was born on the fifth of March in 1957. I was six pounds and change at birth. My parents lived in Sunnyrock, a small town in eastern Oregon.

I don't remember it, but my mom said I was dropped on my head a few months after I officially joined the human race. You know, started living outside her womb.

My father always looked embarrassed when the subject came up. Apparently he was the one who lost his grip.

When I hear a story like that I always wonder if the event had ramifications. Did the incident make me smarter? Dumber? More sympathetic?

Maybe God had created a potential genius with staggering potential. But Bob Hawthorne had fumbled the ball (or in this case, the child) before anybody had a chance to be staggered by me.

I have no real evidence it affected my mind in any permanent way. Maybe it just served as a warning that life was going to be full of bumps and bruises.

My earliest memory is from a day when I was about two years old. I had decided it would be fun to be a baby again.

I spent the day crawling and making baby noises instead of talking normally (or at least the two year old version of normal).

I suppose in some infantile way I represented the "slacker" mindset prevalent among so many males later around the turn of the century. All I was missing was the goatee and the ironic t-shirt.

I got tired of this routine after three or four hours. It was really hard on my knees. Crawling seems great when it's all you can do but quickly begins to suck if there are other modes of self-transport available.

Besides, there was a lot to do if a young fella was willing to act his age and walk upright. There were pots and pans that needed to be pulled out of the lower cupboards. Picture books that needed to be looked at. And the neighbor's cat needed to be picked up and carried wrong at least once a day.

We lived in town the first four years of my life. I got lots of attention from people in the neighborhood, especially the elderly ladies. Everybody called me Jimmy.

It was funny how that name stuck. Some of my older relatives were still calling me that when I was in my forties. It didn't seem to matter I had a beard and grey hair at my temples... on some level they still saw the same little kid who had ran noisily through their house back in 1963 with their own children.

I developed a fondness for television at an early age. It was very basic back then... a black and white screen showing the two channels that were broadcast out of Boise.

The first show I remember watching was "Riverboat". It starred a very young Burt Reynolds.

Not too long after that I discovered "Whirlybirds". It was about a couple of helicopter pilots who got involved in all kinds of adventures. I was also a big fan of "Sea Hunt". It starred Lloyd Bridges as a scuba diver.

It's strange, I feel like the Bridges family have always been in my life. I watched Lloyd on Sea Hunt, in the "Airplane" movies and on Seinfeld. I've seen his two sons Jeff and Beau in too many movies and television shows to even recall.

"Lassie" was my favorite show for a few years. There was just something so majestic about that dog. She was like the messiah of canines. Well, messiah might not be the right word since she was female but you know what I mean.

I often felt sorry for her... the humans she lived with seemed to have limited intelligence and a remarkable inability to predict the consequences of their actions.

They would make stupid mistakes or succumb to some rural temptation and the poor Collie would always have to save them.

“Lassie, Timmy thought it would be fun to play in the quicksand. Go get a rope and save him”.

“Lassie, Grandpa neglected to get his prescription refilled and now he’s had a heart attack. Run to the drugstore and get his pills but make sure you get the generic version because they’re just as good and they cost half as much and he wouldn’t know the difference anyway”.

Thank heavens the show took place before the rural Meth problem started. I shudder to think what that family would have put the dog through if they’d become dealers or tweakers.

Sometimes I got disgusted with that family… it just seemed like they put way too much pressure on that dog.

However, I never got disgusted with June Lockhart. She was my first crush and no woman ever looked better in an apron.

During one special two-part episode, Timmy and Lassie ended up in a hot-air balloon that got loose and headed for parts unknown.

I got pretty hysterical. It took Dad over an hour to calm me down and get me to understand it was just a story.

I kept saying, "Daddy, what do you mean, it's just a story? I can see them right there on the T.V. screen. They're not in a book." The funny thing is, it never occurred to me to wonder why these real people and this real dog were only a few inches tall and lived inside an appliance located in our living room.

It's probably a good thing. Otherwise I would have been checking the oven for little devils and the refrigerator for an Eskimo village.

It took years for me to come to terms with "The Wizard of Oz". I think it would be interesting if somebody polled Baby Boomers to see how many of us watched that film too early in our childhoods and ended up traumatized to some extent.

Like the Lassie hot-air balloon episode, it wasn't just scary. It was Freudian pain-of-separation scary.

It caused me to think if I got separated from my mom in a department store there was a good chance I'd end up having to deal with witches and flying monkeys and tornadoes and little guys who represented the Lollipop Guild.

CBS showed it once a year, usually on a Sunday. I found this very confusing... I thought for a long time that the movie had some religious significance. Like maybe there was a little-known Book of Dorothy hidden between Judges and Ruth and perhaps the Israelites used the yellow brick road at some point during their years of wandering. Who knows, maybe it was a good short cut between Canaan and Jericho.

Year after year I watched a bit more of it, gradually working up my courage. I could totally identify with the lion.

I got past the tornado sequence and then the Wicked Witch and then the trees that could talk and grab you. But those flying monkeys would always send me down the hallway. I might creep back and watch a few seconds here and there but those winged bastards totally scared the crap out me.

Even sitcoms could occasionally freak me out. I always loved "The Dick Van Dyke Show" but one particular episode really got under my skin. Dick had been watching a scary science-fiction show like "The Outer Limits" right before bed and then had a dream where an alien who looks like Danny Thomas lands on Earth and proceeds to use walnuts to destroy our civilization and turn everybody into space zombies. Even sweet, reliable Laura Petrie became a space zombie!

Eventually I started to enjoy being scared a little bit. One of my babysitters went to the movies quite often and I would beg her to tell me the plots of the scary films she'd seen. My favorite was "The Fly". The thought of a tiny human head on a fly's body blew my young mind.

It's interesting how you evolve over time. The terror I felt when I was really young and watched something scary gradually turned into curiosity. By the time I was an adult, I was seriously addicted to that delicious tingle I felt when I read a good Stephen King novel or watched a well-made fright flick.

Chapter 2: Fortunate Son

My father's name was Bob. He was a cattle rancher and he owned about five hundred head of cattle and two ranches when I was born.

I've never understood why ranchers use the term "head" of cattle. Why can't you just say five hundred cattle? It seems like the head should be an assumed part of the deal, much like the steering wheel on a car or the legs on a chicken.

One ranch was fifteen miles west of Sunnyrock and the other (where we moved when I was four) was three miles east of town.

Sunnyrock is located roughly fifteen miles west of the Oregon-Idaho border and sixty-five miles from Boise, Idaho. Many settlers passed through the area on their way to the green forests and fields of western Oregon.

Apparently, some of them decided they were sick of traveling and decided to give eastern Oregon a try. It's not a place that gets much rain but thanks to the wonders of irrigation, the farms are extremely productive. There are lots of bare hills and green fields.

Of course, when the pioneers first came it was just dry and brown and mostly sagebrush. They had to clear the land to make it productive.

There were some Indians living in the area before the White Man came but I've never really heard about any conflicts between them and the settlers. Either they were pacifists or they just didn't feel like that part of the country was worth fighting about.

It was strange when I moved to the western part of the state as a young adult and met people who had been to Europe but couldn't tell you a thing about what existed on the eastern side of Oregon.

When I tried to explain where my hometown was they would get this look in their eyes that told me I might as well be describing the longitude and latitude of Atlantis.

It can be irritating if people have never heard of the place where you grew up. It can be downright disheartening if you sense they think it doesn't even exist.

The day I was born our town was flooded by a quick Spring thaw. Dad didn't make it to the hospital right away because he was busy floating around in a rowboat picking up senior citizens and their pets.

Dad loved being a rancher. He loved walking through the pastures, checking on the cows and seeing how the new calves were doing. He never cared about making a lot of money… he was just happy having a job where you got to work outdoors and make your own decisions and cultivate the land.

It gets very hot in eastern Oregon in the Summer and very cold in the Winter. Sometimes if a calf is born in freezing weather, Dad would carry it down to the basement of our house so it could warm up and survive.

He was in the steer business. If a cow gave birth to a male it would be castrated at around a year old and then sold about a year after that.

Normally they were purchased by somebody who had a feedyard. They'd be fattened up and eventually sold for slaughter.

I never liked feedyards… they were usually just giant corrals where the steers stood around in the mud and their own waste waiting for the next bale of hay to be dropped into the trough.

We always had a couple bulls who bred our females. They were kind of funny… macho and not all that bright. Of course, really no cattle are all that bright.

Whenever they got too close to each other, they'd try to fight. I couldn't understand what they had to quarrel about. They had plenty to eat and way more girlfriends than they knew what to do with.

Sometimes Dad would take me to the weekly Sunnyrock livestock sale on Friday afternoon. I thought it was really exciting, especially the way the auctioneer talked.

When we would pull out of the driveway in the pickup truck he would always say "and we're off like a couple of wild dogs". It always made me smile.

There were always lots of interesting characters at the auctions. Wealthy ranchers, people who worked there, old guys who came to town when they had a cow or horse or a few pigs to sell. Maybe that's the only time they ever had any cash.

I couldn't believe how many people my dad knew. It was like he was the mayor or something.

He would usually say hello to them and make a joke about how hard times were.

"Hey, Fred. How's it going? Just thought I'd bring my boy down here and show him why we're so poor. This is pathetic, they're practically giving these cattle away".

Nobody appreciates the humor of financial despair more than people involved in agriculture. It's like the Catskills with cowboy boots.

He was always really good about making sure I felt included. He would introduce me to different folks and say "my fondest wish is that when this boy grows up he becomes anything except a farmer or a rancher."

I never really believed him because he usually started laughing after making this grand pronouncement. But I also felt like he would support me no matter what I chose to do with my life.

I always sat on my hands during the auction. I was scared to death a fast-talking auctioneer would misconstrue one of movements as a bid. The last thing I wanted was a quick nose pick resulting in my father having to pay for a small group of Holsteins.

Before the sale, we'd usually go to a place called Emma's Cafe. There were always lots of people in there who said hello to Dad. I usually ordered the open face turkey sandwich or a cheeseburger and fries. The waitresses were always very nice to us.

I loved riding in the pickup with Dad. He'd tell me about ranching and farming and how Sunnyrock had some of the best land anywhere in the West.

He'd also tell me stories about what life was like when he was growing up in the area. He and his brother Mitch rode horses to their little country grade school.

Very often he would veer off into political territory and advise me on how the world worked. "You see, son, the Democrats always want to raise your taxes and put all the honest folk out of business. Their main job is spending our money".

They sounded like a pretty scary bunch... maybe not flying monkeys scary but still a bad crew.

Dad was also a World War Two vet. He didn't seem to have any psychological scars from the experience. He said, "Hell, I don't mind talking about it. It was a big part of my life. And some of it was actually kind of fun".

He often told me he joined the service simply because he got tired of being hungry. He enlisted prior to Pearl Harbor.

Like so many young guys, he'd bounced around here and there trying to find work during the Depression. His father had basically ran he and Mitch off the farm when they graduated from high school, telling them they needed to go out in the world and make their own way.

He had originally trained with the ski troops but then got transferred to a unit that used mules in areas that trucks couldn't make it through. He'd spent a lot of time working with mule teams back on the farm and the military was happy to take advantage of his experience.

He'd had a bit of college and the other guys started regarding him as a leader. Eventually he went to Officer Candidate School and became a captain in the Artillery. He would help direct strikes in a lot of campaigns, including the Battle of the Bulge.

He told me about celebrating freedom with the French people and the terrible sadness he and his men felt when they liberated a concentration camp full of starving prisoners.

He even had a sword given to him by a surrendering German officer. I thought it was the coolest thing in the world.

I really put my dad on a pedestal. He was a football player, a cowboy and an officer in the military. A true man of action.

My mother was named Faye. She was a housewife when I was little but she worked in a doctor's office before she married Bob.

She was an attractive woman. There was a picture taken of her when she was in her early twenties and she looked a lot like Grace Kelly. And people seemed to like her a lot.

Dad was also good looking. He was kind of short but strong looking and always in good shape. He had very dark brown hair and a pugnacious chin.

This was the second marriage for both of them. I didn't quite understand the concept of divorce but I was glad they'd gotten together and made me… or asked the stork to deliver me. I was a bit unclear on the concept of where babies came from.

Dad's previous marriage more or less "bookended" the war. He and his first wife met when he was training in southern California, had a brief courtship and got married before he shipped out to fight in Europe. They lived together in Sunnyrock a few years after he got back but things just didn't work out. I didn't learn about this marriage until I was in my 40's.

Mom's first husband was known as Rick the Italian. He wasn't actually an Italian guy but he was part American Indian. Lazy racism often produced inaccurate nicknames where I grew up.

I didn't find out he wasn't really Italian until I was an adult. When my folks talked about him I always pictured this bad guy with a machine gun and a plate of spaghetti.

Rick didn't treat my mom very well. I heard he spent a lot of time hanging out in the bars and gambling away what little money they had.

Faye and Rick the Italian had a son named Roger. He was seventeen years older than me. When I was little he would come stay with us a couple times a year.

He was a really good football player in high school and had a way with the girls. He had jet black hair and wore it greased back like Elvis.

He left town at the end of his senior year. He had gotten involved with a slightly older woman named Cookie. She was a dance instructor. I never did hear how she ended up with that nickname.

Cookie got pregnant so they ran off to southern California to get married. Roger knew some people down there and they figured they'd both find jobs easily and have a great life together.

When I was three, Roger came and stayed two weeks with us. Apparently, things hadn't worked out between he and his dance instructor.

I slept on the couch when Roger came to stay. He always went out with his old buddies at night and then slept in really late. When I would sneak into my bedroom to get some clothes to wear it always smelled like body odor, stale beer and the stench of a million cigarettes.

My mom and dad were very social. She belonged to Eastern Star (a feminine offshoot of the Masonic Lodge), a card playing club and the Sunnyrock Christian church.

Dad was a Mason, an Elk and a member of the county sheriff's posse. They rode horses and occasionally searched for lost people. I suppose they would have looked for bad guys too but I just don't remember that situation ever coming up.

He was also a Shriner later on. He had a fez but I don't know if he ever got to ride one of those tiny motorcycles.

One summer Dad built a barbecue out of cement blocks and they decided to have a big party. It was during the Hawaiian craze and all the men wore flowered shirts. The women all wore the big, colorful dresses known as Muu-Muus.

I thought it was funny that the ladies wore clothing named after what a cow says.

Chapter 3: Who Made Who

I never knew either of my grandfathers.

My mother's father was named George Hansen. I was told he was a quiet, good-natured fellow. He had a little farm over in southwestern Idaho.

My dad's father was a tough old rancher named Jeb. He apparently had little time or patience for his children and was known to cheat on his wife every now and again.

On the plus side, he was a very shrewd businessman and over the years came to own tens of thousands of acres of land in eastern Oregon.

Some of it was fertile but most of it was range land you might run cattle on during the warmer months of the year.

Jeb got cancer in the late 1940's. He blew his brains out.

I've heard he was just a "no nonsense" kind of guy. I think his attitude was if you can't work you have no business taking up space on the planet. At least not above ground.

I've always thought he and Ernest Hemingway would have gotten along well. At least once they stopped arguing about that whole Spanish Civil War issue.

I don't think Jeb would have cared much for me. Of course, I'm just basing that on the way he treated my dad and the fact I ended up pretty darn liberal.

I'm sure he would've considered my life to be full of nonsense. Actually, if he came here directly from 1947 he would've considered the whole world to be full of nonsense.

On the other hand, it's probably not fair to conjecture about whether or not he would have liked me. He was a product of different times.

There's a reason almost nobody is smiling in those old photographs… their lives were really hard. They weren't spending a lot of time thinking about fairness and rights and the environment. They were too busy trying to keep enough food on the table.

Sometimes I wonder what happens after to us after we die. Do our souls rise up out of our lifeless corpses and head off to some other spiritual plane? Could it be a place where we're rewarded for all the suffering we put up with while we were on Earth?

Maybe when they're not playing golf or having sex with that soldier they met at the USO club in 1932, our ancestors really enjoy watching us stumble through our daily lives. Maybe we're their favorite reality t.v. show.

I can just see some of my dead relatives sitting on the couch with a big bowl of popcorn, pointing at the "viewing" screen. Maybe we're their entertainment.

My uncle Kent pointing at the screen and slapping his knee, trying to convince the gang to once again watch a particularly bad date I went on in 1984. He thinks it's hilarious.

Or maybe my cousin Lloyd Jr. tearing up when he watches me having to put my dog Hank down in 2009. It makes him cry but it also reminds him how much he loved his own dogs.

They appreciate being able to do this because I lost touch with most of them during my adult years.

Sometimes when I'm paying for an overpriced, fussy meal in a downtown Seattle restaurant I swear I can actually sense old Jeb slapping his forehead and calling me a goddamn idiot.

My grandmothers couldn't have been more different.

My mother's mother was born in Sweden and her family immigrated to America in the waning days of the 19th century. Eventually they would come out west with a wagon train.

Her name was Anna Hansen. She outlived two husbands and gave birth to eight children (and also had a few miscarriages). She was kind of short and stubby and had a little bit of a lady mustache.

When I was a kid, Anna lived in a little rental house in Weston, Idaho. It's a town located about thirty miles from Sunnyrock. It's just another little farming town but they do put on a pretty decent country music festival every June.

She took in laundry and received financial help from her kids. That's one thing about having a lot of kids, once they're out of the house you have a ready-made network of folks you can guilt money out of when necessary. I've always thought of big families as Mother Nature's Ponzi Scheme.

She wasn't big on progress or modern technology. One time I was trying to talk to her about NASA. She shook her head and said, "I don't like those astronaut guys. What are they trying to do, find Heaven?".

Anna always had a pot of coffee going. Probably because she always had company over... either one of her kids and their family or a neighbor or somebody from her church.

She was a good person but not a terribly upbeat one. I think the struggles of her life ground her down some over the years. Or maybe it had something to do with being Swedish. Maybe those long, dark winters have somehow become part of their national DNA.

My other grandmother was named Leslie. She lived across the river from us in a white stucco house with a redrock chimney on the side.

She had a fat little dog named Cindy. Cindy was sweet but had hair that was so coarse you really didn't enjoy petting her. I always thought of her as a friendly porcupine.

Leslie was tall (at least by the standards of the day) and thin. She had a nice wardrobe and always kept her house up.

Leslie had grown up on the east coast and always seemed a bit more sophisticated than most of the adults I grew up around. She seemed like an odd match for someone like Jeb. Maybe he liked her intelligence and grace.

Unfortunately, whatever it was didn't seem strong enough to prevent him from chasing other women. Dad said Leslie and Jeb had stopped living together a few years before he died.

I felt kind of bad neither of my grandmas had a man in their lives. I guess back then a lot of women felt like it looked bad if they took up with a new guy after a certain age. Or maybe they just didn't feel like taking care of men anymore.

Leslie's biggest claim to fame was serving as a delegate at the 1956 Republican National Convention. I think she and my dad enjoyed talking politics, though she seemed a bit more tolerant of liberals. I don't remember her ever ranting about how the Democrats wanted to put us all in the poorhouse.

There were three things I liked best about going to her house... having orange sherbet, using her TV remote control and looking through her old issues of TV Guide.

Leslie had bought a TV with a remote control because she had a big living room and she hated having to get up to change the channel. Of course, it was kind of funny since there were only two channels.

I liked the TV Guides because they gave capsule descriptions of movies and TV shows, many of which I had never seen or heard of before. It had not only listings for our two Boise channels but also ones for two or three channels we didn't get. I wasn't sure why... maybe they were stations located in cities too far east for us to pick up on our antenna.

I especially loved reading about "The Twilight Zone" and "The Outer Limits". I didn't always understand what the words meant but I figured it must be creepy, exciting stuff. Maybe even creepier than the movies my babysitter went to see. Every week a new ghost or monster or space alien on the television screen, what could be better?

The Fall Preview issue was like a holy book to me. So many new shows, so many possibilities. I probably should have put a big chart up in my room so I could keep track of what was on when.

Chapter 4: He Ain't Heavy...He's My Brother

My uncle Mitch and his wife Evelyn lived about a mile east of Leslie's. He was my dad's younger brother.

Mitch and Bob got along okay but there always seemed to be tension between my dad and Evelyn.

She was from one of the area's wealthier families and always acted a bit aristocratic. Kind of like a character from a 1930's screwball comedy who boards the wrong train and ends up in Buffalo Junction instead of Beverly Hills.

Of course, in those movies the character usually goes through some funny embarrassing situations and ultimately gains some humility and perspective. Evelyn never seemed to go through that process.

They had sheep and chickens and usually at least a couple horses. I think the fact Mitch liked sheep more than cattle always bugged Dad a bit. It's a macho thing that goes back to the range wars of the Old West.

They sold the wool from the sheep, eggs from the chickens and occasionally rented their stallion out for stud services. They also had a roadside stand where they sold vegetables in July and August. They never really seemed to have a business plan, more just a random list of activities that might or might not make money and they were never sure how much.

Evelyn once told me, "Your father worries too much about making money. Sometimes I think he should just slow down and appreciate the lifestyle more. We have these wonderful animals and all this space and you don't hear your uncle Mitch worrying every minute if all the bills are paid on time. It's certainly not a matter of life and death."

I did not appreciate her bad mouthing my dad to me. But I was too young at that point to really stand up to her.

And actually, I always felt like Dad was just trying to make enough to keep his head above water financially and provide a reasonably comfortable life for his family.

I think if they could have afforded it they would have staged a yearly fox hunt, complete with guys in red coats and a hundred baying hounds. Just so she could stand there and proclaim how marvelous it all was.

Of course, they were willing to throw philosophical differences out the window whenever they got into trouble financially and had to ask Dad for a loan. I always wondered why they came to him instead of her family. Maybe she was in the doghouse for marrying Mitch.

Evelyn always scared me a bit when I was little. I think she was probably quite attractive when she was young but didn't really know how to age gracefully.

She wore her hair that extreme black color you see on Goth kids sometimes. She always wore lots of perfume and bright red lipstick, even when she was just doing the chores.

And as the years passed, she refused to get bigger stretch pants. I often wondered what would happen if the waistband suddenly snapped.

Mitch was a big man... actually I'm probably more like him physically than my father. He smoked cigars every day until he started having heart problems later in life. He was always nice to me.

He liked being different, even if it meant being physically uncomfortable. He would always wear the same heavy, black long sleeve shirt when he was out working, even if the temperature was up over a hundred degrees. Sometimes I worried he might end up with a heatstroke.

His farm equipment was always wore out and badly in need of repair. Once when I was 16 I was driving a large grain-filled truck for him and the brakes went out. I was barely able to get it off the road before getting involved in a nasty accident.

He just laughed it off. He said, "Oh, stuff like that happened to me all the time when I was a kid. It's good, it develops your reflexes."

They were considered a bit odd by the local folks. Instead of attending a local church, they listened to something on the radio called the Worldwide Church of God. It was a ministry founded by a preacher named Herbert W. Armstrong. Their Sabbath was on Saturday and they refused to even talk about business on that day of the week.

This was something else that infuriated Dad.

The strict rules of the denomination kept them from socializing much with anybody. The man on the radio told them people outside their religion (even other Christians) were more often than not bad influences and backsliders.

I always felt like this was a big reason why Evelyn liked the WWCOG... it provided her with a spiritual rationale for looking down on other people.

They had three daughters named Karen, Michelle and Carlene. I always felt sorry for them because they weren't allowed to date or be involved in any extracurricular school activities.

They weren't allowed to watch TV (they didn't have one) or go to the movies. As far as I could tell, all they were allowed to do was study, do farm chores and play together. It was almost like they were living on the other side of the Iron Curtain. Or in this case, the Alfalfa Curtain.

It seemed like a miserable childhood to me but I guess it all worked out pretty well. Karen became a successful real estate agent, Michelle ended up being a district attorney and Carlene pursued a career in broadcasting but married a diplomat.

Maybe not being allowed to watch Green Acres or go to school dances didn't damage them so much after all.

Evelyn passed away in the early 80's. Mitch grieved for a while but then started going to the Friday night dances at the Sunnyrock Senior Center. It turned out he was a very social fellow, given the chance. Soon he was dating different ladies and just having a great time. It was like he got his second wind after his wife died.

Dad also had a half-brother named Charlie. Charlie was about ten years older than my father and was married to a woman named Grace. He was also a farmer.

They were really nice to me. Grace knew I liked comic books and would always buy me a bunch for my birthday.

They smoked a lot. Their little house always smelled like an ashtray. The thing that really got me was when we would all get in the car and go for a drive somewhere in the wintertime.

Charlie would smoke with the windows rolled up. I remember sitting in the backseat, seriously struggling for breath. I was surprised it didn't seem to bother my parents more.

Back then, kids weren't allowed to complain. Especially about something adults other than their parents were doing. Better to be unconscious than impolite.

My mother had a brother named Kent and a sister named Ruth. She also had younger half-sister named Ellen and younger half-brothers named Luke, Mike, George and Richard.

Kent and his family lived up in northeastern Oregon, Ruth was up by Portland and everybody else was in southwestern Idaho.

I really liked Luke's wife, Nora. She was a bit younger than most of the adults in the family and had a great way with all the kids.

Chapter 5: Jesus Children of America

Church was my first real opportunity for social interaction outside the family.

Mom and I always went to Sunday school and sometimes stayed for regular church service. The regular church service was always really boring but I did like the little glass of grape juice we got to drink during communion.

Dad was a lapsed Episcopalian but he would join us at the Sunnyrock Christian church on Easter and Christmas.

I was always a little confused why the place we worshipped at was called the Christian church. Weren't Catholics and Lutherans and Methodists and all the rest of the denominations also followers of Christ?

I'm surprised my church got away with it. It was kind of like the NFL allowing a football team to call themselves the Green Bay Football Players.

I liked Sunday school. I met a bunch of kids around my same age, several of whom I hung out with clear through our high school years. Ronnie Felson and I have kept in touch (on and off) our entire lives.

I have a picture taken of the Sunday school kids when we were around four or five years old. We're cute but it seems like we all had heads that were a bit too big for our bodies. Eventually I would have both a big head and a big body.

We usually did some arts and crafts. There seemed to be a lot of emphasis on constructing cabins out of popsicle sticks. I wondered sometimes if Jesus lived in a log cabin at some point, maybe with Abe Lincoln. Or maybe Jesus just came over and watched "The Wizard of Oz" with Abe.

We also sang. We would basically go through the same list of songs every week. Stuff like "This Little Light of Mine", "Down In My Heart" and "Jesus Loves the Little Children". Well, the girls sang and a lot of the boys just yelled out the words.

My favorite was one where you made motions while singing, "I may never march in the infantry, ride in the calvary, shoot the artillery. I may never fly o'er the enemy, but I'm in the Lord's army".

I wasn't sure exactly what the Lord's army was but I was confident we could whip pretty much any other army that gave us trouble.

I was a bit confused why we needed both the U.S. army and the Lord's army but I figured you can just never have enough firepower. I noticed they didn't say anything in the song about stuff you do in the water… maybe the Lord had a big old submarine like the one on Voyage to the Bottom of the Sea.

It's funny, years later when I saw the Village People perform on some TV show I flashed back on this song and our little military dance routine.

Often we would go to each other's houses after church and spend the afternoon playing. I had one friend named Trent who was extremely bright but a bit on the hyper side.

Today he would be on Ritalin or something similar. We were always starting projects but he could never stay focused long enough to finish anything.

His folks really liked me… when we got older his mom and I would actually talk about Trent's problems sometimes.

When he came out to our house my dad would eat lunch and then climb on the tractor and head out to get a little extra work done. He knew there was no hope of relaxation with Trent around.

Chapter 6: My Old School

I've only been to one high school class reunion so far. It was a strange experience.

It was in the summer of 1995. There was an informal get-together on Friday night but we couldn't get to Sunnyrock in time to attend. On Saturday afternoon everybody gathered at the city park.

Most of the women were recognizable. A few had put on weight. Sheila Young actually looked thinner than she had when we graduated... she'd been busy living the Mormon lifestyle in Utah pumping out six kids.

I couldn't believe how she'd aged. Her skin looked like flesh-colored jerky.

Robin Sykes was annoyed because everybody kept telling her how much she looked like Ellen DeGeneres. Robin was married, had two kids and didn't register on my gaydar even a little bit. But she did look a bit like Ellen.

Byron Helms was there with his wife. She was somewhat older than him but she was a woman. I was surprised, I always thought he'd move away and come out of the closet. I guess he was just packing a lot of estrogen.

The women were a bit frustrated because so many of the guys in our class had grown beards to downplay the chubbiness of their nearly middle-aged faces. It was hard to tell who was who.

Several people commented that they were surprised I didn't become a cartoonist. I really liked to draw when I was younger. A few people asked where my adopted sister was and I just had to lie and tell them she wasn't feeling well. Well, I guess that wasn't really a lie.

As I sat there sipping on a beer I thought about what a shock the first days of first grade had been.

My town didn't have a public kindergarten and almost nobody where I lived went to daycare back then. So this was the first time most of us were spending substantial time away from our families.

Children seemed to be doing just fine and suddenly their faces would scrunch up and they'd break down sobbing. It was like their courage would only hold up so long and then they'd remember where they were and lose it.

I'd be talking to some little girl and she'd be happily telling me, "We have a dog at home named Susie and she just had puppies… oh my God, where's my mommy, does anybody know where my mommy is?".

Of course, some kids needed to express their angst through vomiting. The janitor would have to come in and mop up the puke and then spread this powder around that smelled like Pepto-Bismol.

I always thought (on a subliminal level) my specific first-grade class might have been a little extra freaked out due to the fact our teacher was named Mrs. Graves. She was actually pretty nice and not really scary in any way but it was kind of a spooky name and she did have a limp.

Actually, I'm not sure why her limp would scary anybody. Unless maybe she got it because of something that happened to her when she was busy robbing graves!

Surprisingly, being at school really didn't bother me. Being an only child who lived out in the country was boring sometimes. I was glad to have all these new playmates, even if three-quarters of them seemed to be sporadically having nervous breakdowns.

I became friends with a boy named Stan Larsen. We both liked Marvel western comic books. When we played together at recess I would pretend to be the Two-Gun Kid and he would be Kid Colt Outlaw. He was blonde like Kid Colt and I wanted to wear a mask like Two-Gun.

Marvel also had a character named the Rawhide Kid. I always wondered if the company had a policy that stated all their western heroes must have the word "kid" included somewhere in their names.

Maybe it was a way to connect with their young target audience…a character named the Two-Gun Kid would certainly be more appealing to a six-year old boy than one named Roger the Middle-Aged Desperado.

Stan had charisma even in the first grade. He just naturally took charge of situations without ever really seeming pushy. It was weird, it seemed like whenever he showed up other kids would automatically follow his lead.

That's the way it was for Stan clear up to the time we graduated from high school. But over the years I started to get the feeling this power of his was almost like a curse from an old Brothers Grimm tale… maybe he could only be amazing if he stayed in Sunnyrock.

Chapter 7: Heroes and Villains

I eventually switched from cowboy comics to ones featuring superheroes.

I never really liked Archie or Richie Rich or any of the other “funny” comic books. I liked funny comics in the newspaper but they didn’t cost me anything. If I was going to shell out twelve cents for a comic book it better be full of muscular guys who wore masks and punched each other.

I still stuck with Marvel comics. I especially loved anything drawn by Jack Kirby (which back in the early to mid Sixties seemed like two thirds of the Marvel titles).

My favorite comic book was the Avengers. Not the mod British spy duo but a superhero team that seemed to have pretty flexible membership guidelines.

The line-up changed a lot through the years but my favorite was always Captain America, Thor, Iron Man, Giant Man and the Wasp.

Captain America was originally in stories printed in the 1940's. He was a normal soldier who was given drugs that enhanced his speed, strength and intellect so he could fight the Nazis. In other words, a super-patriot on steroids.

His popularity waned after the war and the company stopped publishing his stories. Later when they decided to bring him back for the Avengers, the writers explained he'd been in some kind of suspended animation for over a decade.

Thor was the Norse god of thunder. I thought this was an interesting concept... here was a god (unlike the one I worshipped every Sunday and talked to before I went to bed) who walked around in human form and even had a secret identity.

He was also a bit of a trailblazer hair-wise... he had long blonde locks years before it was accepted by the mainstream culture.

One of his main enemies was his scheming adopted brother Loki. This part of the story puzzled me. If gods are immortal, why would one need to be adopted? Was he so obnoxious his god mom and dad left him in a basket on Odin's doorstep?

Thor's alter-ego was a partially disabled doctor named Donald Blake. Thor's weapon even had a secret identity. When he changed from the doctor into the god of thunder, his cane would change into a large mystic hammer and his hair would grow down to his shoulders

The guys at Marvel even mixed mythologies. They had Thor tangle with Hercules on more than occasion.

Iron Man was a wealthy industrialist who built a special metallic suit that allowed him to fly and shoot different kinds of rays from his hands. In the original story, he built the suit when he was being held captive in North Vietnam. The 2008 movie starring Robert Downey Jr. updated the plot and had the hero taken prisoner in Afghanistan.

Giant Man was a scientist who created a formula that made him gigantic and the Wasp was his wife. She swallowed something that made her shrink down to size of a wasp. He crushed evildoers and she stung them.

They never had children. Apparently the whole size thing was just too much of an obstacle.

Captain America wasn’t one of the five original members. He replaced the Hulk.

Apparently the writers realized after the first few issues that including the Hulk probably didn’t make a lot of sense. The other members would never know when he was going to be the insanely angry green-skinned giant or his reasonable scientist alter-ego, Bruce Banner.

I can see Iron Man telling Captain America, “Hey, we just got a call from the police chief.

Some super-villains are trying to destroy City Hall. It's your turn to piss off Bruce Banner so he'll turn into the Hulk."

Plus, when you stop to think about it, the Hulk would probably be pretty hard on your furniture and crime-fighting equipment. And God help the superhero who drew the short straw and had to remind the Hulk he was behind on paying his membership dues.

"Hulk sure he paid dues in May. You need to go back and check books! Me sick of always having to dig up my old receipts!!". Then he'd storm off and try to wreck the headquarters.

The Silver Surfer was my favorite non-Avenger superhero. He wasn't introduced until 1966. Marvel wanted to bring in a more emotionally complicated type of character, a hero who reflected the angst being felt in the country at that time. And they also wanted to do stories about a superhero who surfed.

He soared around the universe and brooded about the big existential issues when he wasn't having intergalactic adventures. He just always looked so free… no spacesuit, no spaceship, just a shining metallic body and a cosmic surfboard. This was another character Jack Kirby drew.

Marvel superhero comics had an epic quality. Kirby would often create battle scenes that would take up one or two entire pages. Their main competitor (DC comics) had stories that featured villains who might rob a bank or maybe blow up a skyscraper if they were feeling really evil.

Marvel had bad guys who gave magnificent over-the-top speeches and tried to wipe humanity off the face of the planet.

Of course, there were DC titles I read occasionally. Their underwater guys were pretty cool. When I was at the public swimming pool I would pretend to be Aquaman or one of the Sea Devils.

Marvel also had an underwater character named Sub-Mariner. He didn't appeal to me as much as Aquaman… he had a bad attitude about humans and pointy ears. I always thought he looked like Mr. Spock in a bathing suit.

Aquaman was the king of an oceanic kingdom and the Sea Devils were a team of expert scuba divers. While other kids were trying to dunk each other, I would be down swimming along the bottom of the pool, pretending I was in the middle of some great underwater adventure.

It's funny, when I was a kid I thought it would be awesome to live in a city located underneath the ocean. Of course, this was when I lived in a place that had at least some sun over 300 days a year.

Later, when I moved to the west coast I would often grumble about how cloudy the sky was from mid-October to April.

Of course, Superman was DC's superstar. But he always bugged me. I felt like he was a cheater… nobody should get to have that many superpowers.

They might as well have put a red cape on God and had him rescue Lois Lane. And the whole Kryptonite deal seemed silly… you're telling me there's only one thing that can hurt this guy and it's not even produced locally?

DC also had some good war comics. Sergeant Rock was terrific and they also had these great stories about soldiers who ended up on remote Pacific islands and fought dinosaurs.

My cousin Jeff would give me his old comic books when he was done with them. He was a couple years older than me. His younger brother Darrin was my same age. They lived in the same town as my grandma Anna.

Their mom was my mother's younger half-sister Ellen. Their house always smelled like cigarette butts and Ellen always seemed to be feeling under the weather. She seemed older than her age. Their dad was named Leonard. He was a big guy who played football in college.

I didn't like hanging out with Darrin. He used to pull tricks on me or talk me into doing stuff that would end up getting us both in trouble. I hated getting in trouble but for him it was just the price you paid to have a good time.

I was a naïve only child who lived out in the country. In other words, I didn't stand a chance when he wanted to manipulate me into doing stuff. I was a gullible Thor and he was my Loki.

I was always hearing stories about him from other relatives. When he was eight he took his parents' station wagon for a joyride around town. I'm not sure how he reached the gas and brake pedals. Maybe he had an eight-year old accomplice down on the floor taking care of that part.

When he was nine he faked drowning at the city pool and got banned from swimming there all summer.

I have to admit, I was a bit of a baby when it came to Darrin. A couple of times I talked him into wrestling with me and when I didn't win I ran to his mom and claimed he and his friends had tried to beat me up.

Of course, it was easy to frame him… by this time his family rap sheet was so long his mom would have believed me if I told her he was downtown robbing the supermarket.

We played against each other in sports from time to time but he was much more of a star than me. He was Weston's starting quarterback in junior high and high school and their starting point guard in basketball. I guess at a certain point he managed to harness that reckless energy and put it to good use athletically.

Ironically, I was in Weston in 1998 and it just so happened it was the day of his daughter's wedding. She was getting married because she was pregnant. I couldn't help feeling like this was a nice moment of karmic justice.

I stopped by the reception and Darrin was really friendly and glad to see me but his brother Jeff sort of gave me the cold shoulder. Funny how these things turn out.

I've never really bought into the idea of reincarnation or the "past lives" theory. But I have to say, it's certainly an odd coincidence I've ended up having issues with three different guys named Darrin during the course of my earthly existence.

Chapter 8: Paper in Fire

By the time I was in the first grade, we'd moved out to the country. Our place was about three miles east of town.

My dad built a new barn. I was really excited because I figured that's where the men of the family (Dad and I) were going to be living. It wasn't like I was trying to get away from my mother… I guess I was just going through a phase where I identified more with my male parent.

Or maybe (as was so often the case), I was just confused.

To compensate for my disappointment, my parents decided I should have a bigger bedroom. Of course this would require I sleep down in the basement of our house.

At first I was truly excited. However, during the first night I spent in my new room I had a panic attack. I lay on my bed, looking up at the ceiling and thinking, “Come on, Dracula… if you’re going to bite my neck and turn me into one of the undead let’s just get it over with”.

I was always trying to impress my dad. Showing him how far I could jump or how fast I could run or maybe even how good I could cuss.

One day there was a horserace on the television and I bellowed out, “Wow, look at those sonofabitches go!”. I wasn’t even sure what the term meant but I’d heard Dad use it one day when we were branding cattle. My folks looked at me with amused horror on their faces and then explained that it probably wasn’t something I should go around saying.

My parents were very patient with me. One summer Dad was going to a place over in Idaho called Sand Hollow. He was going to help some friends round up cattle and he asked me to come along.

The past couple months had been brutally hot and everything was extremely dry. There had been a lot of concern that if there were lightning strikes in the area they might set off massive range fires.

When we got there I discovered there was a separate bunkhouse. I thought that was so cool. I hung out there while Dad visited with his buddies in the main house.

I looked at some old paperback books but after a while I got bored. Then I happened to see a box of wooden matches sitting on a table. I had never lit a wooden match before... when I struck it against the side of the box I was amazed how much more satisfying it was than the flame produced by those wimpy paper matches we kept in the junk drawer at home.

It was kind of addictive. I lit one and then another and then another and then another. And then I accidentally dropped one into a garbage can full of paper. The paper burst into flames.

I ran around trying to find some water but there was no sink or toilet in the bunk house. I finally got scared and ran into the main house where I saw Dad sitting in the living room.

I tried to appear nonchalant. Dad looked at me and said, "How's it going, son? Did you find anything interesting in the bunk house?".

I replied, "Oh, not really. By the way, if there was a fire in a garbage can what would be the best way to put it out?".

He thought about it calmly for a second and then got a look of horror on his face. He jumped out of his chair and ran outside to get the hose so he could put the fire out. Fortunately, he was able to catch it in time before there was any damage.

He was shook up but didn't jump all over me about what had happened. He could tell I felt bad and probably figured this was just one of those learning experiences kids have to go through.

A couple times he saved me from angry cattle. Cows are pretty docile animals except when you get between a mother and her young calf.

Occasionally somebody would forget to close a gate and some of our cattle would wander into an area near the house where we kept the bales of hay. One day Dad asked me to go out and drive them back into the corral and then close the gate.

Things were going fine but then I got stuck between a mother and her calf. She really got pissed and started chasing me. She had horns and I didn't know if I could get to the house before she ran me down. I started yelling for help.

Dad came flying out of the house in his bare feet. He grabbed a pitchfork that happened to be lying by the hay bales and managed to put himself between me and the homicidal bovine before she could run me down.

He was yelling at her and waving the pitchfork and she finally turned around and ran through the gate with her calf. I'm sure he saved my life that night.

One of my best friends when I was young was our dog Ranger. He was what I would call a handsome mutt... he looked like a cross between a Coonhound and a Rotweiller. He was mostly black with tan markings on his face and feet. He had a sleek shiny coat and was always ready to run.

Ranger was a wonderful pal. He'd follow me all over the ranch. If I got hurt and started crying he would sit down next to me and howl until one of my parents came to see what was wrong.

I had to walk about half a mile through a field to catch the school bus every morning. Ranger would always go with me and then run home.

He was scared of loud noises like thunder and gunshots. Pheasant hunting season was a miserable time of year for him. Hundreds of hunters would descend on the Sunnyrock area for a few days every October and make our neighborhood sound like a war zone. Ranger was a basket case while that was going on.

We also had a black and white cat named Champ. He and Ranger curled up and slept together every night.

I've had quite a few dogs since becoming an adult. Not long after my wife and I got married, we decided it would be nice if we rescued one from a shelter.

I found a seemingly friendly, light-colored cocker spaniel at the Seattle city pound. The tag on his cage said his name was Jo Jo but we didn't feel like that really fit him. He had an air of quiet intelligence. We decided to call him Elliott.

Elliott was fine for a couple days and then started going after people when we least expected it. He also ran off a couple times. It was frustrating trying to catch an animal who's main goal in life was to bite friends, family and strangers who might end up suing you.

I ended up taking him back to the pound. I wanted to get him out of the house before he bit one of the kids in the neighborhood.

It was a bad experience but we still wanted to get a dog. We decided to go the puppy route instead. We bought a female beagle and named her Betty.

Betty had a very strong-willed personality. She was very affectionate but also manipulative. She would run to the far end of the yard and start baying. She'd only stop once you said "doggie bone" and then gave her one. It was daily extortion, plain and simple. But I really didn't mind because I admired her chutzpah.

I've always been sort of funny that way. I guess I tend to see our dogs as furry little humans. I go kind of easy on the training stuff because I don't want to break their spirits. I won't tolerate destructive or aggressive behavior but I'm pretty flexible about other idiosyncrasies they might have.

Betty was always working food scams. One time we were just about to start eating a pizza and she came running up the stairs, barking furiously like there was something seriously wrong in the basement. We followed her down there and then she ran back up the stairs, jumped up on the table and began gobbling down pizza.

Very often I would find half-finished tunnels where she'd been digging under the fence that separated our yard from our neighbor's. These were often very ambitious projects she would quietly work on when we weren't paying attention. I started to feel like the hapless Colonel Klink from "Hogan's Heroes".

Next came Hank, a lovable yellow lab who was part of our lives for thirteen years. Everybody loved him.

He was a great watch dog. He had a thunderous bark and when strangers walked up to the front door they always looked very apprehensive. But once we let them inside he was immediately their friend.

He liked kids and was enthralled with babies. One time a couple brought over their infant daughter and Hank started walking around on his hind legs so he could smell her better. We called him "Nanny Hank" for a while after that.

Chapter 9: Jungleland

I spent a lot of time watching old movies and short subjects when I was a kid. Tarzan, the Three Stooges and the Little Rascals were my favorites.

The local TV stations would show them after school and often on weekend afternoons. They didn't seem that old to me… but then again everything on our television set was in black, white and assorted shades of gray. A murder mystery from 1943 didn't look all that much different than the CBS evening news (and sometimes better).

Tarzan was kind of confusing because he was played by several different actors over the years. And his speaking ability seemed to vary, depending on which actor happened to be wearing the loincloth and what decade the film was set in.

The first actor to play Tarzan in a film was named Elmo Lincoln. I love that name… it sounds like he was raised by rabbits in the middle of a cornfield. It seems odd that the studio didn't ask him to take a different stage name when they cast him to play the king of the jungle.

My favorite was Johnny Weismuller. He starred in the movies during a big chunk of the 1930's and 1940's. I would say he is by far the Tarzan people remember best. Of course the number of people who even remember those films has been greatly reduced over the years.

He was the first one to do the famous yell in the movies. He really seemed (at least to me) like someone who could have been raised by apes.

His Tarzan had an innocent, childlike nature and was barely articulate. I knew a couple football players in college who could have been his understudy.

On the other of the spectrum, there was Ron Ely (Tarzan #15). He seemed more like a brilliant swimsuit model who got bored studying at Oxford and decided to take a sabbatical swinging through the trees of darkest Africa. He was a little too well-groomed for my tastes. He also played Doc Savage in a later movie.

Mike Henry was another weird choice. He was a former pro football player and used no accent of any kind in the movies. Here was a character who supposedly had been raised by apes and he sounded like a guy who manages a tire store in Muncie, Indiana.

Jane seemed like a really good sport. I know she loved Tarzan but it had to get old living in a tree and wearing clothes made out of giant leaves. She probably could have related to women of the Sixties and early Seventies who got talked into joining communes and ended up having to eat porridge made out of parsnips.

In one of the Weismuller films, Cheetah the chimp finds a white baby boy in the jungle (he had survived a plane crash). Cheetah delivers the baby to Tarzan and Jane. They name him Boy and raise him as their own.

When I was a kid I felt sorry for Boy. I thought he got stuck with a pretty silly name. But it didn't seem so bad as the years passed and I heard about celebrities cursing their offspring with monikers like Moon Unit and Pilot Inspektor. Tarzan and Jane might have been a bit lazy when it came to naming their kid but at least they didn't use him as a prop for expressing their "creativity".

It was all pretty racist when you stop and think about it. Here you have a massive continent inhabited by tens of millions of black people. Who did the studios make movies about? Three white people. All the black people got to do in the movies was carry stuff and occasionally throw a spear.

I was glad I didn't live in Africa. I thought it would be fun to have a chimp for a pal but it hardly seemed worth it when you considered all the man-eating plants, quicksand and angry witch doctors that family had to contend with.

There also seemed to be multiple sets of Little Rascals. My favorite was Spanky, the little mastermind who organized their various schemes and directed the shows they would put on to raise money for whatever Depression-era crisis had come up.

Robert Blake also appeared in some of the later episodes. He really had to be one of the cutest kid actors of all time. He later starred in "In Cold Blood", a couple different t.v. series and his own real-life Hollywood murder scandal.

I've always been surprised there weren't more accidental child deaths blamed on the Three Stooges. The "pretend" damage they inflicted on each other was amazing.

Their stuff wasn't exactly After School Special material. The only lesson I ever learned from watching them was make sure you poke the other guy in the eye before he can drop an anvil on your foot.

Chapter 10: The First Cut is the Deepest

My early childhood was happy for the most part. I laughed a lot and made friends pretty easy. But (like all kids) I occasionally stumbled into situations that roughed me up physically, emotionally or both.

I saw an ad in a magazine that said I should try to sell packets of seeds to our neighbors. I must have been trying to win a toy of some kind. I sent away for the seeds and when the order form arrived in the mail I jumped on my bike and headed down the road.

The only problem was that in my neighborhood the houses were approximately a half a mile apart. And it was a dirt road and that's never a particularly fun bike ride.

The lady at the first house I rode my bike to turned me down. The second house was really scary but nobody was home and I breathed a sigh of relief. The kids from that family always seemed to have warts all over their hands. Sometimes I wondered if they had a bathtub full of toads.

The last neighbor on the road was named Mrs. Culver. She also turned me down. She said she wished she could help me out but she was on a fixed income and couldn't afford to buy anything extra like that. I had no idea what a fixed income was and what it had to do with me. Was there such a thing as a broken income?

On the ride home I burst into tears. I had been so excited about the toy I could earn selling these seeds. It had all seemed so simple when I was reading the ad. I was sure if I was a town kid I could have sold lots of seeds. Town kids got all the breaks.

A couple months after that I was watching a show about the Alamo and decided I wanted to build a small fort. I was so excited about my project I didn't even bother put on socks or shoes before I went outside. It was the middle of summer so I wasn't worried about my feet getting cold.

I was walking around out behind the barn and it was almost dark out. All of a sudden I felt a sharp pain in my right foot. I had stepped down on a nail sticking up out of a board and it had gone deep into the bottom of my foot.

I pulled the board away from my foot. There was a bloody hole where the nail had gone in. I limped to the house, screaming for my mom. I was sure I was a goner.

A couple years later I was over at Uncle Luke and Aunt Nora's house playing with their kids. The sliding glass door had been open all day and we were chasing each other.

At some point (while I was inside the house) one of the adults decided to shut the sliding glass door but didn't let us kids know. I ran into the glass door at pretty much full speed and stunned myself. I felt like Wile E. Coyote after one of his failed Roadrunner catching attempts.

I've never broken a bone. I guess drinking all that milk when I was a kid paid off. I did suffer some gruesome sprained ankles in junior high and high school while playing sports. I think one bruise was purple, orange and kind of greenish.

I found out fairly early that sports is an arena where some kids first decide to try out their power-grabbing skills. I had no idea this was going to happen… I had always thought if you showed up and you were a boy, you would get to participate in whatever game was being played.

One day there was a baseball game being played at recess. It was weird, it looked like there was about twenty kids on each team. There were kids in the infield, kids in the outfield, kids further out in the outfield and even more kids standing around behind them.

A boy named Tony Chavez seemed to be in charge. He went to the Catholic church and it seemed like the guys who went to that church always felt like they had a God-given right to be in charge of anything to do with sports. I always thought of it as the Notre Dame complex.

I asked him if I could play. He said, “Sure, but you’ll have to be a utility backup guy in the outfield. And you don’t get to bat.”

I should have objected. I should have said that was stupid and there was no reason he should get to be in charge. But I turned that righteous anger inward and a voice in my head said there was something wrong with me and I didn’t deserve to get what I wanted.

And in Tony’s defense, I have to admit there were already a lot of kids in that outfield.

Chapter 11: Everyone's Gone to the Movies

I have this weird habit when I go to see a film in a theatre. When it's starting I always think "maybe this will be one of the best movies ever".

I have no idea when I started doing it or why I started doing it. Athletes do stuff like that before a big game to help them focus. Of course, a lot of them also throw up before the big game.

I guess it just shows what a big part of my life movies have been. I don't know anybody else who has a movie mantra. Or maybe they do but don't want to talk about it.

Art is a strange thing. Sometimes I'll hate an album or a film initially but then over time I'll start to understand what the artist was attempting to do and end up loving it. And other times, stuff just grows on you and you really have no idea why. But you're happy it's happened.

Books are a different animal... I'm not willing to keep re-reading a novel over and over. You don't have to win me over right out of the gate but a person only has so much goodwill.

The first time I saw "Pulp Fiction" I was outraged. I felt like this movie was was a sign our culture had left the tracks and was headed for a total collapse.

I'd had too much coffee that morning. That is not a good film to see when you're jacked up on caffeine. I've watched it in bits and pieces over the years since then and come to realize it's a work of genius in its own twisted way.

Another example was the first "Matrix" movie. I was really looking forward to seeing it but I almost got up and walked out halfway through because it just felt like a high-budget kung fu film. But I gave it another chance about a year later and realized how amazing many of the sequences were and how much the film had to say about the current state of humanity.

The only time I seriously considered asking for my money back was when I went to see "Ocean's Twelve" starring George Clooney and Brad Pitt. This may seem odd considering it's just a harmless little caper flick but I didn't feel like I was actually watching a film. I felt like I'd paid seven bucks to watch a bunch of celebrities stand around and mug for each other.

The movie theatre in Sunnyrock was called the Ideal. Looking back, I would hardly say it was ideal but it wasn't bad considering how small the town was.

It wasn't really big but they stayed pretty current. And best of all, when I was young they only charged kids under twelve a quarter to get in.

I saw my first movie there. I don't remember what the feature was but I do remember it was at night and I was with my mom.

One of the coming attractions was for a Godzilla film. I was only two or three at the time and the sight of that giant lizard stomping Japanese people and shooting flames totally freaked me out. I was practically climbing on top of my mother before she calmed me down.

When I got a bit older I started going to the Saturday matinees. My dad normally went to town to play cards in the afternoon and I would ride in with him.

He would give me a dollar. That was enough to pay for my ticket and a couple candy bars at the movie theatre and also a comic book or two at the drugstore.

The Saturday and Sunday matinees were always a bit of a free-for-all. Sometimes it felt like a daycare in the dark.

Kids were always running up and down the aisles and throwing food at each other. Occasionally it got so rowdy one of the theatre's owners would have to go up front and lay down the law. They never actually went through with their threat to shut down the show but I do recall a few especially bad kids being told to leave.

The owners were a nice older couple. They also owned a ranch. I don't think they made a lot of money off the theatre. I always got the sense they just kept it going out of a sense of civic pride.

Or maybe they just liked people and this was a good way to see a big chunk of the town's population on a regular basis. Kind of like having a party every Thursday through Sunday.

I thought the movies were magical. I got over my Godzilla-induced trauma and started to understand the big screen was like a doorway that allowed me access to an unlimited number of alternate worlds. I'd purchase my ticket and walk through the door and that first whiff of popping popcorn always put a smile on my face. I don't even particularly like popcorn but I love the smell.

Sometimes I went with friends and many times just by myself. It didn't really matter… when you live in a small town there's a good chance you'll know a lot of the kids in any given movie audience.

I started to check the little ad the theatre ran in the weekly Sunnyrock newspaper. Was it going to be cowboys vs. Indians this week or spacemen or a kid's movie or some icky adult drama? I was lucky… I pretty much got to go any Saturday afternoon I wanted.

It seemed like right around the time I started going to movies on a regular basis, subtle changes were starting to occur.

The Disney stuff was still pretty innocent but the movies being produced for adults were getting incrementally edgier all the time… a little more cleavage here, a few more double entendres there, horror movies that were a bit more horrifying.

The older stars were starting to seem a little stale. There were still lots of movies starring John Wayne and Lucille Ball and Bob Hope and all the other usual suspects of that generation but their fans weren't filling the theatre seats on a regular basis like they used to. They were home watching television.

Some stars had reached a point in their career where they knew they needed to alter their image a bit. Jerry Lewis was desperately trying to remain relevant but the results seemed increasingly painful.

"The Nutty Professor" seemed to be the turning point. Lewis was getting too old to play the innocent idiots of his earlier films and was now trying to figure out a way to be both a goofball and a greasy-haired hipster. Buddy Love was here to stay.

There also seemed to be a new screenwriting rule… if you couldn't come up with a fresh idea, just show a girl in a bikini. Or better yet, dozens of them.

It didn't matter if it was a movie about spies, surfers or Elvis swinging his hips at a clambake. You could count on seeing lots of girls with long straight hair and minimal flesh coverage. Whatever it took to keep those young males buying tickets.

I always felt sorry for Elvis. For the most part it seemed like he was just going through the motions in his films.

Here Elvis, put on this suit of armor. You're a swingin' knight who wins the jousting competition and then breaks into song at the big mead party. Hey Elvis, put on this astronaut outfit. You're a swingin' spaceman who defeats the aliens and then breaks into song at the first teen dance on Mars.

Even westerns were changing. It was getting harder to tell the good guys from the bad guys. Everybody was sweatier and dirtier and the shootouts were a lot bloodier.

I remember sitting through "For a Few Dollars More" and thinking I didn't feel like rooting for any of the characters. Instead of good versus evil it was just bad versus evil.

On the other hand, some of the stuff coming out was really powerful and almost prescient. "Fahrenheit 451" haunted me with it's depiction of a society where firemen burn books and the citizens are controlled with drugs and non-stop interactive television.

Ironically, the two films that bothered me most when I was a kid were ones I watched on t.v. The first was “Seconds” starring Rock Hudson. It was about a wealthy man who learns of a secret organization that can help you fake your own death and change your appearance through plastic surgery. He goes through with it but then tragically learns that his new life isn’t really any happier than his old one and the organization demands a very high price when their clients fail to make a go of their new life.

It’s extremely dark and disturbing, filmed in black and white and using cutting edge camera techniques that create an atmosphere of surreal horror.

Apparently I wasn’t the only person it bothered. Brian Wilson of the Beach Boys went to see it when it was initially released in the theatres. He was starting to deal with schizophrenia, taking lots of drugs and stressing about how to complete the “Smile” album. He arrived after the movie had started and the first piece of dialogue he heard was, "Come in, Mr. Wilson". Due to his state of mind at the time, he assumed the voice onscreen was talking to him.

He alternated between being horrified by the film and fantasizing about the film’s premise that you could somehow escape your own life. At one point he told someone he thought maybe rival producer Phil Spector had convinced Columbia Pictures to make the movie to “mess with his mind”. He wouldn’t see another film in a theater until 1982.

The second was “Suddenly Last Summer” starring Elizabeth Taylor, Montgomery Clift and Katherine Hepburn. I was too young to understand the veiled references about homosexuality but the moments of insanity and cannibalism were all too vivid.

Hollywood seemed to be having an especially hard time figuring out how to deal with the emerging counterculture. You got the feeling the studio executives didn’t know whether to just humor the kids with some banal piece of crap starring Sonny and Cher or let young directors take a shot at sincerely portraying their generation’s visions, hopes and fears.

Sometimes they just couldn’t keep up with how fast the culture was changing.

I remember seeing a film called “What’s So Bad About Feeling Good?”. It starred George Peppard and Mary Tyler Moore as depressed beatniks who (along with everybody else in Manhattan) are infected with a virus that makes them happy and generous.

The movie features a really bad musical sequence that shows what happens to the characters after they get the virus and regain their zest for living. It almost made me wish they’d go back to wearing their black turtlenecks and whining about how bad everything was.

The strange thing was, that film came out in 1968. The Hollywood studios and mainstream media were still trying to figure out why Maynard G. Krebs wore black and played the bongo drums.

Meanwhile, his younger brother had grown his hair down to his shoulders and started tripping on LSD.

Chapter 12: Girl From the North Country

When I was six my parents adopted a little girl six months older than me.

I had a very hard time grasping this concept… why would my parents need another kid?

I had actually met her a year earlier. She and her parents lived in Bellingham, Washington and had come down to visit my folks. Her mother and my mother were old friends. The little girl's name was Janet.

The couple had adopted her when she was still an infant.

We'd all gone to a rodeo. I remember somebody took a picture of Janet and I dressed in our little cowboy and cowgirl outfits. Everybody kept commenting on how cute we looked together.

Sometime in the past year, my mother's friend had died and the father didn't feel like he could do a good job of raising a little girl. My parents felt bad for him and said she could come live with us.

I was furious when my folks told me I was suddenly going to have a sister. It just seemed like such a strange concept.

I could probably accept a new baby brother or sister but this really threw me for a loop... I'd always thought life was perfect with our family just being the three of us (well, five if you counted Ranger and Champ).

I pouted for a couple days when she first arrived. But slowly we got to know each other a bit and I began to realize it might be fun having another kid around full-time. Luckily she was nice and seemed grateful my parents had taken her in.

I showed her around the place, introducing her to my horse and some of the more prominent cows (Dad had a few favorites we named).

Then we walked down to the river that divided our place from my grandma Leslie's. It was the Malheur river. It wasn't all that deep where it cut through our place. Actually, during the hottest part of the summer you could drive the tractor across it.

It did have quite a few fish in it, mostly just carp and catfish and sucker fish. They weren't very good to eat because they'd been living in dirty water for so long. But they were fun to catch because a lot of them were big and put up a good fight.

We were throwing rocks into the water and I said, "Hey, I know this is all kind of weird for you. But everything will be okay... this is a pretty fun place to live".

She smiled and said, "Thanks. I think it will be fine. I'd like to get a horse some day and maybe that's something I could do here."

I could tell she was scared to be changing families. But I also sensed she was excited to be living out in the country, like maybe it was something she'd always dreamed of doing.

And Dad did end up buying her an Appaloosa colt a couple years later.

It was so weird going to school with her that first day. All of a sudden I had a sister to introduce to everybody. But kids are really flexible at that age and nobody gave us a hard time.

I remember one of my friends saying, "Wow, you got a new sister just all of a sudden? I didn't know that was possible".

Of course, he was kind of gullible. If I had told him we grew Janet in our garden he probably would've believed me.

For the most part, Janet and I got along surprisingly well. I liked girls and never really felt a need to pick on her. She teased me sometimes and I would chase her and inevitably she would run into the bathroom and lock the door. We performed that ritual roughly eight thousand times.

The only time she made me really mad was when she would "girlify" one of my projects. For example, when I made a spaceship out of two lawn chairs and some old blankets and she brought out an old coffeepot and some plates and said she wanted to have a tea party inside it.

We were a couple of pretty goofy kids at times. One time Dad had a pair of coveralls hanging on the clothesline and put baby kittens in all the pockets and made Mom take a picture of it.

Another time we decided to run away from home. We weren't mad about anything, it just sounded like fun. We just got up really early and rode our bikes down to the river and ate Pop-Tarts. We were back at the house by 10am.

We were both crazy about the Batman television show. During one episode, the Catwoman drugged Batman and ended up kissing him. Janet and I went crazy, running around the house and screaming just to be silly. Dad finally got mad and made us turn the television off.

He was also a bit aggravated when I mowed the Bat symbol into the lawn. But that was an easy thing to fix.

We also made up story about a criminal named Big Man Fatso. We said he came to town every May 20th so you had to be really careful on that day. We wrote it on one of the inside walls of the barn and later when either of us mentioned it we had a good laugh.

She never talked about her former family much. I guess it was just too painful.

She ended up having four different mothers by the time she reached adulthood.

Chapter 13: I've Seen All Good People

Something that's always bothered me is how many people we lose in the course of our lifetimes.

I don't just mean people who've died. I'm also talking about all the folks we encounter at some point and then lose contact with them. The numbers really start adding up when you've taken up space on the planet over half a century.

When I was a kid it seemed like the night sky was almost always clear. I would look up at the stars and sometimes imagine what it would be like if they started to go out one by one. That's sort of how I see relationships that end for whatever reason… lights up above me that burn for a while but then suddenly disappear.

Facebook has brought me back into contact with quite a few people I grew up with. People I was sure I would never communicate with again.

It's weird, though. Like a friend of mine said..."okay, you're back in touch with some guy you hung out with in the fifth through eighth grades... now what do you do?".

Good question. You might tell them what you've been up to since 1975. Give your little life resume, where you went to college, where you ended up living, the name of your spouse, what you do for a living. All of a sudden you realize there's more actual human contact in a job interview.

But it's not all bad. On another level you're slapping each other on the back via the Internet, saying in not so many words that you're glad they survived this long and visa versa. It's almost as if you and all your long-lost acquaintances were lost at sea thirty five years ago and now you've all miraculously washed up on the same beach.

Your "friends" are now in their late forties and early fifties for the most part. Not old enough to be dead but old enough to have started feeling the chilly breeze of mortality blow through their lives every so often.

Some of them have become odd. One woman says her favorite cause is called "We Need Legal Horse Slaughter". I'm certainly no expert on the subject... maybe we do need this. But it sure threw me for a loop the first time I saw it on her Facebook page. I live in Seattle now and we tend to be against slaughter. Or at least we don't try to convince strangers we need more.

The truly amazing thing is that all these people I know have found a way to come together through time and space and what do they talk about… what they had for breakfast, what time they're going to the dentist, how much they love bologna. It's all trivial all the time. But maybe people find a kind of comfort in sharing these moments and thoughts.

Martin Rhodes became my "friend" today. He was actually a very good friend back in the mid Sixties. His mom was our Cub Scout leader and we had our meetings at their house every other Wednesday after school. One time I accidentally walked in on her nursing her baby. I quickly turned around and walked out of the room, experiencing a mix of horror and awe.

Some of the people I used to know are still married to someone they met in high school. Sue Larsen does the Facebook thing but my old buddy (her husband) Stan Larsen does not. Well, I guess he does do the Facebook thing in the sense that every time she puts something on there I see a little picture of the two of them.

He has the same crew cut he had in the first grade and no facial hair. I have somewhat long hair and a full beard. I assume our political differences are symbolized by the way we look now. I should send Stan a message but something holds me back… I don't want the reality of today screwing up the good memories of yesterday. Of course, yesterday wasn't all good either.

Dina Everly is on there too. A little heavier but still very, very pretty. I had a huge crush on her in high school.

Crush doesn't even adequately describe it... I pretty much just melted when I was around her. She was two years younger than me but it didn't make any difference, I was still tongue-tied and scared I might say something really stupid.

Of course, it really didn't make any difference because she was head over heels in love with one of my best friends.

Robert Diaz is on there. He was a couple years younger than me and we played on the tennis team together in high school. I always tried to look out for him when possible, he was a gentle soul and I didn't want to see him getting picked on. It was fun, kind of like having a younger brother.

David Peters is on there. Nice guy I guess but he always had the personality of a potted plant. Seems like he would have had to searched coma wards for someone to settle down with.

I became "friends" with Tom Hayes about a week ago. I never particularly liked him in high school but what the heck, maybe he's an interesting person now. He ended up looking a lot like the actor Ron Perlman. Poor bastard.

His dad was a basketball coach. The old man seemed to live on peanut butter sandwiches, taught bonehead math and generally threw two practice fits per season, one in December and one in February. It normally involved a lot of yelling and throwing basketballs really hard against the bleachers.

Trent Paxton is on there. He was my ADD church friend. He was making some comments on there praising Glenn Beck… apparently he traded in one kind of mental illness for another.

Jeremy Robin Reed was another interesting classmate. He had always seemed kind of effeminate when we were in grade school and middle school but our sophomore year he got a girl pregnant. They were both Mormon.

Suddenly they were both taken out of school and whisked off to some magical birthing clinic in Utah. I bet there are Israeli commando raids done less efficiently.

I'm assuming after the baby was born they were probably settled into some house in a bland Provo, Orem or Salt Lake City neighborhood.

Her name was Patty. I don't know what happened to her but here he is on Facebook pictured with another woman. I have no idea how hard it is for a Mormon person to get a divorce. I mean, aren't they supposed to be married for eternity?

At least Facebook is free. Rackets like Classmates.com just like to torture you… "Jim, do you want to know who your illegitimate half-sister is? Just sign up for our Gold membership…”.

Chapter 14: Cowboy Song

We had two ranches located eighteen miles apart. During October, Dad and his buddies would drive the herd down to where we lived and then in April move them back up to what we called the Bully Creek ranch.

We had to drive the cattle through Sunnyrock on a backstreet. There were generally four to five hundred animals.

It was a lot of work. The first time I participated was when I was seven. I had a slow old horse named Bonnie. She dutifully trudged along but was sometimes a bit obstinate about going the direction I wanted her to. I'm sure I didn't contribute all that much to the success of the cattle drive but Dad wanted me to experience what one was like.

The Bully Creek ranch was fairly rugged. It stretched out over approximately a thousand acres of hills covered in sagebrush and whatever grass managed to survive the wind, heat and cold.

During the summer we always had to be on the alert for rattlesnakes. I remember Dad shooting a big one that got too close.

The house was built over a natural hot spring. It was nice in the winter because the floor always stayed comfortably warm no matter how cold it got outside.

My uncle Richard and his family lived up at that ranch for a couple years. He was one of my mom's younger half-brothers. Richard was a nice guy but had serious emotional problems and later had to be institutionalized.

Eventually Dad had to sell the Bully Creek ranch because it was costing him too much tax-wise. I wonder how many times the place has been sold since then.

Chapter 15: Holdin' On to Yesterday

It's funny now to think about how naïve most Americans were about drugs once upon a time.

I remember sitting in Janet's room playing a 45 of "Mother's Little Helper" by the Rolling Stones. It was a birthday present from our aunt Ruth.

A little explanatory side note here for you younger readers: a 45 was a small vinyl record with one song on each side. Clearly, by today's standards it was a very inefficient way to store and manage media. But when we were kids we thought they were really cool.

The song "Mother's Little Helper" is about housewives getting hooked on amphetamines. I'm sure Ruth thought it was a musical tribute to boys and girls who kept their rooms clean.

I had a good laugh about it later when I figured out what Mick and the boys were actually singing about.

My aunt Ruth and uncle Lloyd lived in a suburb of Portland, Oregon called Oregon City. Lloyd worked for the telephone company and Ruth was a homemaker. She'd been an operator back before they were married.

They had a son named Lloyd Jr. who was eight years older than me. He was Lloyd's son by a previous marriage. Ruth and Lloyd never had kids together because right before they were to be married, he slid down a pole too fast and crushed his pelvis. He was rendered infertile.

He eventually healed up and was able to lead a very active life. When he wasn't at work he played golf, bowled or worked in their big, beautiful yard.

Lloyd was funny. He always acted normal around other adults but was playfully gruff with us kids. When he'd first see us he'd always says something like, "Oh, are you still living at home? Boy, when I was your age I was already out earning a living. I guess I need to have a talk with your folks".

You could never get a straight answer out of him but he was always generous and happy to take us places when we came to visit.

Dad and I always played hours and hours of horseshoes with him out in the backyard. By the end of the visit my right arm would be pretty sore.

Ruth was like a spokesperson for the suburban 50's mindset. I'm surprised she and Lloyd didn't have a framed picture of Dwight Eisenhower on their fireplace mantle.

I'd always felt like her devotion to housework bordered on the fanatical.

Of course, I suppose if a person doesn't have a job and they don't have children to take care of, they might get really serious about housework.

She didn't drive so if Lloyd wasn't around to take her somewhere she would put on her scarf or plastic rain bonnet and go catch the next bus coming through the neighborhood. I had a hard time understanding why she didn't get a driver's license… it seemed like some sort of weird, self-imposed handicap.

I never got the impression Lloyd was against her learning how to drive, maybe she just felt like it wasn't something women should be doing.

I thought riding the bus with her was a great adventure. Mom and Janet and I would go with her to downtown Portland and go to the big department stores. Janet and I especially loved the escalators and elevators. They were like carnival rides that didn't cost anything.

Every time we went to visit, the highlight was always Ruth's blueberry pancakes. Or at least she considered it the highlight. The berries were from her yard and she was very determined that if you stayed at her house you would at some point wolf down a pile of those pancakes. And I will admit, they were mighty tasty.

If anybody ever brought up a subject that was the least bit provocative she would immediately try to steer the conversation back to a "nice" one.

For example, if I said, "Aunt Ruth, do you ever worry that the Russians might drop an A-bomb on Portland?", she would reply, "Oh, that's not something an 8 year old boy should be talking about on a nice, sunny day like this. You should be thinking about getting good grades, helping your folks and eating some more of these delicious blueberry pancakes".

She didn't even like it when family members talked about each other. And hey, that's half the fun of belonging to a family.

I think as the 60's progressed it got harder and harder for her to make sense of the changes occurring in American culture. No matter how much she might deny it, the Eisenhower era was over and people were going to have honest, sometimes unpleasant conversations about the world they lived in.

She (and probably a lot of other people) felt cheated. They'd survived the Depression, World War

Two and Korea and now they just wanted to enjoy living in the suburbs with other middle-class people

Why did all these young people and minorities have to start complaining about how bad things were? If everybody just worked hard and went to school and started their day with a nice plate of blueberry pancakes, everything would work out fine.

I always felt bad she couldn't have kids with her husband. I knew she loved Lloyd Jr. but I always got the sense she felt like she'd been deprived of something really important. Maybe that had something to do with how she approached life.

But she did have a good heart. She would spend a lot of time taking care of Janet and myself over the next few years while my parents contended with my mother's health issues.

Chapter 16: We Are the Champions

My dad loved football. And I'm sure as soon as he knew he had a son, he was mentally picturing me wearing shoulder pads, cleats and a helmet.

He'd been a defensive lineman in high school and played two years of college ball. His freshman year he played on the University of Oregon junior varsity team. His sophomore year he transferred to Eastern Oregon College and played a season.

He was amazingly tough. He was only five seven and weighed roughly two hundred pounds at his heaviest.

This was back when helmets were made of leather and the guys were always getting their teeth knocked out because they didn't have face masks.

Come to think of it, this must have been before they invented that rule that says you can't grab somebody's face mask. Maybe back then the rule was you weren't allowed to grab somebody's face.

When I was a kid he watched college and pro games on television and attended most of Sunnyrock's home high school games. Mom went once in a while but it was usually just we two fellas.

I loved going to the games with him. He was a very intense spectator, marching up and down the Sunnyrock sideline, sniffing and snorting and cursing under his breath if our team screwed up or if the ref made a call he disagreed with.

His cursing was generally pretty mild. More often than not, he would use the term "judas priest".

That's not a swear term you hear much anymore. Back in the old days I think it was sort of a way to swear without really swearing. Now it's the name of a heavy metal band with a gay singer who wants to be your turbo lover.

He'd done some boxing in the Army and had his nose broken a couple times. Whenever he got stressed out about something, it seemed like he did a lot of pacing and sniffing. It was kind of like living with Rocky Graziano if he had a coke habit.

His favorite pro team was the Denver Broncos. Back in the 60's and early 70's, they were the only pro team in the western United States outside of California.

He seemed even more nervous watching football at home than when we'd go to games. He was like a caged animal, pacing around the living room, stopping only to yell at the television when Denver made a mistake or cheering when they scored. It was almost more fun to watch him than the game.

As we watched the games, I would ask him questions about the rules and the different players. He was pretty old school… he liked the tough guys with crew cuts who didn't show off much. Jim McMahon of the Chicago Bears always drove him crazy.

As far as he was concerned, the coaches could do the talking. All the players needed to do was run, pass and knock somebody down.

Years later, he told me the first time Denver won a Super Bowl he was so happy he opened a can of Coors and went outside to dance a jig in the street. I wish I could have been there to see it.

I'm glad he could lose himself in the games. He went through a pretty rough stretch after my stepmom died in 2004.

He told me watching football on the weekends and on Monday night helped him deal with his loneliness and depression. Watching football was the only thing he had to look forward to for a while.

My favorite pro team was the Dallas Cowboys. I think I started liking them simply because of the name. All my friends were Green Bay Packer fans and they gave me a pretty bad time. It was a good learning experience, though… it was the first time I had to stand up for what I wanted and take a little heat for it.

I especially liked the quarterback Don Meredith. He wasn't the greatest quarter- back but he had a nice, easygoing personality. He always seemed like he could be a real cowboy but decided to mess around with the whole football thing for a while.

I thought Roger Staubach was a bit bland in comparison. He wasn't funny and always seem to exude the charisma of an insurance agent trying to sell you on the benefits of term life.

Football was a religion in Sunnyrock. It was like the Super Denomination that took priority over all the weaker ones that merely worshipped a supremely powerful universal deity.

You might be a Baptist or a Mormon or a Lutheran or even a Buddhist but it didn't really matter because deep down, being a loyal Sunnyrock football fan was what was truly important.

There were several big families that supplied a large number of the star players, year after year, decade after decade, generation after generation. These families were either Catholic or Mormon… it was kind of weird, you could see why those churches instructed their faithful to keep cranking the kids out. It was their way of dominating everything from local politics to athletic programs.

If you weren't born into one of those families it seemed like you had to try a whole lot harder to get much playing time.

They were like brand names. If you were a Jordan, a Yankovitch or a Carlson it was assumed you would eventually take your rightful place in the annals of Sunnyrock sports history. I will admit they were all good athletes but they definitely also had a step up on the rest of us. And it wasn't just Sunnyrock, I'm sure this happens in small towns everywhere.

Dave Wilson was from Sunnyrock. He eventually ended up becoming an all-pro linebacker for the Los Angeles Rams.

The whole program had a Spartan seriousness about it. Our school colors were black and white. I was never sure how the town's founders had come up with that color scheme. Perhaps they thought anything less basic would cause the players to lose focus.

I almost felt like those uniforms sent a subliminal message to each of us that said we were winners no matter what we wore and would do just fine without all the fancy extra touches like color.

I'm just glad the league rules dictated the school had to let us wear face masks.

We were called the Sunnyrock Raiders. We were the smallest school in our league but nearly always in contention to win the division title and go on to the state playoffs.

Looking back on it now, it seemed like Sunnyrock belonged in Texas or Oklahoma. If you've ever seen "The Last Picture Show" you've got a good idea how important football was to the folks I grew up around.

It was always so exciting on game nights, especially early in the season. The field would be filled with the long shadows of the players as they warmed up and the air would be crisp with the first cool air of autumn. The school band was playing and people were filling the stands, greeting each other and politely making room so everybody had a place to sit.

And not long after that, the night sky would be ink black and all the big field lights would be on and the announcer up in the box would be telling you what down it was and how much yardage the team with the ball gained on the last play. I felt like all my senses were amplified… I couldn't imagine being anywhere more exciting.

The fans were pretty boisterous. My all-time favorite comment was made by an elderly woman who yelled, "Fight 'em and kill 'em!".

I would usually follow Dad around for a while and then go get a hamburger or a candy bar at the concession stand. There was just nothing better than the smell of that meat grilled out in the open.

Sometimes there was other stuff to do besides watch the game. A bunch of us would often go to an adjoining park and play our own little football game. Or you could go underneath the bleachers and pick up empty soda bottles and turn them in for money.

I was very excited. Here was a way to earn cash for comic books! Stan Larsen and I spent a lot of Friday nights picking up those bottles.

I loved Sunnyrock football but I loved comic books even more.

Chapter 17: My Hometown

When I was young, my favorite sitcom was the Andy Griffith Show. I think a lot of rural people could relate to it's gentle humor and quirky small town characters.

Andy seemed to possess a common sense chromosome found lacking in pretty much all the other adults who inhabited Mayberry. No matter what kind of trouble the townspeople got themselves into, he would come up with some kind of wise and heart-warming solution. He was kind of like Lassie except he could also drive and didn't have to explain things by barking.

Griffith was an interesting actor. He could play the nicest guy in the world or the nastiest.

His deputy Barney Fife created a good deal of the problems Andy had to fix. He was full of false bravado and always itching to control other people.

I feel like I've known a lot of Barney Fifes over the course of my life.

I was always amazed how often Andy and Barney got dressed up in their suits. I wouldn't be surprised if they put on a tie when they went bowling. And I don't think Thelma Lou and Helen Crump were even putting out.

I was pretty fond of Floyd the barber. He was always remarkably confused. It was like his thoughts were bouncing around in his head like soap bubbles. He was somewhat like Mr. Kimball on "Green Acres". He would start talking about something and then get easily distracted over and over again and completely forget what his point was.

But it didn't matter. He lived in small, sleepy town and he had the only barber shop and everybody liked him. Life was good for Floyd.

Later on in life I was able to do an impression of Floyd several of my male friends thought was hilarious. Women found it utterly creepy.

The secret was to ramble on incoherently from subject to subject. "Oh, that's true, Andy…why just the other day I went fishing and… oh wait, was that the other day, I…hey, did you fellas…ooooh, that's a nice piece of pie".

A similar impression my women friends found repulsive was Billy Bob Thornton's character in "Slingblade". When I would do that one they would back away like they were worried I was about to stuff them in the trunk of my car.

The show took a strange turn after Andy and Don Knotts left. Andy and Helen got married and Barney became a police detective and they all ended up moving to Raleigh.

Otis the drunk also left the show… I don't know if his character sobered up or decided to start sleeping them off in some other town's jail. They never really tied up that loose end.

I felt like I'd suddenly lost a whole host of good friends. Goober was still around but he was more less just the Mayberry village idiot. Which in Mayberry was really saying something.

I think CBS figured since both Griffith and Knotts were leaving it was a good time to make the show less home-spun and a bit more relevant. They brought in a bureaucrat named Howard and a crotchety fixit guy named Emmett.

I found Howard especially annoying. Sheriff Andy always found a way to resolve problems using country charm and an understanding of human nature. Howard, on the other hand, exemplified the kind of guy was utterly helpless if he wasn't given a mandated government program to follow.

And even worse, he wore bow ties. Few men can wear a bow tie and get away with it. Maybe an intellectual heavyweight like George Will, but that's about it. Don't even get me started on guys who sing in barbershop quartets.

Bow ties are like berets when worn by artsy guys… they say "I'm telling you right up front I'm a pompous douchebag and there's a very good chance I will annoy you a great deal. There's a sign-up sheet if you plan on beating me up".

I didn't mind Emmett so much. I always got the impression that given half a chance he would've clubbed Howard to death with a pipe wrench.

Howard would always learn the error of his ways by the end of the episode but I just didn't care. I kept hoping he'd get fired for embezzling funds or filling out too many forms in triplicate.

Then they brought in Ken Berry and he was even less appealing than Howard. He was a good dancer but that's not really a necessary ingredient for a show about a rural sheriff.

The show just didn't seem funny anymore. I was starting to grasp the concept that nothing good lasts forever. I realize most people learn this from critical moments in their own lives but at that point in my life I was more tuned into what was happening to the folks inside my parents' black and white TV.

That feeling of loss would come back to haunt me many times in the years ahead. Dealing with change was always hard for me but I think I did get a bit better as time went on. I would put a little blame on my dad for this… he really hated change.

There was an older gentleman in Sunnyrock I always thought would fit right in with the Mayberrians. His name was Elmer Martin. He didn't have much income or inclination to launder his one black suit. His white shirt always had sweat stains around the collar, he wore thick black glasses held together with tape and he always had a couple days worth of beard growth.

Actually, on the beard thing he was just ahead of his time. He would have fit in really well on "Miami Vice" twenty years later.

He wasn't homeless. He had a nasty old shack somewhere outside of town. And he drove a beat-up old car that coughed up oily smoke every time he started it.

Every time our church had a wedding, funeral or celebration that featured free food, he'd be there. He'd eat as much as he could and then sneakily wrap pieces of cake or whatever in napkins and stuff them in his coat pockets.

We also had a pair of elderly spinster sisters in our church. They were always very sweet to me. One had gray hair and the other blue.

Our town drunks weren't funny like Otis. They were just kind of sad. It was a father and his son. We had other drunks too but these were the guys who would be having trouble walking down the street at two in the afternoon.

Things moved pretty slow in Sunnyrock. There was never all that much traffic and I don't think anybody ever worried about using the crosswalks. Even the town dogs pretty much went where they wanted, when they wanted.

The two main streets were one going east to west and another one a block away, going west to east. Once in a while a stranger would accidentally drive the wrong way down one of these streets and any kids who happened to be around would excitedly run after them, yelling for them to stop and turn around.

Sunnyrock has always had a lot of community spirit. There's always been a lot of support for the sports programs and charity benefits. And they have a surprisingly decent three-day rodeo there every July second through the fourth.

On one of the nights they always have what they call the Suicide Race. My dad rode in it one time.

The riders and horses start at the top of a fairly high, steep hill located above the rodeo arena. Somebody sets off some dynamite and the riders come flying down, hanging on for dear life. At the end of the race the riders and horses have to cross a river but it's not all that deep in July.

Part of the Fourth of July celebration is a parade that goes through downtown.

When I was eight I joined the Cub Scouts. I never really liked it all that much but it was cool having a uniform.

My Cub Scout troop was going to be riding on a float in the parade, waving at the crowd and throwing out candy to the kids.

My folks got a late start that night and rushed me to the part of town where the parade was supposed to start. I saw a float with Cub Scouts standing on it and assumed that's where I should go. I leaped aboard and my parents drove off to find a place to watch the parade from.

About thirty seconds after the float began moving I realized I was on the Mormon Cub Scout float. I knew all the kids but I was still mortified. They were all looking at me with puzzled expressions.

And I became more mortified as more and more people (including my bewildered parents) pointed at me and mouthed "what are you doing on that Mormon float". Mom and Dad weren't virulently anti-Mormon but they seemed shocked I had converted without first discussing it with them.

It was like that scene at the end of the 1978 version of "Invasion of the Body Snatchers" where Donald Sutherland is alerting the other pod people that Brooke Adams is still human.

On a positive note, this story really reflects what a tolerant country America is most of the time. I got on the wrong religion's float, we all had a good laugh about it and now I'm telling you the story.

I wouldn't be surprised if I had made this mistake in some Middle Eastern countries it would have cost me my head.

Chapter 18: Hello, It's Me

Here are some brief flashes from my first few years of grade school.

Nothing good ever happens on a school bus. Some days are okay and the worst thing that happens is that the driver gets irritated and yells "you kids better sit down and shut up". There are also days when somebody gets their hair pulled and they in turn punch the puller in the arm very hard.

Or it could be a very bad day, like the one when my neighbor Terry Mason decided to inform me there is no Santa Claus. He was one of those kids who lived on our road and had warts all over his hands.

I was in the second grade so it was probably time for me to learn the cold, hard truth but still it would have been nice to hear it from my parents.

When I got off the bus I was almost shaking. I began thinking about who else might not exist… the Tooth Fairy, the Easter Bunny, Rudolph. This was really traumatic stuff.

I don't have a lot of phobias. But when I was a kid I was really scared of heights.

A couple times our teachers took us on field trips to Owyhee dam. We were up on top of the spillway and kids are running all over the place. Stan Larsen was also scared of heights and so we're both standing back behind the group, encouraging our classmates not to hang over the edge and look down. We were sure somebody was going to get careless and fall to their doom.

I've always been husky. I tell people I was thin in the fourth grade for about half an hour. It was the one time my height genes were a lot more active than my weight genes. Or maybe it was the one time my height genes were able to stay ahead of my healthy appetite.

When I was in the third grade, a new kid named Robert Targen moved to town. A bunch of us went camping out on their place during the summer. Robert started telling us how he and his sister had made up a game they called "Naked City". There was a t.v. show called that from 1958 to 1963 but I doubt what Robert and his sister were doing had much to do with the NYPD's 65th precinct.

I had tacos for the first time at Robert's house when I was eleven. I really liked them. I think I had ten or twelve.

I nearly ruined one of my mom's friendships. She and I were having lunch with an old friend of hers and I decided to participate in the conversation. I looked at the woman and said "You're not nearly as fat as Mom said". I was trying to be complimentary but I'm sure that's not the way she took it.

I'm severely unhandy. My dad wasn't all that great either but I am a true idiot when it comes to putting things together. I only built one model the whole time I was growing up and it was Batman. I never saw the fun in trying to assemble a plastic battleship or a miniature 1957 Chevy.

Assembling the Batman model is the hobby equivalent of doing the TV Guide crossword puzzle. It's not much of a challenge.

When I look at an instruction sheet, all the words start to blur.

I'm really grateful I live when I do. I'm good on the computer and I'm good at dealing with people. Thank God I don't have to build houses or repair car engines. There isn't enough duct tape in the world to fix the mess I would make.

Ironically, I've always loved buying new cars. I don't know much about how they work but I do know a few things about makes and models and such. Of course, they're so computerized now hardly anybody can work on one at home.

One of main jobs as a kid was serving as a weight. I would sit on a piece of equipment called a "ditcher". It's like a blade you pull behind a tractor and it clears out the weeds in an irrigation ditch. There could be some rather violent jerks and after three or four hours my rear end would be awfully sore.

We had a strange teacher in the fourth grade. He wanted to teach us about electrical conductivity so he had everybody in the class stand in a circle and hold hands. Then he used some kind of crank-powered generator to send a small charge through us.

I hated electric fences. My dad installed some and told me one of my jobs was to go around and make sure they were working. I had a little tester thing but I was always accidentally getting shocked.

When I was in the third grade I thought I was a pretty good baseball player. I was out sick one day and when I got back I found out the better athletes in the class had joined with some other guys in our grade and formed what they called an all-star team. They hadn't included me.

This made me pretty mad so I decided to form my own team. I gathered together all the other boys who hadn't been invited to join the all-star squad. Our first and only game was against a team of girls and we lost.

Chapter 19: Time Passages

I decided to start creating my own comic books.

It's funny how the creative process works sometimes… you enjoy some type of art and gradually you end up thinking you might be able to do it just as well or possibly better.

Or maybe you feel like there's a niche that hasn't been filled, such as pictures of birds dressed as pirates. Or maybe you're just overwhelmed by a creative hunger and you decide you're willing to do whatever's necessary to satisfy it.

Art was definitely not my strong suit when I started school. I remember getting reprimanded by a teacher for coloring a kitten purple.

Of course, if I had attended grade school ten years later I probably would have been rewarded for my funky creative spirit. I probably would have been encouraged to draw a purple bird dressed as a pirate.

Well, probably not in Sunnyrock in 1973. After all, this was a town where the school colors were black and white.

My initial attempt to go public was a series of short stories called “Pistol Pete and His Sister”. I think the plots generally revolved around Pete engaging in shootouts with bad guys while his sister rooted him on. They had a very simple, violence-based relationship.

My friend Robin Sykes liked them and paid me a nickel for each little book. It doesn’t sound like much but in those days I could buy a real comic book for twelve cents. I got very excited about this new venture… if I could retain Robin and maybe pick up two or three other steady customers I would soon be swimming in nickels!

I even started fantasizing about using the mimeograph machine in the principal’s office.

I’d heard somewhere that if you were gonna dream, dream big. Sounds like something you’d hear somebody say in one of those boring old movies where everybody sings and dances and puts on a show. But it was still good advice.

I wanted every child in our school to own a copy of “Pistol Pete and His Sister”. I wanted it in the school library. I wanted it mailed to children who were sick at home for more than three days. I wanted it sent in CARE packages to starving children in Africa.

Unfortunately, my grand dreams of publishing glory were abruptly shattered.

After I had raked in a mere fifteen cents, our teacher found out and prohibited me from engaging in further capitalism during school hours. I was really mad when she told me this. What was she, some kind of Communist?

This setback didn't dampen my passion for cartooning. I became obsessed, using every piece of scrap paper I could get my hands on. I think one Christmas I said all I wanted was a box of typing paper. Fortunately, my mom ignored this request and bought me toys.

The characters I created were basically knockoffs of my favorite Marvel and DC superheroes.

Fire Guy was my version of the Human Torch, Mister Steel was my Iron Man. And Captain Northwest was my regional alternative to Captain America.

Captain Northwest didn't really have any superpowers, per se. He did have a mask and a cape, drove a Jeep and was friendly almost to a fault. I don't think he actually fought anyone but he was always ready to rescue lost hikers.

Looking back, he seems more like a flamboyantly gay park ranger than an actual crimefighter.

A book about a character named Timehunter was my most ambitious project. I'd done a couple shorter stories about this intrepid time traveler but in this one he ventured back to the days of ancient Egypt and got caught up in a war. It was an epic tale, going on for more than twenty pages!

I even tried emulating my cartooning hero, Jack Kirby. The book featured several full page battle scenes. Of course, doing full page battle scenes also helped me cut me back on the amount of plot I needed to create.

The plot was pretty simple. Timehunter shows up, some bad Egyptians get mad at him, some good Egyptians rescue him, a lot of heroic stuff gets said, there's a big battle and he comes back to the present.

I didn't do much research... for example, it didn't occur to me that altering events in the past could lead to horrible consequences in the present. You know, like leisure suits or the election of George W. Bush in 2000.

I even tried my hand at a Mad magazine knockoff. I called it "Let's Take a Vacation From Education". I asked my parents to read it.

Mom was amused and complimented me on the artwork. Dad seemed annoyed that I was spending so much time thinking about stuff besides football and farm work. I decided to hold off telling him I wanted to be a cartoonist when I grew up... I still remembered how annoyed he seemed when I mowed the Batman symbol on the lawn.

I don't think he necessarily felt like I had to be a farmer or a rancher. But he did want me to be something serious.

I was confident about my ability to draw male heroes and villains. They all looked like they were spending way too much time at the gym. But I never really mastered the female form.

Sadly, all the women in my cartoon universe looked like men with long hair and breasts.

Perhaps I should have done a book about a transsexual superhero.

Chapter 20: Everybody Hurts

It's amazing how quickly kids have to start dealing with cruelty and sadness.

Some of my saddest childhood memories are of a girl named Bonnie Schmidt. She was from a poor family and her brother had accidentally shot her right eye out with a pellet gun.

She didn't wear a patch and the eye often looked messy. Some of the meaner kids would torment her about it during recess, calling her Cyclops or Pirate Girl.

At first she acted hurt but eventually their taunts turned her hard and just generally hostile to all the other kids. It's terrible when a kid has turned bitter by the third grade.

Or maybe it's a situation where the kid is from a really poor family and the parents are lax about their kids' hygiene.

There was a girl named Darlene in our fourth grade class. She was a little overweight and she always had kind of an odor. And even though nobody in Sunnyrock was particularly wealthy, Darlene's family was considered pretty trashy.

But I think up to this point in her life, Darlene still thought there was a chance she could fit in with the other kids.

We had a custom where you brought treats for the class on your birthday. Darlene brought home-made divinity candy but none of the kids wanted to eat it.

Poor Darlene just sat at her desk and silently cried. Our teacher wasn't sure what to do... it's not like she could force us to eat that weird-looking stuff.

When a lot of people hear about stuff like the violence at Columbine, they ask how could this happen. I've always sort of wondered why it doesn't happen more often. Every school has Bonnies and Darlenes who are being tormented for one reason or another and lots of Jimmies who don't have the courage to walk away from the herd and reach out to them.

One of the strangest things I ever witnessed happened to a girl named Tina Peters. A bunch of us were playing on a merry-go-round out on the playground and she was standing on it while the rest of us were pushing it. She had a very long ponytail and somehow the end of it got caught in the mechanism located in the middle.

Meanwhile, we continued to push the merry-go-round, unaware why she was screaming. Finally, somebody realized what was happening to her and got us to stop pushing. She wasn't seriously injured but the pain must have been horrible and she ended up having to get a very short haircut. It was like something out of a horror novel or a bad dream.

Death also came knocking pretty early. I suppose some kids had experienced losing a grandparent or some other older relative at some point. But when a kid your own age dies it sort of knocks the wind out of you.

Max Richter was the meanest kid in our grade. He had a square head and a very short crewcut and claimed his German Shepherd was a killer dog. I could easily picture him wearing a Nazi uniform.

It seemed like he never missed a chance to pick on smaller or more timid kids. He'd figured out early how to get what he wanted through intimidation.

One day I came to school and learned he had drowned. It was the first time I heard someone I knew had just died.

I felt bad for his family but a little relieved he had gone away before he had gotten around to beating me up. If someone was going to die I preferred it be a bully. I know that sounds terrible it was the truth.

My mother was diagnosed with cancer in 1966. She had to go to the hospital for a couple days and when she came home she only had one breast. One day I happened to see the foam breast form lying on her bed when she was taking a bath.

I could tell she was feeling self-conscious. Janet and I felt really bad for her. It was bad enough she got sick but also terrible she felt bad about the way she looked.

We didn't really understand what cancer was. We just hoped she wouldn't ever get sick again.

Chapter 21: God Only Knows

My grandma Leslie bought us a series of books called "My Bible Story". They covered both the Old and New Testaments.

I was pretty surprised. She attended the local Episcopal church but I'd never really heard her talk about religion much.

Sometimes you would see one or two volumes sitting around in dental or medical waiting rooms. We had the whole set.

I was already acquainted with a lot of the stories in the Bible. But for some reason I had never heard about the Book of Revelation. I'm pretty sure the teachers had never mentioned it to us… we were too busy making popsicle stick cabins and doing our military dance routines.

I was comfortable with Adam and Eve and Noah and Moses and the walls of Jericho and Jesus. I understood they were like historical stories with some supernatural elements mixed in and they were meant to teach us how to be good people.

I took the fantastic stuff on faith, basically because I couldn't think of any reason why my mother would drag us to church every Sunday just so the teachers and the minister could fill our heads with lies.

When I became an adult I would start to wonder how people could totally accept the miraculous aspects of their own religion and then turn around and totally mock what somebody else believed. Like it or not, everybody who buys into the supernatural is riding in the same car to a certain extent.

This last book of the New Testament was unlike anything I'd ever seen before. It sounded like a horror movie made by Walt Disney if he was taking drugs with H.P. Lovecraft.

It talked about all the scary stuff that was supposed to happen in the future prior to Jesus returning to Earth. And this wasn't standard Biblical fare like somebody turning into a pillar of salt or being swallowed by a whale.

The "My Bible Story" book showed monsters and the moon turning bloody and talked about some guy named the Beast branding your forehead. And if you didn't let him brand your forehead, you wouldn't even be able to buy a loaf of bread.

It was weird thinking about the future being preordained. It made life seem like nothing more than a moving sidewalk... you just keep moving along and one of these days a bunch of bad stuff happens and there's really no way you can avoid it.

Of course, a lot of people would describe disease and old age that same way but those conditions don't necessarily involve all-out war in the Middle East.

This new information petrified me. Anytime I heard a news report about Israel I got very, very scared. I was sure Jesus was on his way back and I had no idea if I'd get picked to be on his team.

One hot summer night I was watching Billy Graham on television giving a sermon about Judgment Day. A thunder and lightning storm started and I became extremely agitated.

It was like I was having a spiritual panic attack. I was sure Gideon's trumpet was gonna blow any minute.

It was interesting over the years to see who people thought might be the Anti-Christ. Hitler, Bill Gates, Saddam Hussein and many others were considered at different times. Of course, most of the discussion occurred on the pages of rags like the Weekly World News, a publication for people who believed in Batboy and the Bigfoot diet.

I've had a couple bosses I thought might be in the running but the scope of their evil turned out to be pretty limited.

Those little Jack Chick cartoon pamphlets scared me even more. You would often find them left at Laundromats or bus stations or in public restrooms. I wouldn't be surprised if Larry Craig (the former senator from Idaho) had a collection of them.

I found one in the bathroom at our church. And of course, since it was a comic book I had to read it.

They always seemed to have essentially the same storyline… some guy is just living his life but then gets mixed up with the wrong crowd and instantly becomes an alcoholic or a drug addict.

Then he dies before he can commit his life to Christ. He gets judged and sent to burn eternally in the lake of fire. I wondered if that was going to be my story.

Years later, the arrival of the new millennium put a lot of people in an apocalyptic mood. My dad and stepmother and uncle Mitch laid in a supply of food and water and candles in case the Y2K catastrophe came to pass.

Even though the church I attended as a kid was pretty mellow, we still had our odd moments here and there.

The Sunday school classes were taught by volunteers. They generally followed some kind of approved lesson plan but you never knew when somebody would come up with a zinger like the fact that children are born retarded because God is punishing their parents for past sins.

And he wasn't talking in the politically correct sense where the child has problems because the mother drank or smoke when she was pregnant or the parents did a bunch of acid and it messed up the kid's genetic makeup.

"These children are born cursed with low intelligence because of sin. The sins of their parents. Their fathers drank liquor and played cards and listened to rock and roll. Their mothers fornicated and betrayed God in all kinds of other ways. The Lord sees that kind of behavior and exacts a terrible vengeance."

This little gem came from a guy who was dating one of the pastor's daughters. I told the pastor what the guy said. I didn't want to be a tattletale but I just didn't feel like it was right for him to be laying that crap on a bunch of impressionable kids. I knew and respected the pastor and was pretty sure he would agree with me.

I actually heard about a new version of this story lately. A right-wing politician in Virginia made remarks implying that a woman who has an abortion will run the risk of birth defects in later pregnancies as a punishment from God.

Another time we got on the subject of evil and the Sunday school teacher started talking about demons and ghosts and modern-day supernatural events. I think he was trying to warn us about stuff we shouldn't get involved in but I just thought it was cool he was talking about something exciting for once.

It was the first time I'd ever heard of ectoplasm, this stuff that supposedly floats around in haunted houses or comes out of the mouths of possessed people. It sounded like Silly Putty for spirits.

Sometimes people would try to use the church as a place to push their own agenda. One middle-aged man hated long hair on men so much he said he could prove that Jesus had a crew cut.

I suppose there may have been a slight possibility the son of God had short hair at some point. But a crew cut? That's definitely overselling it.

The bad thing about our church (and this is very common) was how there always seemed to be a small group of families that were always trying to run things.

One of the main ways they held on to their power was by never letting any pastor stay too long. It seemed like just when the guy was starting to get comfortable they would always find some lame reason to criticize him publicly. Like he failed to wave at them when they were driving by or he wasn't strict enough about what his daughters wore.

I don't think these folks consciously sat around and made plans about how to torment and get rid of their pastors. It was more like a reflex, something they'd done all their lives, probably an attitude that had been passed down from their parents and their parents before that.

The next thing you know, the elders are meeting and voting to give the poor pastor the boot. He and his family would have to pack up and move on to the next intolerant little town. Some of these poor guys got moved around more often than pro basketball players.

I think this constant bickering and division was one of the main reasons I lost interest in going to church later on. It could often be a fertile environment for pettiness and jealousy. Just the opposite of what you would hope to find in a place where people worship God.

But there was also a lot of good in the church. People really looked out for each other. That's something I miss sometimes.

I may start attending some kind of church again someday. I haven't shut that door completely. Maybe a new denomination will start up that I feel comfortable belonging to.

Janet and I attended church camp five years straight. It was always held at the same place up in the Idaho mountains.

It was pretty fun. You had to go to classes in the morning and attend a service at night but during the afternoon you got to go swimming or hiking or boating or whatever. I met a lot of cool kids who came from lots of different towns in Oregon and Idaho.

I developed a pretty serious Mountain Dew addiction when I was at church camp one year. That stuff was so loaded with sugar and caffeine it was like crank for kids.

Each year the staff would pick a Best Boy Camper and a Best Girl Camper and announce who won at the end of the week. Those two kids would get to go to camp for free the next summer.

My third year I decided I really wanted to win the award. I pandered shamelessly, answering more questions that anybody else in the classes and constantly volunteering to help clean up in the kitchen. I'm sure a lot of the other kids found me kind of sickening.

It worked. I won the award that year and Janet won it the following summer. I was really happy for her.

Chapter 22: Masters of War

Walter Cronkite was bringing the Vietnam war into our house every night. The whole thing seemed pretty confusing but my basic understanding was that we were helping some good Asian guys fight some bad Asian guys.

There was a casualty count every few days. They talked about how many Americans were killed or wounded in the fighting. I remember feeling encouraged if our numbers went down and discouraged when they went up.

Eventually it didn't seem to matter all that much. The war started to feel like it might not ever end and the statistics were no important than a win-loss column on a daily newspaper's sports page.

It always seemed like ten times more North Vietnamese died than Americans and South Vietnamese. I was amazed they could sustain those kind of losses and keep on fighting us.

I began to get the feeling maybe this wasn't a black-and-white-no-questions-asked conflict like World War Two. Or at least that was always my impression of WW2.

There were news stories about people actually protesting the war. I had a hard time wrapping my mind around this concept. If the president said we should fight somebody, how could you have a different opinion? Didn't American presidents basically receive their orders from God and then pass them on down to the rest of us?

The war started to feel like a dark cloud hanging over everybody's lives. High school boys either made themselves feel better with commie-killing bravado or just learned to live with the dread and hoped they could figure out a way not to get drafted.

I think the government started to get the feeling maybe a little cheerleading was in order. John Wayne made a movie about the war called "The Green Berets".

Duke wasn't happy with the growing anti-war atmosphere and social discontent in the country and for some reason figured the kids would all settle down and cut their hair if they saw him swaggering through the rice paddies with a green beret on his head.

David Janssen from "The Fugitive" TV show played a reporter. You know, one of those pesky guys who always get in the way and ask a bunch of stupid questions instead of just taking Wayne and LBJ and Robert McNamara at their word and believing everything is just gonna work out fine.

Conservatives always seem to underestimate the insight and intelligence of teenagers and young adults. Instead of rallying the public to support the war, "The Green Berets" came and went and was regarded by most people as nothing more than the lamest kind of propaganda. It was a lot like Nancy Reagan's "Just Say No" drug program of the 1980's... not only ineffectual but downright mockable.

My older cousin Lloyd Jr. served in Vietnam. It was so ironic... his stepmother (Ruth) had always restricted his activities growing up out of fear he might get hurt. No football, no basketball, no track team.

But as soon as he graduated from high school, he headed down to the nearest Army recruiting office to enlist. He was desperate to get out from underneath Ruth's thumb. So desperate he was willing to risk his life slogging through the jungles of southeast Asia.

He came to visit us one time when he was still in the Army. He and I took a walk down towards the river and I asked him what it was like in Vietnam.

He said, "I hate it over there. It's always hot and there's lots of weird bugs and you spend practically every day marching through the jungle. And you can never let your guard down... if it's not some gook trying to shoot you it's the damn monkeys in the trees throwing rocks at your head".

"A lot of these gung-ho types back here at home really have no idea what they're talking about. This whole war was a big goddamn mistake".

Talking to him really shook me up. It was at that moment I stopped seeing the war as a romantic adventure and started thinking of it as a bloody mess that was wasting thousands of young American lives.

I prayed it would end before it wasted mine.

The U.S. always seems to be involved in a war or on the verge of going to war with somebody. Eventually we got out of Vietnam but we still had to deal with the Russians and the Cold War.

I was in college when the Russians invaded Afghanistan in late 1979. It looked for a couple days like we might be creeping toward a real honest-to-God shooting war with them. My friends and I watched the news and worried about our futures.

Fortunately, the U.S. government was feeling pretty run down at the time and decided not to do much more than make speeches.

Some people say Jimmy Carter was a bad president but I believe his decision not to take action against the USSR at that time potentially spared the world from a nuclear war.

I was amazed how quickly guys on campus started organizing anti-war rallies and making plans to head for Canada. It was like a reflex that had resulted from all of us watching the news every night all those years and the stories we heard from older brothers and cousins and friends.

The pain of the Vietnam era still burned like a hot coal in our collective consciousness. Nobody was going to get caught flat-footed this time.

Then the Soviet Union fell apart and we all thought there would be a peace dividend. Maybe we could build fewer bombs and more housing for poor people.

Chapter 23: Tie Dye On the Highway

Rock music was a mystery to me in the Sixties. I didn't understand the lyrics and I didn't understand why anybody would like a song if they couldn't tell what the singer was singing about.

I liked country music. I lived out in the country so I assumed that's what I was supposed to like.

Sometimes when I was having a hard time falling asleep I would lay in bed and make up country and western lyrics. I didn't know much about cheatin' or drinkin', so my songs were sort of on the tame side.

I worked all week
And I bought a new shirt
I really liked the old one
But there was too much dirt.

I was pretty hostile about the long haired performers initially. I was living in a pretty hard-core Barry Goldwater political environment and automatically assumed these guys and gals were all weirdo communists just trying to confuse us so they and their overseers in Russia and China could enslave the country.

Later on, I lightened up a bit and started to enjoy their antics.

Kids born in the late 1950's initially grew up with what I call "the gown and tuxedo people". Rock 'n roll was around but prime-time television was still dominated by Frank Sinatra, Judy Garland, Perry Como, Dean Martin and all those other showbiz legends who seemed perfectly happy to keep asking Bill Bailey to please come home. No dope (at least that we knew about at the time) but lots and lots of booze and cigarettes.

Apparently I was a Sinatra fan during my toddler years. My mother said the first time she ever heard me sing was on a long car trip. I did a duet with Frank on "All the Way". Or at least I helped him out on the chorus.

Of course, those performers at least had glamour. My folks (and it seemed like everybody else's) watched "The Lawrence Welk Show" every Saturday night. It made "Hollywood Palace" look downright decadent.

The Welk show served as a weekly reminder that everyone should conform and be as boring as possible.

Tens of millions of American adults tuned in every week, confident in the knowledge they would never be offended, puzzled or even a little bit surprised.

The only thing worse than boring is boring pretending to be hip. In the late 60's and early 70's the younger guys on the show started wearing "styled" long hair and weird pastel colored suits. They and the gals and the orchestra would proceed to drain all the passion out of recently popular songs, turning them into the musical equivalent of a tuna hotdish you'd find being served at a South Dakota grange hall meeting.

Janet and I grew to hate that show. It represented everything we thought was boring about adults. Of course, our main gripe was more personal… Welk and his cronies were on the same time as "The Green Hornet".

Of course, I will admit a part of every generation fights to hold on to the culture and feelings they loved when they were young. Today people in their 50's will pay good money to go see Styx or some other old group even if there are only one or two original members left in the lineup. The desire to hold on to some small fragment of your youth can be a very powerful one.

We ridiculed our parent's reluctance to accept change and then we started listening to Classic Rock stations where it's always 1976 and Peter Frampton is forced to play "Do You Feel Like We Do" over and over and over again through all eternity.

It will be interesting to see how well formats like Classic Grunge or Classic Gangsta Rap do in the years to come. You never know what somebody out there might be waxing nostalgic about.

The new music was an unstoppable tidal wave in the 60's. The Baby Boom teenagers were becoming a huge source of disposable income in the country and the television networks reacted accordingly.

Sunday mornings we went to church but Sunday nights we were watching new rock and soul performers on the Ed Sullivan and Smothers Brothers shows.

It was strange watching Ed Sullivan introduce some of these acts. He just seemed really disconnected from the youth culture. He seemed comfortable with somebody singing a song from a Broadway play or some guy spinning plates, not the Doors or the Byrds. But you have to give the guy credit… he would stand there with that wooden face and introduce the rock bands and do his best.

I always wished he could say what he was really thinking… "and now here are five overpaid, hairy brats from England playing some annoying song I would never listen to if I wasn't stuck hosting this stupid fucking show".

It seemed like the whole country had a sliding scale. My dad couldn't stand Elvis back when he first came on the scene but then started liking him a whole lot better when the Fab Four started getting popular.

A lot of them were tame but every so often an act would come along that would make the whole country tense up for a day or two.

You always wondered if this was the band that had taken things a little too far out there, the act that would so outrage the Silent Majority they would rise up off their couches and out of their recliners, demanding that the National Guard go house to house searching for joints and forcing teenage boys to get crew cuts.

But it didn't happen. Some people got mad, some people gave speeches and some people burned records. But the bands just kept coming and the songs just kept on playing. The music got in our blood.

Burning the records always seemed silly to me. After all, somebody had to purchase the record before you could throw it on a bonfire.

One big advantage this new music had was that often it's energy came from people's pain and despair. There was stuff you could listen to when you just wanted to forget your troubles but there was also a new kind of music that actually talked about what bothered us and what was going on in the world and what we could do to change things.

Folk music had carried those same messages but it lacked something. It was too earnest and dry, a corny white guy with short hair playing a banjo and asking if he might take a moment of your time to talk about nuclear weapons testing.

Rock and soul music had heart and anger and sex and heat and religion. You didn't need to make an effort to like this kind of music… it grabbed you and made you sweat and made you want to shout out loud and dance. And sometimes it made you think about stuff in a whole new way.

The Beatles were more than musicians. They were deities… the Smart One, the Cute One, the Quiet One and the Goofy One. It's hard to explain to a kid today how completely and utterly they were idolized. They were like explorers and every album they created was a doorway into yet another new country they'd discovered.

They went from playing simple songs about holding some girl's hand to ones about weeping guitars and yellow submarines and ladies named Madonna.

Of course, even they couldn't hold on to the spotlight forever. I remember hearing a celebrity tell a story about how his teen-age daughter came home from school one day during the late 70's and asked him if Paul McCartney was in any famous groups before Wings.

The Stones were cool in a different way. They were skinny and slightly menacing… like a bunch of longhaired alleycats, always looking to provoke a little sensation with their suggestive lyrics and wildly creative album covers.

Every time I heard the introduction to “Gimme Shelter” I would get a wonderful chill running up and down my spine. It was like they captured the sound of an entire world questioning everything it’s ever been told.

There’s a funny scene in the movie “Almost Famous” when the character played by Jimmy Fallon is ridiculing the idea Mick Jagger would still be performing at the age of 50.

Ironically, the first rock song I remember absolutely loving was called “The Rapper” and it was performed by a group called The Jaggerz. I always wondered if these guys were related to Mick somehow. Actually, they were from Pittsburgh and nobody in the group had the last name Jagger.

The first time I saw the Who I thought they were lunatics. I loved watching them on the Smothers Brothers show, smashing their instruments and stalking off the stage like they could care less what anybody in America or anyplace else thought of them. Of course, in this new upside-down counterculture that was exactly the right attitude to have if you wanted to sell a lot of records.

It was almost like a mathematical formula…multiply the band’s talent times the amount of dismay on your parents’ faces and you could get a good idea how successful the group would be (at least in the short term).

Of course, there were also dozens of second-tier groups who often had more hair than creative energy.

There was a definite pattern to follow… you get together four or five people, write at least one good song and call yourselves something surrealistic like Moby Grape, Iron Butterfly or the Strawberry Alarm Clock. Then sell enough records so you can get booked on a variety or talk show and play in front of a screen filled with psychedelic images. Then sell some more records.

I always thought it would have been funny if a group had called itself the Lawrence Welkomwagon. They could have done songs like “I Hate Champagne Bubbles” or “Getting It On With the Lennon Sisters”.

Rock music was starting to change the way young people looked at the world. We began to realize weird was fun. There had always been a small segment of the population who felt that way but now the philosophy was spreading far and wide.

Pink Floyd puts a picture of a milk cow on their album cover? Sure, why not. The Beach Boys used an electro-theremin on “Good Vibrations”? Hey, that’s cool. I like music that makes me feel kind of strange. Alice Cooper is a guy? Wow, that is freaky but I guess if I like the music I can live with it.

I was fascinated by album covers. There were so many provocative ones.

The Stones had Their Satanic Majesties Request and the infamous Sticky Fingers cover. The Velvet Underground's debut album simply featured Andy Warhol's painting of a banana on a white background. Santana went both sensual and spiritual with the cover of Abraxis. Frank Zappa and the Mothers of Invention joked around with Weasels Ripped My Flesh.

During the early 70's I was particularly taken by the first two Blue Oyster Cult albums covers. I was young and naïve enough to think maybe this music actually was being produced by a mysterious cult of some kind. The black and white covers depict mysterious objects, one out in space and the other some kind of tower sending out waves of some kind. They looked like illustrations from some obscure black magic text.

I actually became a pretty big BOC fan years later. I saw them play three or four times in Seattle. They were amazingly loud, in fact the last time I saw them I think the volume caused me to hallucinate a little bit.

Like pretty much every other act, over time the venues they played at got smaller and less glamorous. They went from stadiums to theatres and then casinos and finally county fairs. One day you're on top of the world with "Don't Fear the Reaper" and thirty years later you find yourself on an outdoor stage asking the farmers and 4-H members of Grant County if they're ready to rock.

Actually, county fairs aren't even the worst gigs. One time in Seattle I went to a club to see the singer-songwriter Elliott Murphy play. There were only ten people there and two of them were the bartenders. I have to give Elliott credit, though... he didn't pout and he graciously thanked the tiny audience for coming out that night.

I watched Dick Clark every Saturday on American Bandstand. He had on every kind of pop, rock, soul and funk act. It was interesting to watch the groups and the studio audience change through the years. The hair got longer and the skirts grew shorter.

As time went on, Clark definitely started to seem more and more out of sync with what was going in the culture. He was like a capitalist robot.

If a singer or a group was selling records, he liked them and said he hoped they'd have a lot of success. Hitler and the SS would have been welcome on that show as long as their latest single "Fatherland Blues" kept moving up the charts.

Things were changing quickly and most Americans were having a hard time getting their bearings. Especially the kids.

Chapter 24: Paranoid

The media of the mid and late Sixties began to obsess about the burgeoning drug culture spreading throughout the country. There were more and more reports about it in magazines, newspapers and on the evening television news.

One of the amazing things about television was how it could pull you into humanity's shared consciousness. Or at least the country's shared consciousness.

Other forms of media had done this to some extent in the past but now you had a magic box sitting in your living room, ready at a moment's notice to put you next to a soldier walking through the jungles of Vietnam or an astronaut during a space launch or a zonked out kid on a street corner in Haight-Ashbury.

It always tickled me how these apparently straight-laced reporters in their blue suits and white dress shirts would approach drug users and other counterculture folks. They almost sounded like English explorers making contact with some kind of lost tribe. You almost expected to hear them say something like, “Doctor Feelgood, I presume?”.

The kids (if they were reasonably coherent) genuinely seemed to enjoy messing with them. The reporter with the sport coat and slicked back hair would stick their microphone in the hippie’s face and cautiously ask where they were from and what being high was like.

Sometimes the kid would pull out a joint and try to get the newshound to experience it for himself. Or he would give some rambling diatribe that made the prose and puns of Alice in Wonderland sound like the height of seriousness.

I always thought it would have been funny if they’d pulled the same thing with big-time celebrity alcoholics. Yeah, go ahead and ask Frank Sinatra how he feels after he gulps down five martinis. Hey, Richard Burton, do you ever wonder if drinking a fifth of Scotch a day might be harmful to your health?

Of course, these guys probably wouldn’t stand for that line of questioning. Frank would call a guy he knows and have you whacked. Richard would punch you in the bloody face, drink some more Scotch and then go either marry or divorce Elizabeth Taylor again.

The ironic thing for us was that drugs (as far as I knew) weren't a big problem yet where we lived. But there were all these people on t.v. warning us about them and it made you kind of curious.

At first it all seemed kind of terrifying. You would hear stories in the media about people who took the wrong drug, had a bad trip and were never quite right in the head again. Or maybe they got high and hallucinated they had wings and ended up falling out a tenth story window. There were lots of rumors and exaggerations and hysteria.

Of course, the hysteria had begun roughly thirty years earlier, not long after Prohibition ended. Harry Anslinger, then America's commissioner of the Federal Bureau of Narcotics, ranted that "Marijuana is as dangerous as a coiled rattlesnake … how many murders, suicides … and deeds of maniacal insanity it causes each year, especially among the young, can be only conjectured".

I've been on the planet over fifty years and have yet to witness any deeds of maniacal insanity performed by a person high on marijuana.

However, I have seen people get stoned and eat entire boxes of Captain Crunch without milk while laughing way too hard about an old Mr. Ed episode where he decides he wants to re-decorate his stall in a Hawaiian theme.

And it seemed like the harder the government and the media worked to discourage young people from getting involved with drugs, the more attractive the whole thing seemed.

The "Dragnet" drug episodes were downright hilarious. If you were a kid, would you want to be a groovy dope smoker or Joe Friday, a repressed cop who probably hadn't enjoyed himself since that one night with the Filipino hooker during WW2? Even when I was ten years old I sensed that old Joe probably spent too many lonely evenings contemplating eating his gun.

The shows eventually even showed their heroes taking drugs, albeit not by choice. I remember watching an episode of Mod Squad where one of the heroes got kidnapped and turned into a heroin junkie.

The episode really freaked me out… I'd never even smelled marijuana but now I had to worry about the possibility a heroin dealer might someday pull me into an alley, plunge a needle into my arm and transform me into a desperate, hollow-eyed addict who would do anything for his next fix.

I could have probably used a little more supervision when it came to television. Life is hard enough without those kind of worries.

Of course, after a while everything becomes more familiar and less frightening.

There was a recurring segment on the television show "Laugh-In" where the cast and guest stars were supposed to be at a party of some sort. I always got the feeling half the people in front of the camera were stoned to some degree.

Years after the show went off the air, Dick Martin told Entertainment Weekly there were seven pot jokes in the pilot episode alone but the network censors didn't catch them because they weren't hip enough to understand the references.

One winter my friends and I built a snow fort out on the school playground. It gradually started to melt down and turn into a pile of dirty snow and ice. We came up with a game called "LSD party".

Well, it wasn't really a game. We were just imagining what it would be like to trip on acid. I remember waving my arms and yelling, "I'm a banana! I'm a banana! Please don't peel me!".

I don't know if the previous generation ever played "drunk party". I kind of doubt it.

I always thought it was funny when people talked about "acid rock". Most folks erroneously thought this was music that was so ferocious and crazy it would literally turn your brain to mush.

Originally the term just meant music it was fun to listen to when you were high, especially if you had taken acid (LSD). If an entire side of a record consisted of one song, there was a good chance this is what the artists had in mind. Either that or they weren't very prolific songwriters and they put a lot of filler on their records.

I think a lot of parents worried that exposure to long guitar solos might end up sending their children to the state mental institution. Nonsensical lyrics were also a potential danger... be on the lookout for surrealism and non sequiturs!!

Of course, there were also bands that deliberately filled the soft rock niche. The Moody Blues were interesting because they were exploring psychedelic themes but still playing gentle, romantic music for the most part. Visiting Timothy Leary on a Tuesday afternoon, if you will.

I always thought the group Bread's advertising slogan should have been "they play rock, but you know, not acid rock". They were a band you could bring home to meet your parents.

The occult also started showing up in the pop culture landscape. The film "Rosemary's Baby" was a sensation. I remember looking at an article in Look Magazine where they showed how certain scenes were filmed.

These weren't the funny witches on "Betwitched". This was a coven of Manhattan Satanists drugging poor little Mia Farrow so she could be impregnated by their master. This was pretty dark stuff.

Then the band Black Sabbath came on the scene. The name alone made people uncomfortable.

Of course, this was the band fronted by Ozzy Osbourne. Years later he would end up in reality show hell with his screechy wife, two unpleasant children and a bunch of annoying small dogs.

There was even an occult-themed soap opera on television. Janet and I loved watching "Dark

Shadows". Barnabas Collins and the rest of the assorted werewolves, witches and monsters were so much more fun than the usual shows.

One time when we went to visit aunt Ruth in Portland we made up a game we called "Dark Shadows". We were playing with one of the neighborhood kids down in the basement. We'd turn off the lights and one of us would be a human and the other two would be vampires trying to get them. We scared ourselves silly.

Chapter 25: Everybody Knows This is Nowhere

My dad was a great guy. However, he did have a few faults and one of them was that he lacked travel empathy.

He'd been quite a few places, mostly during World War Two. If you asked him what Paris was like he'd say, "Oh, it's just another city. No big deal." If you asked what skiing in Colorado was like he'd say "Oh, it's just cold. No big deal."

I suppose if he'd been an astronaut and you asked him what the moon was like he would have said, "Oh, it's just another lifeless celestial body circling the Earth. No big deal."

He was like most farmers and ranchers. They generally don't enjoy traveling because when they're away all they do is worry if everything is okay back home on the place. And he really didn't like driving in cities.

I will give him credit on the driving part. He nearly always got lost when we went to Portland but he was willing to disobey the Man Code and ask for directions.

We normally went to Portland and the Oregon coast on our vacations. One year we did drive up through Glacier Park in Montana and on up to Canada. I remember being really scared on the high mountain roads as we drove through Glacier.

He didn't like crowds much and usually did his best to avoid them. A prime example was when we went to the Seattle World's Fair the day after it ended. He was trying to avoid the crowds but still see the buildings. Sort of what you would call a Neutron Bomb vacation, I suppose.

However, his worst crime occurred the summer we were supposed to go to Disneyland.

When I was a kid, it seemed like no place on Earth could possibly be better than Disneyland. It was the place where all your kid dreams would come true. There were rides and spaceships and the Nautilus submarine and parades and all those Disney characters walking around.

I've often thought that pastors and priests would have had more success connecting with American youth back in those days if they had said heaven was basically Disneyland with angels working at the snack bars. Of course, the downside is that we might have ended up with an epidemic of impatient kids jumping off buildings so they could go see Mickey and Pluto.

When our parents told us we were going there, Janet and I must have jumped up and down for two days straight. We drove our parents crazy, asking over and over how soon we'd be leaving for Disneyland.

We were going to drive down. Back then gas was cheap and flying was expensive. We loaded up our silver Pontiac Catalina and headed south into Nevada. It was going to be a long, hot trip due to the fact the car didn't have air conditioning. But Janet and I didn't care... we would have ridden on a stage coach all the way to Anaheim if necessary.

Dad was in kind of a weird mood from the very start of the trip. I think sometimes he had a hard time just relaxing and having fun with us.

Maybe being in a state with legalized gambling was getting to him. I'm sure he had to promise Mom he'd try to get through Nevada without going on a betting bender.

He tended to be kind of a philosophical guy and that was usually fine. But this was one of those times when we needed him to just leave the troubles of the world at home and try to have a good time.

We stopped at Lake Tahoe and he and I went for a walk. At some point he turned to me and said, "Take a good look, son. Someday all this will be gone".

I was too stunned to ask for further details… I'd never seen him do this scary Old Testament prophet routine before and it kind of scared the crap out of me. I didn't know if he was talking about a war or the lake drying up or space aliens taking over the gambling industry in Nevada.

Dad was generally a pessimist about things but he also had a sense of humor. He often told me his philosophy was "hope for the best, plan for the worst". Of course, who could blame him for feeling that way? He'd survived the Depression, World War Two, an abusive father and a divorce.

And being a rancher was no picnic either… one year you're making good money and the next you have a bunch of sick cattle out in the corral and there's a good chance you're gonna lose everything.

Janet and I hated Nevada. This was before the state decided to get "family friendly" and it was really hard to find a place where a kid could go in and use the bathroom. Apparently they were worried that if we even saw a slot machine we'd end up being corrupted for life. Maybe they had to be that strict in order to maintain their arrangement with the other forty-nine non-gambling states.

Our next stop was Salinas, California. We were supposed to stay one night with a couple named Rex and Rhonda. They were old friends of my mom's.

They seemed weird. They both had wrinkled, leathery skin and paid very little attention to me and Janet. I immediately got the sense they saw our visit as some kind of opportunity, maybe a chance to sell Mom and Dad something.

Rex and Rhonda were heavily involved with the John Birch Society. It was an ultra-conservative political organization that saw Communist conspiracies lurking in every aspect of American life, from fluoride in the water to the Civil Right movement.

The organization's influence was probably at its height around the time Barry Goldwater won the 1964 GOP presidential nomination. He wasn't a member but he agreed with a lot of their policies, especially when it came to state's rights.

They seemed particularly obsessed with the subject of race. They drove us down to a local public swimming pool just so they could show our folks how many black children were splashing around in there. I couldn't understand why it made them so angry… you would have thought the pool was full of alligators.

They started trying to recruit Dad. They knew he was politically conservative and figured it wouldn't be that hard to bring him farther to the right and into their organization.

Rex said, "Hey, Bob, we need to get busy and straighten this country out. Everywhere you look there's niggers and spics running around like they have the same rights as you and I do. And you know there are Communists behind the scenes putting them up to it. A lot of Jew Communists."

It was horrible. It was like being trapped at a timeshare presentation being put on by the KKK. I was amazed how much hate that guy could spew in any given thirty second period.

They somehow talked our folks into staying another night and then another. Janet and I were starting to get desperate. We were in California! We were so close to Mickey and Donald and the animatronic talking Lincoln head!

Dad finally told Rex and Rhonda he would think about joining the JBS but wasn't ready to commit to anything at this particular time. They accepted this but then proceeded to finish off our Disneyland dream by telling Dad how horrible traffic and the crowds were down in Anaheim.

Maybe the John Birch Society was against people visiting Disneyland too. After all, this was an organization that one time more or less accused Dwight Eisenhower of being part of a secret Communist conspiracy.

Apparently even winning World War Two and serving in the White House honorably for two terms wasn't enough to ease their suspicions.

I hated Rex and Rhonda. I not only hated how they'd ruined our vacation but also how they'd kept after my dad days on end trying to lure him into their web of hatred and imaginary political plots.

Dad decided we needed to get back and check on the cattle. It was a long, hot, sad drive home. For the next few years whenever I saw a commercial for Disneyland it just seemed like a cruel joke.

Janet and I eventually forgave Dad but I still teased him about it from time to time. I didn't get to Disneyland until I was 26.

Chapter 26: Poor, Poor Pitiful Me

My grandma Leslie passed away in 1968. She'd been living in a nursing home for a while prior to that. It was sad, she had to move there after she fell and broke her hip.

This was the first time I had lost someone I really cared about.

Dad inherited her place and so now we had property on both sides of the Malheur river. I'm sure it aggravated Mitch and Evelyn a great deal that my dad got Leslie's place but they were having trouble managing what little property they already owned.

He and Mom decided we should move into Leslie's house. It was nicer than ours and it was located right next to the highway that ran between Sunnyrock and Brisco. Now if somebody was going to Brisco or even Boise and they wanted to invite us to come along, all they had to stop was on the way and pick us up.

Janet and I were happy to move. We were tired of living at the end of a dirt road. The only thing I would miss would be the sound of the freight trains that ran nearby. I always liked that for some reason.

We went into the sixth grade in September of 1969. It would be a great year for me.

We had a young, attractive teacher named Mrs. Peirce. She was only about 25 or 26. I immediately had a crush on her.

Our class was considered the “smart” one because we’d gotten the highest scores on some reading test all the kids had been given a couple years previously.

Human nature being what it is, we were quick to accept the idea we were just a bit better than the kids in the other two sixth grade classes.

Over the course of the school year, several of us coupled up. I had a girlfriend named Sherry. She was tall, shy and pretty.

Our “romance” wasn’t very serious. I think we mostly ended up together because three of my friends (Stan Larsen, Robert Targen and Ronnie Felson) were going steady with three of her friends and they all wanted Sherry and I to be a couple so the eight of us could hang out together.

Everything was very pleasant and we all felt very cool. We were smug little elitists secure in our sixth grade superiority.

But the first day of Middle School (seventh and eighth grade) quickly gave my friends and I a new perspective on things. The eighth graders were hungry to dish out the same kind of misery they 'd suffered the previous year.

It was a real slap in the face for me and my friends. We were used to thinking of ourselves as being sort of special. Now we had bigger, older kids slamming us up against lockers and screaming in our faces.

The teachers didn't intervene much. There was a long and proud tradition of hazing in Sunnyrock.

I think some adults felt like this behavior helped toughen our athletes emotionally and contributed to our amazing high school football win-loss record over the years.

We didn't have a Pop Warner league or anything similar in our area so Seventh grade was the first year I could play football.

The first practice was pretty traumatic for me. I was nervous and couldn't get the football pants to button correctly. When we were doing the warm-up drills I had to use one hand to hold them up, making for some very awkward looking jumping jacks.

And it was hot. I was used to 95 degree weather but I'd never experienced it exercising while wearing a football uniform before. I was sweating before I got out of the locker room.

Our coach was named Mr. Griffin. I'm pretty sure he was an ex-Marine. He kind of looked like Robert DeNiro with a crew cut and when he got mad his face would turn an angry shade of red. You know, like Satan.

He assembled the seventh graders in a big circle and started yelling at us.

"Welcome to football, fellas. The eighth graders can tell you I expect a lot. We're gonna work really hard out here. We're gonna run and then we're gonna run some more and then we're gonna hit those sleds. And then guess what? We're gonna run some more."

"Somehow I have to get you miserable lumps of dough into some kind of shape. If you want to play football for me, you're gonna have to work harder than you've ever worked before. You're gonna start by giving me a one hundred and ten percent effort and then we'll raise the bar from there. It's my hope that you'll all be sore as shit tomorrow morning."

"Right now you look like a bunch of little girls dressed up in football uniforms. Maybe after you sweat and bleed and puke a little, you'll start to resemble a goddamn football team."

This was him, calm. What really scared everybody was when he would get frustrated with us and start grabbing people by the face masks and throwing them around. Then he would get in their face and launch into a tirade unlike anything I'd ever seen before.

He was the meanest adult I'd come across up to that point in my life. He never smiled and he always looked at us like we were stuff he'd wipe off the bottom of his shoe.

We'd all start to get kind of depressed during our last class of the day. The girls and non-football players all seemed so carefree, looking forward to walking out into the bright autumn sunshine and enjoying their hours of freedom after school was done for the day.

The football players (for the most part) sat at their desks and anxiously watched the clock on the wall count down the minutes left until our next two and a half hour torture session.

I'll admit I had probably been a bit sheltered. I'd never been in trouble much and I wasn't all that used to being yelled at. Occasionally Dad might yell at me if I was spacing out while we were working with the cattle but that was about it. I never knew that being a good kid might eventually prove to be a detriment.

The assistant coaches weren't so bad. You could at least ask them a question without worrying if you'd survive the experience. I got the impression they were both pretty intimidated by Mr. Griffin.

The formula I'd always lived by was that adults yelled at kids who did bad things... now I was dealing with adults who yelled at you for not doing something correctly. Or just yelled at you because that's how you turn a bunch of goofy, spoiled kids into some kind of cohesive athletic team.

He coached to win. If you happened to have fun while playing for him it was purely an accident.

As the days went by we learned how to tackle, block, catch passes and deal with pain. Rule number one of dealing with pain was to not talk about it.

We ran wind sprints, did the three man roll coordination exercise and pushed the blocking sled hour after hour after hour. One especially muggy afternoon I puked before I could get my helmet off.

After the first couple weeks I was feeling pretty miserable. Every part of my body ached. Both my arms were covered with bruises.

I sat down to dinner one evening and started complaining about how Coach Griffin was treating us. My dad looked at me and said, "Well, if you don't like it you should quit".

I was stunned. First the horror of football practice and now I was being betrayed by my own father. I said, "I don't want to quit. I was just telling you what the practices are like."

He replied, "I don't want to hear it. You need to make up your mind... either toughen up and act like a football player or get off the team. Whining about it isn't an option."

I staggered off to my room after dinner. I lay on my bed and stared at the ceiling, trying to sort out my feelings. Apparently I had never really understood how much hard work and self-discipline playing football would require. This was a situation that required a gut check.

It was strange... the next few days I didn't hate practice quite so much. The exercises were still exhausting and the hits still hurt and I actually saw stars one time but now I felt like I was there by choice. Dad had given me the option to quit but I'd chosen to tough it out.

I was reasonably big and athletic and about three games into the season the coach put me in as a starter on the defensive line. I had a decent season and the experience boosted my confidence a lot.

Mr. Griffin was the head coach for all the boys' Middle school sports. He had a rule that seventh graders had to go through a four-week wrestling program before they were allowed to be on the basketball team. I guess he wanted to expose everybody to both sports since joining the wrestling team would actually be an option in High School.

At the end of the four weeks we had a tournament. Fortunately, I was assigned to wrestle my old buddy Stan Larsen. We both hated wrestling so we agreed to just go through the motions well enough to satisfy Mr. Griffin's requirements.

Mr. Griffin also taught the Health classes for boys. We had a textbook that covered all kinds of teen-age issues, everything from acne to unintended pregnancy. One chapter was about dating and it featured a cartoon with a teenage boy saying, "Oh my gosh, I can't believe what a boner I pulled". We all thought that was the funniest thing we'd ever seen.

Right after basketball season started, a new kid moved to town. He was six four and we were all really excited about how much he might help the team. His name was Brenton Samms.

Unfortunately, his growth had far outpaced his agility. He couldn't seem to make any kind of shot consistently. But that didn't stop him from thinking he would be the star of the team.

He also had a bit of a speech impediment, the kind that makes people say the letter "w" instead of the letter "r". He told us an easy way to remember his name was by thinking of England. We asked him why and he got a big, goofy grin on his face and replied "Gweat Bwenton".

Chapter 27: All We Have is Now

The team bus dropped me off at home after a basketball game in December of 1969. I saw our minister's van parked in our driveway. I didn't remember him ever having come out to our house before.

When I walked in, I saw him standing in the living room comforting my mom and dad. Janet was in her room.

It turned out my mom's cancer was back. It had spread to her colon. She was scheduled for surgery in a few days. My parents were trying to be brave but it was obvious they were both devastated.

I lay in bed that night thinking about how unreal life suddenly seemed. All I had ever wanted was a normal childhood. Now the harsh reality of my mother's condition threatened to plunge our whole family into a nightmare.

The next morning I woke up feeling good. Then I remembered what had transpired the night before and my heart sank.

My mom's illness was like a cloud that would block out the sun no matter where I stood.

Chapter 28: The Seeker

My mom began her chemo treatments and the rest of us just did our best to maintain a positive attitude and comfort her. I could tell the situation was taking a heavy toll on my dad. He was a lot more quiet than usual and I often saw him staring off into the distance, obviously worrying about what might lay ahead for our family.

We got a lot of support from the folks at our church and other people in the area. My aunt Ruth came down and stayed with us from time to time. It was easy for her since she didn't have a job or little kids to worry about. I think it especially helped Janet that Ruth was spending time with us.

But I also began to understand that no matter what's happening in your life, the world continues to spin and life goes on. The rest of humanity is being born, going to school, working, retiring and dying. No matter how special you might think you are or how tragic your circumstances might seem, you're just one soul among the billions.

At this particular point in time, humanity in America was busy having a loud discussion about change.

I think it's hard for younger people today to appreciate how different things were when I was growing up.

I realize every generation makes statements like that. But in terms of how we looked at each other and the resulting social repercussions, the 60's and 70's were a social earthquake. Things were happening fast and once repressed groups were suddenly finding the courage to stand up for themselves.

Blacks, Latinos, Asians, Native Americans, women, gays, disabled people and a host of other groups all asserting their rights and demanding fair treatment.

You can hear about it in a History or Sociology class but sometimes that paints a picture that seems dry and distant.

During the first ten to fifteen years people had televisions, the medium basically just reflected the white, heterosexual viewpoint. White men were in charge, white women supported them, racial minorities knew their place, disabled people didn't complain and gays would be tolerated as long as they didn't have sex and hated themselves.

Even the silly sitcoms perpetuated this hierarchy... Wally and the Beaver living in their seemingly perfect suburban neighborhood. Rob and Laura Petrie sleeping in separate beds. The jokey sexism of I Dream of Jeannie.

But society was changing and television started to reflect that. It was slow at first but then they started spreading ideas that helped break down the old barriers.

For example, the population of my little town was nearly all white and race never seemed to be much of an issue (at least as far as I knew). But we all had televisions and got exposed to the same shows that generated discussions everywhere else in the country. The sitcoms and dramas were far more effective at changing attitudes than any news documentary would have been.

My dad and I always watched "All in the Family" together. It wasn't just a television show... it was a weekly challenge to most people's prejudices and pre-conceived notions.

Archie Bunker (the main character) wasn't a cross-burning Klansman. He was just a regular white guy who lived in the Northeast. He went through life assuming he was just a little bit better than anybody who differed from him racially, sexually or religiously.

In other words, he represented a huge chunk of the American population.

Dad and I would discuss the show after an episode ended. I always looked forward to that almost as much as the show itself.

It wasn't like an "official" discussion time. Maybe he would ask me what I thought about whatever issue came up on this week's episode. Or sometimes I would just put an opinion out there and see how he reacted to it.

I was starting to develop some moderate political opinions and he considered himself a Goldwater conservative.

Looking back, I think that meant he believed in low taxes, a strong military and the right to be racist as long as you more or less kept it to yourself and didn't actually harm anyone. Kind of like the Republican version of "Don't Ask, Don't Tell".

But I gave him credit for at least talking about the issues with me. He never demanded that I think the way he did... he wanted me to form my own opinions, even if they ended up being somewhat different than his.

The show also caused me to at least stop and think about the racist and sexist jokes I laughed at along with the rest of my friends. And some prejudices were more resilient than others. I would need to live several more years and move to a more urban culture before I could even consider the possibility that gay people were just born that way and weren't making a choice.

Archie Bunker and the other characters on the show opened the door and suddenly primetime was filled with thought-provoking shows that not only made you think but also laugh out loud.

I always thought George Jefferson was a pretty remarkable character. He was black and smart and far from perfect. In fact, he was downright unpleasant most of the time.

We'd gone from bad black stereotypes to good black stereotypes (see Sidney Poitier) and were now being presented with a flawed, complicated, intelligent human being. What a concept!

The main character on the Mary Tyler Moore was another big step forward. She lived alone, she had a good job, she dated and I always assumed if one of her fellas appeared on multiple episodes then they were sleeping together.

I had a weird habit of imagining what went on in television character's lives between episodes. Not all of them (that would have been exhausting) but just certain ones I really liked a lot. For example, I didn't think about Jed Clampett spending an afternoon out whittling by the cement pond or Mannix shopping for a new gun.

Mary Richards lived for Mary Richards. She wasn't Samantha Stevens sitting at home waiting to make Darrin's nightly martini. Or the gals in Mayberry that you just knew only worked because they weren't married yet.

I could see the sexism in my own little world. Girls had almost no sports programs at my school and couldn't wear pants.

I also loved "Room 222". It was about a black guy who teaches history at a Los Angeles high school. I really considered becoming a history teacher for a while, especially if I could count on all my students being groovy.

When I was younger, I just listened to Dad and assumed all his opinions represented the undeniable truth. Now I was actually starting to think for myself and disagreeing with him once in a while.

Some fathers and sons share a passion for fly fishing and others share a love of golf. We shared a fondness for driving around in our old dirty pickup and arguing about how the country should be run.

My literary and film interests really matured that first year of Middle school.

I liked reading the newspaper and I'd see all the provocative ads for movies playing over in Boise. It was even more exciting when we'd go to visit Ruth and Lloyd in Portland and I could check out the Oregonian's movie listings.

I was so curious about films like MASH, Barbarella and Brewster McCloud. The ads were so intriguing and there was all this symbolism I didn't understand.

I wondered why the one for MASH (a war movie) had a hand holding a peace sign and it was connected to two sexy female legs in high heels. What kind of soldiers were these? What kind of war was this?

I had so many questions...what was Andy Warhol's "Frankenstein" about? Was it scary or just weird? Who was Andy Warhol?

These movies even started to present counterculture characters in a more sympathetic way. Bikers had always been pictured as crazed marauders who wanted nothing more than to rob you and rape your girlfriend. Peter Fonda and Dennis Hopper in "Easy Rider" weren't model citizens but on the other hand they were a whole lot less threatening than the one-dimensional psychos presented in the earlier movies.

There seemed to be a artistic shift that said not everything was black and white, right and wrong. Sometimes you ran into gray areas.

I read as many movie reviews as possible so I could find out what all these amazing, forbidden R and X rated movies were about. "Parents" magazine was an especially good source of information. I'd go to the public library in Brisco at least once a month and check out what they had to say about the new releases.

I was amused later in life when I saw some of these movies at college or on TV and realized how tame (and sometimes lame) they actually were. But, as someone once said, everything is relative.

I was always interested in popular culture and what it had to say about the country and the world in general.

When I was nine I had a letter published in the Boise newspaper's TV supplement. I was defending superhero cartoons like Space Ghost and Jonny Qwest because I had heard on the news some group had said the shows were too violent for children.

It must have been a reasonably coherent letter. I ended up receiving a reply from an adult who thought I was old enough to bother arguing with.

Occasionally I actually got to see a film that stimulated my burgeoning sex drive. My friend Robert invited me to go see "Butch Cassidy and the Sundance Kid". The scene at the beginning where Katherine Ross is partially undressed practically made me break out in a sweat. I kept wondering if there was any way we could stick around and sit through that scene again during the next showing.

A couple years later, Stan Larsen and I managed to sneak in to see "The Godfather". It was another big step in my cinematic sexual education. Katherine Ross removing her corset was small change compared to James Caan and his horny bridesmaid going at it standing up.

It was always exciting when you'd go to a G-rated movie and they'd show a preview of something with a more mature subject matter. One time Janet and I went to see "The Odd Couple".

The film “Wild in the Streets” was of the movies featured in the coming attractions.

It was more or less just a silly teen exploitation film but I was just naïve enough to believe the events in it could happen any minute.

The plot is about what happens to the country after the voting age is lowered to fifteen. The kids eventually make thirty the mandatory retirement age and anyone older than thirty-five is sent to a re-education camp.

I was especially mesmerized by the scene showing members of Congress trying to conduct business while high on LSD.

One film from that era I’ve always felt was overlooked is “Cold Turkey”. It starred Dick Van Dyke, Bob Newhart, Tom Poston and a lot of other fine comedic actors. It was a satire about what happens when a tobacco company offers a 25 million dollar prize to any small town that can give up smoking for thirty days.

It was a pretty radical film considering the power of the tobacco industry at that time and the fact cigarettes had always been a prominently used prop in Hollywood.

The movie stated in no uncertain terms that smoking was physically addictive and that there was no level the tobacco companies and their P.R. people wouldn’t stoop to in order to keep people hooked. It was way ahead of its time… smart, cynical and subversive.

I also found myself drawn to books about more mature subjects. I started getting into Kurt Vonnegut. I didn't always understand what he was talking about but I loved the way he wrote and the way he exposed hypocrisy and foolishness.

I was fascinated by the "Slaughter-house Five" concept that declared all the moments of your life are happening simultaneously. You might be making toast in the present but you're losing your virginity in the past and meeting your new grandson for the first time in the future...

I especially liked the fact Vonnegut created Kilgore Trout, his marginally talented science-fiction writer alter-ego. It just seemed like just a cool idea.

I was also very moved by Arthur C. Clarke's novel "Childhood's End". My religious upbringing always taught me all that really mattered was the relationship between God and humans. But here was a novel that said we were just another form of life and if we disappeared the universe would get along just fine without us.

Claude Brown's "Manchild in the Promised Land" exposed me to the hard lives of black kids growing up in the ghetto. This wasn't "Julia" or "Fat Albert"... this was pimps and whores and having nothing to eat because your mom is out trying to find some heroin.

I found a used book store and started hanging out there whenever possible. I always told my parents I was looking for science-fiction novels but more often than not I was fervently thumbing through books looking for sex scenes. It seemed like a good way to educate myself.

Actually, I think Dad would have probably been relieved to know I was in there reading about sex. He really had no use for science-fiction.

Recently published Westerns actually had some great sex scenes in them. There was usually just one about halfway through the novel, I guess kind of an intermission between gunfights. I could usually locate it in under a minute.

During one visit to my brother Roger's I discovered a copy of "The Happy Hooker". I would sneak upstairs every so often, devour a chapter or two of Xaveria Hollander's sexy memoir and then rejoin the rest of the family downstairs. It was kind of fun knowing Roger really couldn't get mad at me since it was his book.

Being a thirteen year old sex maniac really helps you develop your acting abilities.

Chapter 29: (Don't Fear) the Reaper

We lost Ranger the summer after seventh grade.

On the night of the Fourth of July, Janet and I were shooting off bottle rockets and apparently at some point he got scared and ran out on the highway.

We discovered him the next morning. It was the saddest day I'd ever experienced up to that point in my life… I felt so bad we'd caused him to panic. We hadn't even considered how he might react to the fireworks.

To be honest, when we moved to the house by the highway we should have found a new home for Ranger. He needed room to roam and it wasn't a big surprise he'd run out into traffic.

He'd been a good and loyal friend to all of us and it felt like his passing was a hole in our lives that could never be filled. But it was nothing compared to the pain waiting for us in the not too distant future.

The next few months Mom's health continued to decline. I could tell she was getting a little weaker every day. We all made an effort to stay optimistic but it was obvious she was losing the battle.

Our church decided to put together a directory that would contain pictures, names, addresses and telephone numbers for all the families and single individuals in the congregation. We went to the church on a bitterly cold Sunday afternoon in January.

Mom was feeling pretty miserable but she wanted to get this family picture done while she still had the strength.

It's so strange to pose for a picture like that. We all knew it was the last one that would be taken of our full family. Nobody's really smiling in the picture… it's a pretty accurate representation of what we were all feeling at the time.

The cancer had continued to spread and the radiation treatments had aged her a lot. We knew she wouldn't be with us much longer. She finally went in to the hospital for the last time.

She told Janet and I to take good care of Dad. I felt so bad for her, she'd been through so much pain the past few years.

She died in mid-February of 1971. She was 52.

I heard years later that she and Rick the Italian had lived in the Tri-Cities area for a while back in the 40's. That's where the Hanford nuclear plant was located. They both died of cancer… maybe they were exposed to radiation at some point. Maybe a lot of people were.

Or maybe the cancer cells had always been in her, waiting for the right time to start connecting and spreading and laying waste to this woman I loved so much.

I feel bad I can't tell you more about her. It's due to the fact I can't really recall much about her. I'm not sure why this is.

I have different theories, my favorite being that my mind made a secret deal with my emotions… the pain of losing her would be lessened if most memories of her were blocked or wiped away.

But that's just a theory. I also have a theory that losing her at this young age greatly contributed to the depression problems I would experience later in life. My brain is full of theories that can't be proved or disproved.

I remember her comforting me when I was very small and chastising me for being overly sensitive when I got older. I think she worried sometimes people were going to take advantage of me if I didn't toughen up some.

I remember loving the taste of pretty much everything she ever cooked and how good she was about helping out folks who were having a hard time one way or another. She was nice to our animals and patient with Dad.

Years later I would sometimes think about the moments we'd been cheated out of experiencing together. My graduating from high school and college, my getting married, my introducing her to a new stepson.

It all seemed so unreal. I wanted to cry so badly at the funeral but no matter how I tried, the tears wouldn't come. There seemed to be a part of my psyche that refused to recognize that she was gone forever.

I got a raw deal. I didn't cry at the funeral but I felt that emotional pressure in my head at some point pretty much every day for the rest of my life.

I was very touched by something my grandmother Anna said at the graveside service. She made the comment "no mother should ever have to go through the pain of burying their own child".

When Janet and I went back to school, everybody was really nice to us. I think a lot of the kids were unsure what to say or how to say it. But I was surprised how many at least made an effort. I think it shook up a few and maybe they started to wonder how they would manage if suddenly they lost one of their parents. Janet and I were just normal kids… this was living proof it could happen to anyone.

Even Mr. Griffin told me he was sorry for my loss. That was a shock. I really appreciated him dropping the tough guy stance for once.

Not long after the funeral we discovered how Dad was going to deal with his grief.

He really, really liked to gamble. He usually worked in the morning and played Pinochle in the afternoon. Sometimes the afternoon started around 10 a.m.

I'd heard rumors over the years he'd been involved in some really high-stakes games. He and Mom had fought about his card playing a lot.

After she died, Dad went on a gambling bender. He would still work in the mornings but then he would head to town and play cards from noon until midnight.

I guess that's how he dealt with his grief. He needed something else to focus on and when he looked at us I think it just made him think about Mom and how badly he missed her.

We didn't have to sell any land or extra cattle so I assumed he was winning or at least staying even. I was happy about that at least.

I worried about him. He looked exhausted and I could tell his nerves were shot from the endless hours of playing cards. I asked him if everything was okay and he said yes but that didn't comfort me much.

Janet and I more or less took care of ourselves. We were used to it since Mom had been in the hospital or sick in bed so much the past few months.

Our aunt Ruth continued to come stay with us from time to time and the people from our church were good about checking if we needed anything.

That first summer after Mom died felt really strange. Dad was gone most of the time and neither Melody or I could drive yet so we spent a lot of time watching games shows and Star Trek re-runs. We especially liked the Match Game and Hollywood Squares because the featured actors and comedians were always joking around. Sometimes the game and the contestants almost seemed sort of irrelevant.

I became a big Tonight Show fan. I especially liked it when he had Burt Reynolds on and they got real silly.

I felt bad for myself and even worse for Janet. There had been some tension between she and our mother toward the end. Mom had hurriedly been trying to give her some training so she could help Dad run the house after Mom was gone. There were times when Janet was stubborn and Mom was impatient and things got pretty loud between them.

After a couple months, Dad seemed to relax a bit. He got the card playing under control and the three of us settled into the next phase of our lives together.

Chapter 30: Calling Elvis

I always felt kind of uneasy around my half-brother Roger when I was growing up. He wasn't a bad guy but he did seem to have some emotional blindspots.

It just seemed like he was talking at me, not with me.

And he's always assumed that since he's older than me he should always be giving me advice. Ironically, I don't remember ever once having asked for it.

Maybe I was the problem. Maybe I was supposed to be asking him for advice about stuff and upset the natural order of things by not doing so. Not fulfilling my end of the unspoken older brother-younger brother contract.

The problem was I decided at a pretty early age that maybe he wasn't necessarily qualified to be giving me or anybody else advice, at least about how to manage your personal life. He was married four times by the time he was forty.

That seemed like a bad thing to me. Maybe movie stars could get away with it but Roger was just an ordinary guy and I thought it was strange he couldn't figure out how to stay married.

He'd helped conceive three sons (one with each of the first three wives). His M.O. was to marry the women, get them pregnant and then leave once the baby was born. I never really understood why he did this… maybe he suffered panic attacks when the responsibility got to be too much. Or maybe he just refused to share his women with another male.

The fourth marriage stuck. Maybe it was because he never got her pregnant. Or maybe at that point in his life he was just too tired to go through the whole sad process again.

He was living in Portland during the 60's. He was just old enough that he ended up on the reactionary conservative side of that decade's culture wars.

He wore his dark black hair slicked back like Elvis, drove a big red Cadillac and got a Doberman Pinscher to guard his house. He loved the song "Okie from Muskogee" and telling people even Bill Cosby wouldn't rent apartments to black people.

Surprisingly, he did support the Palestinian cause. He'd been friends with one back when he was going to college.

His first marriage was to Cookie the dance instructor. I never knew much about his second wife and his third wife was named Maria. She was an attractive Mexican-American cocktail waitress who wore spidery looking false eyelashes and chain smoked Benson and Hedges 100's. She'd actually grown up in a town down near Sunnyrock.

Maria was always very nice to us. I did get the feeling she was a bit high-strung but on the other hand I understood how Roger could drive people crazy.

When she got mad at him she would start out speaking English but then drift into what I liked to call "buzzsaw Spanish".

She got pregnant in 1976. They split up not long after she gave birth. He married his fourth wife in the 80's and moved to Spokane.

One fond memory I have is of Roger coming to see me participate in a talent show in high school. A group of us lip-synched "The Loco-Motion" by Grand Funk Railroad. I remember several people coming up to me later and asking if I was related to that "Elvis guy" sitting in the audience.

He was always touting a new get-rich scheme but he normally worked as a waiter in upscale restaurants. He loved to brag about the time he got a hundred dollar tip from the pro basketball player Wilt Chamberlain. I guess he didn't mind black celebrities.

You could tell he wasn't happy with the career he ended up in. But instead of taking the boring but necessary step of going to school he obsessed on finding investors who would bankroll his big ideas.

One time it was renovating an old boarded-up Sunnyrock hotel. Another time he was all revved up to go make his fortune in Australia. There were many different plans and his sales pitch to my dad invariably began with an anecdote about having met some guy who got rich overnight or how he read a book that convinced him you should do what you love and not just work for the money.

Dad was always nice to him and acted interested but (as far as I know) never gave him a cent for his schemes.

The dreams came and went and he actually did try to open a restaurant down near Brisco but that didn't go too well. Paying for the different schemes thru the years must have taken a toll on his finances because he's almost 70 now and as far as I know is still working as a waiter.

One thing he never lost his passion for was Sunnyrock football.

When I was a senior, he came for a visit. The last day of practice before school started in September, the coaches had a scrimmage game and sometimes alumni came back to town and participated. Roger heard about it from one of his old cronies and was eager to suit up and pretend it was 1958 again.

"Hey, Jimmy. Won't it be great when I get out there with you guys and smash some heads? I can't wait."

He's always called me Jimmy. I'm 53 now and he still calls me that.

The voice inside my head was saying no, no this is too weird. He needs to be stopped somehow. I just want to be part of the crowd and blend in. I don't want to play next to a guy who went to high school before anybody heard of the Beatles.

For some strange reason I was mortified by the idea of my 34-year old sibling coming out and knocking heads with us. Part of it was probably normal teenage anxiety and part of it was me wanting him to grow up and start acting his age. I pleaded and pleaded with him not to do it and he finally relented.

He really loved Dad. Roger kind of fell apart at my father's funeral in 2004 and after the service I took him aside to console him. Dad may not have invested in Roger's schemes but he was always willing to listen and support him any other way.

Of course, two days later Roger was giving me unwanted advice on the best way to sell Dad's property. I just wanted to use a Sunnyrock real estate agent I'd known my entire life but Roger kept insisting I let him contact some guy down in

California who could put together some kind of amazing deal. Roger wasn't in the will but he figured he'd help me out.

I said fine, go ahead and call your buddy. I figured what could it hurt?

Of course, I also went ahead and enlisted the aid of the local guy. I knew exactly what would happen… I would never hear anything more from Roger about the California guy and I sure wasn't going to just sit around and do nothing about Dad's estate. It takes a while to sell farm land.

It took the Sunnyrock real estate agent three years but he finally got it sold for me.

During the pre-season practices before the start of my sophomore year, I hurt my hip the second day. We weren't even hitting yet, just doing calisthenics and running.

One of the assistant coaches noticed I was running funny. He recommended I go into the locker room and take a whirlpool bath. Unfortunately, he didn't tell me how long to stay in it.

I sat in the hot water for close to an hour and then decided I wanted to get out before the rest of the team came in.

I found getting out of the tub to be really hard. I was pretty dehydrated before I'd got in the tub due to exercising in the 95 degree heat and now the hot water had relaxed my body to the point where I almost felt paralyzed.

Eventually I struggled out of the tub and basically fell on the concrete floor. I was desperate to get my clothes on before the other players returned. I slowly crawled to my locker and then pulled myself up on the bench.

My hip stayed sore for a couple months. I didn't play football that year. I went to see a sports doctor but he couldn't exactly pinpoint what the problem was. He surmised it was probably a combination of growing pains and a badly pulled muscle.

Some of the guys gave me a bad time about it, figuring I was just trying to avoid the rigors of football practice. The two most aggressive were Dave Johnson and Darrin Desmond, two new kids who had attended grade school and junior high at a little country school outside of Sunnyrock. I was never sure why they chose to give me such a bad time.

I figured someday I'd have a chance to pay them back.

Chapter 31: # 9 Dream

I had a strange dream not long after my mother died.

I was walking down a dirt road and the day was sunny and warm. The sky was full of colorful hot air balloons and a few of those big cartoon ones like you see in the Macy's Thanksgiving Day parade.

I could hear happy music playing and off in the distance there was a beautiful blue lake. The sunlight sparkled on the water.

The road was next to an immense green lawn and there were thousands of happy people there, playing and picnicking and enjoying the day.

I saw a few faces I recognized, mostly kids. Some of them looked normal and some looked older. A few even looked elderly. I thought that was so weird.

My mom was there. She was healthy and full of life. She waved me over and we hugged when I went to her.

I told her I knew I'd see her again someday. She said she was glad to see me and that she needed to tell me something very important.

Suddenly, the people on the lawn began disappearing. There was a popping noise each time somebody vanished.

Mom grabbed me by the shoulders and said, "Listen closely. There isn't much time left. I want you to know you're going to live a long time and get to know a lot of people. But you need to be strong because it's so hard to hold on to them".

I started to tell her I didn't understand what she meant but there was a popping noise and she was gone. I couldn't believe it, I'd lost her again.

There was a mad cacophony of popping and then everyone else was gone. I was all alone. Even the balloons were gone from the sky.

I got back on the road and started running but my legs would barely move. The sun set and this dream world went totally black. Then I woke up.

Chapter 32: What Makes You Think You're the One

My dad was always pragmatic. As much as he loved my mom, I always figured he would eventually start dating and more than likely get remarried. He was only 52 when she died and in very good health. I fully expected him to live a long time yet.

This really didn't upset me. I knew one of the main reasons he was considering getting re-married was so my sister and I would have a mother again. He thought it was especially important for Janet at this point in her life.

And I certainly didn't want Dad to be alone… after all, in a few short years my sister and I would be leaving home. I wasn't sure what her plans were but I was planning on getting out in the world and figuring out what I was good at.

I never really thought much about my dad having a sex life. When you're a fourteen or fifteen year old male you're pretty much just focused on your own needs.

Well, focused isn't really the right word... your needs suddenly just take over. It's like your brain is a television set and the Playboy channel is on twenty four hours a day.

You more or less walk around in a hormonal haze, thinking about sex and girls and breasts and halter tops and tight little shorts roughly ninety percent of the time. You're so horny you might get an erection if the wind blows just right.

He was gone a lot of evenings during this time and was a bit vague about what he was doing.

One night during the summer of 1972 he didn't come home until six in the morning. I thought maybe he'd been out at some hardcore all-night card game. But then I saw a motel room receipt on his bedroom dresser.

I was pretty religious at the time. I was going through a weird phase where my body was yelling "Go! Go! Go!" when it came to sex but the Youth Group leader in my head was telling me people shouldn't sleep together unless they're married. Especially if one of them is your surviving parent.

Later that day I confronted Dad about the receipt. He was stunned by my anger but reacted calmly. This was the first time I'd ever yelled at him about anything.

He told me, "I went to Boise with a lady friend of mine and on the way home the car broke down. Fortunately, we were able to get it fixed and get home last night."

I knew he was lying because the car was sitting right out there in the carport and I seriously doubted he'd been able to get the problem fixed sometime between two and five a.m. Not a lot of all-night auto mechanic shops located out there between Brisco and Boise.

I'd been feeling pretty good about the fact Janet and I had been grown up enough to accept the fact Dad would get remarried sometime in the near future. But for some reason I had never considered the possibility that he and the next potential Mrs. Hawthorne would want to take each other out for a test drive.

I eventually calmed down and decided to cut him some slack and try to just forget about it. After all he'd been through the past couple years I felt pretty uncomfortable trying to stay mad at him. He deserved to go out and have a little fun.

Apparently, he took our discussion as a sign it was time to check how I was doing when it came to the birds and the bees. A couple days after I confronted him, he asked if I had any questions about sex.

I knew the basics. As far as anything else goes, I didn't what I didn't know.

He also showed me a newspaper clipping of a flamboyant guy on a float in a Gay Pride parade and asked me if I knew what the term "gay" meant.

I told him I didn't have any questions about heterosexual sex (the kind I planned on having) and knew what the word meant.

I wasn't completely sure why he showed me the gay parade picture. Maybe he was worried that if I wasn't prepared, some guy would try to pick me up someday.

Or maybe he thought that since I mistakenly got on a Mormon float that one time, there was an outside chance I might somehow accidentally end up on a float in San Francisco wearing nothing but a pair of buttless chaps.

I've often thought those Gay Pride parades did a lot of damage public relations-wise. They scared the hell out of older people. They saw those parades on the news and got the idea any gay man they met would be wearing S & M gear or impersonating Liza Minnelli. Any lesbian they met would be topless and riding a Harley.

Not true and not fair but that's how a lot of people felt. People who would vote against gay rights and gay marriage again and again and again during the years to come.

I talked to Janet about Dad dating. Even though we both loved Faye very much, we wanted Dad to be happy and we knew that would involve him finding a new wife. We had a family meeting and told him he had our blessing.

He dated a widow named Marian for a while. She was an old family friend. She and her husband hung out with my mom and dad back in the mid Sixties.

Janet and I were both really comfortable with her. We both remembered spending time at her house when we were younger.

She still seemed really nice and we were rooting for them to get together but for whatever reason the relationship only lasted a couple months. Maybe there wasn't much of a spark since they were old friends.

Then he started dating a woman named Trudy. She seemed pleasant but Dad was concerned about some of her family members, including a developmentally disabled adult son who would be living with us if they got married. I just don't think Dad was up to taking on that challenge so soon after Mom's death.

Eventually he was set up on a blind date with a lady named Nona. Her husband had died a few years ago and she owned a little women's clothing store over in Idaho.

Nona was a little older than Dad but very attractive and stylish. She had two grown children named Russ and Doris. They were both considerably older than Janet and myself so we ended up with two nephews and a niece who were older than us. They were all really nice people.

Dad and Nona were married in a small ceremony at our house in January of 1973. It was officiated by Mick Roberts, the same minister who'd been there to comfort my folks roughly three years earlier.

Mick was somewhat hard of hearing and often got names wrong. He kept calling Nona "Nora" and Janet and I were having a hard time not giggling.

They went to Acapulco on their honeymoon. Nona wasn't prudent about the sun and got a terrible burn that forced her to stay indoors most of the time they were there.

Nona had a tendency to go overboard. Sometimes she'd go on housecleaning binges and work until she was so exhausted she got pneumonia-like symptoms.

And she had quite a lead foot on the highway…a couple years before she and Dad met, she was driving her Mustang to Boise, got going too fast and ended up in a rollover accident that almost killed her. Another time she was late getting to a church social and a state trooper pulled over for going a hundred in her Thunderbird.

When they got back from Mexico, the four of us settled in and tried to create a sense of family. It felt pretty strange.

She did bring a nice, big console color t.v. when she moved in. That was pretty cool. Electronics were not something Dad ever thought about spending money on.

I actually felt kind of sorry for Nona. Teenagers are hard to deal with in the best of circumstances. Taking two of them on as a stepmother had to feel a lot like walking through a minefield blindfolded.

She and I got along okay. She went out of her way to cook things I liked and I appreciated it. She was a really good cook and after enduring my dad's cowboy cuisine for two years it was a treat to eat what she made us.

Teen-age boys are really pretty simple creatures. I had access to a color television and decent food. I was content.

Teen-age girls are far more complicated. They fight older women for freedom and territory and sometimes they don't even know what they're fighting for because their hormones are rushing through them like a herd of cattle headed over a cliff.

I've actually known young women who hope they don't have daughters because they remember the nasty fights they had with their own mothers when they were teen-agers.

Unfortunately, it didn't take long for she and Janet to lock horns. Part of it was the fact that Faye trained Janet to run the household and then Nona came in and started doing things her way. It wasn't anybody's fault... just an unavoidable collision of wills.

Dad did his best to play impartial referee. I did my best to stay out of their squabbles.

After a while I noticed there were things about Nona that got on my nerves too. She seemed to nag my dad a lot about trivial stuff, she had a funny way of chewing her food, she had some gaudy decorating ideas. Nothing all that important but it took some getting used to.

I wasn't completely innocent. Teenagers can be like wolves... once the smell of blood is in the air it's hard not to get caught up in the frenzy, especially when it involves a stepmother or stepfather. You feel like whatever crap you do is justified because by tearing down the new parent you're somehow paying tribute to the old parent.

The first time the four of us went on vacation, Janet and I really started giving Nona a hard time, contradicting her here and there and generally being brats. Just a couple of snickering teen-agers in the backseat doing their best to make an adult feel bad.

Our biggest beef (though not one we actually confronted her about) was how much makeup she wore. In retrospect, it probably wasn't that much but we just weren't used to it. Faye always had a softer, more natural look. We started calling our new stepmother Nozo the Clown behind her back.

We went to the Oregon coast with Roger and his third wife, Maria. One night after dinner, Janet and I went for a walk and when we came back we saw Nona outside the motel having a cigarette.

Oh my God, we were horrified... and also very, very excited. We thought we had caught her doing something terrible behind Dad's back. He'd always hated smoking and it didn't seem possible he would knowingly marry anybody who enjoyed lighting up.

We didn't rush right in and tell him. We kept the info to ourselves for a bit and enjoyed it. We were the Woodward and Bernstein of stepchildren and Smokergate was about to hit the family front page.

How long did this conniving smoky Jezebel think she could lead this double life? We were convinced he would kick her out and the three of us could go back to our uncomplicated smoke-free existence.

Of course, that didn't happen. Later that night we told him what we had seen and he calmly explained that Nona just smoked once in a while and we should give her a break since she'd had to meet a lot of new people on this trip and was probably somewhat stressed out.

We were stunned. Up to this point, we never realized how much he really cared about her.

Chapter 33: Trouble Man

Later that summer, Dad and Nona decided to go visit some friends. Janet wanted to hang out with her friend in Sunnyrock and I asked if I could go up and stay with Roger and Maria in Portland for a few days.

I boarded a Trailways bus and headed north on my big adventure. I was really hungry to get out on my own and prowl around a bit.

I was really getting into music at this point. My income was pretty limited so I tried to buy records that had a lot of different stuff on them.

One was a double album of movie themes and another was a K-Tel record that featured a wide variety of artists including James Brown, the Stylistics and Lobo (singing Me and You and a Dog Named Boo). They packed ten songs on each side of the record so they were pretty much all slightly shortened versions.

The James Brown cut cracked me up. It was either about hot pants or a hot tub or maybe both, I don't really remember.

Top 40 radio was great at that time... there seemed to be very little emphasis on demographics or target audiences (other than maybe in terms of age). We all listened to a Boise station with the call letters KFDX.

It was great. They played songs by everybody from Elton John to Deep Purple to Jerry Jeff Walker. We got exposed to all kinds of stuff and for a kid like me it was a musical education.

I didn't know it was great at the time. That's just the way radio was before everything got divided into specialty stations that only played rap or heavy metal or country or what I always liked to call "secretary rock". I either liked a song or I didn't and I never felt like I had to commit to one genre or another.

One thing we probably shouldn't have been exposed to was seeing the KFDX DJs in person.

They came to our school one night to play in a charity basketball game and I was amazed what an odd looking bunch our radio heroes were. Of course, I'm sure I'd be much more tolerant of their physiques now.

That station also played a lot of great soul and funk music. It didn't matter that Boise had a very small black population. We were still getting to enjoy Al Green, Earth Wind and Fire, the O'Jays and all the rest.

I loved the fact those songs were often (pardon the pun) just a little bit dark. There were tunes about affairs (If Lovin' You is Wrong, I Don't Wanna Be Right), tunes about racial despair (The World is a Ghetto) and tunes about people daring to love someone of a different color (Brother Louie). The words were powerful and the music was exciting.

"Brother Louie" was actually released by four white guys who called themselves Stories. The lead singer reminded me of Rod Stewart on that cut and I thought it was pretty terrific.

Years later when my son got into rap music and culture, I could relate. I never felt like rap was anywhere near as good as the black music of the Seventies but I could understand the allure. When you're sixteen, it doesn't matter if you live in the city or in the suburbs or on a farm... you want to feel like you might be just a little bit dangerous.

For a short time I was obsessed with the "Superfly" movie starring Ron O'Neal and "Shaft" with Richard Roundtree. I was still too young to get in to see these movies but their theme songs totally inspired me.

I started fantasizing about what it would be like to live in a city. I'd drive a big black car and wear a fine leather jacket and go to all the best clubs. I'd have several ladies and they wouldn't mind sharing me if necessary.

I'd walk down the streets of my hometown and people might see just another naïve white farm boy from eastern Oregon.

But on the inside I was a misunderstood black private eye/street hustler trying to find his way in the world. I was outnumbered, outgunned and way too pale.

When I got a little older I moved on to films about misunderstood cops who refused to play by the rules.

I dragged my friends to see as many gritty crime films as possible... Serpico, The Seven-Ups, Freebie and the Bean, the Dirty Harry movies. I just couldn't get enough of that stuff but after a while they started to get pretty sick of it.

Now I was an eastern Oregon farm boy on the outside and a wisecracking white cop on the inside. I had an imaginary drinking problem and an imaginary ex-wife who was always trying to squeeze more alimony payments out of me. If I didn't give her some money soon they'd start to garnish my imaginary wages. But the more life kicked me in the guts, the harder I fought back.

It was odd, for some reason I enjoyed fantasizing about having all these adult problems. I was a strange kid.

It was the era of the anti-hero in movies. You had to either be a bad guy who really wasn't all that bad or a good guy who was kind of rough around the edges. Or in the case of Serpico, a good guy who other cops considered a bad guy because he busted seemingly good guys who were actually being paid off by bad guys.

If it featured car chases, corrupt politicians or a scene where the rules of search and seizure got bent, I was ready to pony up the money for a ticket.

The first order of business when I got to Portland was buying a black fedora. You know, the kind of hat generally worn by the pimps and gangsters of that era. I didn't like pimps and gangsters but I still wanted to look cool. This hat would make it possible for me to be misunderstood.

Roger and Maria really didn't care for the current music all that much. He liked some country music and she was crazy about Tom Jones and Englebert Humperdinck.

Tom and Englebert basically had two outfits… either a black tuxedo or if they were feeling casual, a pair of skin tight pants and a shirt unbuttoned clear down to their navel. That's so you could see the huge, gaudy crosses hung around their necks.

I kind of admired Englebert... how you could pull off being a sex symbol with a name like that was beyond me.

On the negative side, his biggest hit was called "After the Lovin" and it just always kind of grossed me out. I could handle songs about attraction, seduction and even lovemaking. But I really didn't want to hear about the cleanup phase.

Later in the week I asked Roger if I could go see a double feature showing in downtown Portland. Both he and Maria had to work but he said I could take a cab and he'd pay for it.

I was so excited. I made small talk with the cabbie and eavesdropped on the conversations going back and forth on his radio.

It was warm out but overcast and it started raining lightly. I liked the Portland rain. Where I came from, moisture tended to come down hard but not for too long. Up here in the coastal Northwest, the rain is often soft and misty and sometimes just keeps drifting in off the ocean for days and days.

The theatre was big and ornate and had a great screen. The movies were just so-so but the experience was something special. I was out on my own in a city, making strides toward becoming a man. Maybe even an urban man.

I wasn't afraid... in fact I was energized by the solitude of my adventure. This was the kind of place where I was meant to be.

When I went outside to get a cab I drank in the atmosphere. The shiny, wet streets added to my sense of danger.

I was alone in the urban jungle, unarmed but wearing a very cool black hat.

Chapter 34: The Fire Down Below

I was getting to the age where I thought about girls and sex constantly. Constantly and intensely.

Many times when the bell rang to signal the end of a class period, I would have to stay behind for a minute and try to mentally calm down that crazy man inside my pants. It might be 11:30 on Tuesday morning but as far as he was concerned it was always two a.m. at a rock star's mansion and the owner had just announced there were more groupies on hand than the band needed.

Sometimes I didn't even know for sure what was arousing me. My hormones were raging so much I think it's possible certain algebra equations might cause me to stiffen up.

Geez, even listening to a teacher talk about the Lewis and Clark expedition could spark sexual fantasies… was Sacajewea attractive? When would I achieve my Manifest Destiny and have sex with a girl?

I was concerned that looking at a Playboy magazine or Penthouse magazine might potentially send me into a sexual seizure of some kind. Some kind of horrible condition where I wouldn't be able to stop salivating if I saw an attractive female.

Actually, at this point I was wondering when I would even make out with a girl. I went on a hayride in the eighth grade and didn't hook up with anybody. Janet was grappling with a friend of mine and got really annoyed when I tapped her on the shoulder and asked her what I was doing wrong.

It's truly a wonder boys between the ages of 12 and 16 can function at all. You're so distracted you walk into doors and forget your own name. Half the time you're awake you're fantasizing about females, chasing after females, working up the nerve to talk to females or checking out females as you drive by them.

It gets a lot better when we get older but most of us are still dogs at heart. That instinct to chase the ladies is a hard one to give up. I am never surprised when a rich or powerful guy gets caught cheating. I'm not saying it's okay, I'm just saying I'm not surprised.

It's no wonder young males have to pay sky-high auto insurance rates… it's like handing your keys to a dog and sending him down a highway lined with squirrel-filled trees.

I didn't discover masturbation until I was 15. It was still a fairly taboo subject back then and there was no mention of it in the Happy Hooker book. Apparently she was so busy inventing new sexual positions and organizing orgies she didn't have the time or energy to fly solo.

I was introduced to the concept by my friend Larry Smith, pretty much the smartest guy in the school. He was always building radios and primitive robots and other cool stuff. We'd known each other for four or five years at this point.

We were in the school library one day whispering about sex stuff and he asked me if I knew what masturbation was. I replied, "Isn't that another word for chewing food?".

Larry laughed his ass off when I said that.

He explained the fundamentals to me. I thought it sounded pretty weird but later I figured out the rest through trial and error.

I always appreciated the fact Larry made the effort to tell me about this wonderful form of release. It kind of made up for the bad Santa Claus news I got from the warty kid on the school bus back when I was seven.

I was pretty obsessed with this new hobby for a while. Not as bad as some guys… one friend told me he hit it out of the park seven times one day.

Let's just say I was taking a lot of baths there for a while. I was very, very clean.

So while I now had a small measure of sexual release, I still longed to hook up with someone emotionally.

It's ironic that even though boys that age are obsessed with sex, many are also constantly falling in love or wanting to. Maybe it's because they're inexperienced and haven't figured out there's more to relationships than simply being attracted to each other.

I was a romantic son of a gun. I listened to love songs, enjoyed movies about people falling in love and eagerly watched "Love, American Style" and other gooey sit-coms on television.

I'd develop a crush on somebody who already had a boyfriend and never let anybody know. Sometimes I enjoyed just sitting around feeling sorry for myself. I became a champion brooder.

I really, really wanted to get involved with somebody.

Unfortunately, I seemed to be a victim of the Nice Guy curse. Up to this point in my life, I thought it was great being considered "nice". Teachers thought I was nice, people at church said I was nice, my parents and relatives all thought of me as nice. My friends thought I was nice.

However, nice in high school is bad if you're hoping to get a girlfriend. Nice is vanilla ice cream covered in vanilla sauce with a side order of vanilla wafers. High school girls don't want vanilla unless maybe it's a starting varsity quarterback made out of vanilla and even then there has to be at least some chocolate sprinkles.

I've always assumed that being too nice was my problem. Maybe it was something else but nobody ever said anything.

Looking back, I can see now I should have probably just done something outrageous so girls knew I had it in me.

Everybody liked me but nobody was particularly interested in becoming my girlfriend. I was nice, they'd all known me most of their lives and even though I was an athlete, I wasn't a star.

Nobody was interested except Nancy Benson. She was nice but kind of plain and almost as tall as me. She asked me to the Sadie Hawkins dance and I spent the evening trying to have fun without letting things get too romantic. She liked me a lot but I didn't want to lead her on.

She just wasn't what I was looking for. I'd always imagined I'd end up with some petite little blonde who would make me feel big and strong, not a girl who could possibly beat me in a game of one-on-one.

It sucked. We were both nice people and I wished I was more attracted to her.

Her liking me just made things worse. Now I not only didn't have a girlfriend but felt kind of guilty for rejecting someone who seemed to really like me. I was unhappy and I was making somebody else unhappy.

In retrospect, I'm probably lucky I never ended up in a serious relationship while I was still living in Sunnyrock. I knew a lot of kids who ended up marrying their high school sweetheart and never had a chance to go out and experience romance and passion in the world outside our little town.

My parents were starting to treat me like a young adult. That made me feel good.

On my sixteenth birthday, Dad and Nona took me out to celebrate. First we went out for a steak dinner and then then we were going to take in a movie.

My dad was never big on going to the movies. He just didn't see too much value in fiction, especially if it was the least bit fantastical. He didn't even like listening to music on the radio unless it was Peggy Lee singing "Is That All There Is?".

By the way, that is not a fun tune. If depression has a theme song it might just be "Is That All There Is?"

I do remember him liking "Patton" quite a bit. I think it brought back a lot of memories.

We'd also gone to see "The Poseidon Adventure" as a family. That movie was a lot of fun.

He got really aggravated whenever he heard news reports about inexperienced hikers getting lost in the woods and having to be rescued at the taxpayers' expense.

So when he heard about the movie "Deliverance", he actually got excited. It had just been released and people weren't really talking about it yet.

He assumed this would be a film that supported everything he ever said about what happens to unprepared people in the great outdoors. For once, he said, Hollywood had made a movie that people could actually learn something from.

I was happy to go see it. I pretty much always liked Burt Reynolds movies and the commercials made it look really exciting.

Things were going along fine until Ned Beatty got raped. Watching that scene was really rough. I'd seen violent movies before but this was something else all together.

Watching it with my parents was nearly unbearable. I was sure they were going to jump up and rush me out of the theatre. I looked over at them, worried they might be having dual heart attacks right then and there.

But I have to give them credit, they got through it and didn't even seem outraged by how graphic the film ended up being. Actually, my dad seemed almost pleased... now he had another horror he could add to his list of potential hiker woes... horny hillbillies.

A few years later I would take them to see "Raiders of the Lost Ark". Nona thought it was fun but Dad didn't care for it. I was just grateful nobody in the movie got raped or were told they had a pretty mouth.

Chapter 35: All the Young Dudes

One of my favorite memories from my teen-age years is a week I spent hanging out with my cousin Will over in Weston, Idaho. His dad was my mother's half-brother.

Will was a year older than me. I always felt like he and I were a little disconnected from our other male cousins.

I was never sure why the other guys didn't like us. I thought it was because I lived in Oregon and wasn't into being a cowboy. Will was just kind of strange, had a bad complexion and looked like Richard Belzer.

When he was a teen-ager he was tall and thin. It didn't seem to matter how much he ate, he could never gain weight. He would get up and eat a mixing bowl or two of cornflakes and milk every morning.

The week I spent in Weston was during the hottest part of the summer and the national old-time fiddling contest was going on there. Some of the stuff was held in school gymnasiums but a lot of the musicians drifted into local bars after dark and played.

It was great, Will and I were able to sneak into a bunch of clubs and watch people perform. There were lots of country singers who'd come to town to watch the fiddling contests and they would join up with the other musicians and do impromptu shows.

We didn't order any liquor but it was such a festive atmosphere nobody hassled us about being in the clubs. We were all clapping and singing and having a good time and it was so warm out you just felt like you wanted to stay up all night and live every minute to the fullest.

I lost touch with Will after high school. He never left Weston and I heard from relatives that he drank himself to death when he was in his forties. I guess maybe he had trouble fitting in with anybody much so he crawled inside the bottle.

Toward the end of my sophomore year, I'd started to develop some new friendships.

I'd been feeling a bit lost earlier in the year. I played sports but just being a jock wasn't enough.

To qualify as a true jock at my high school it seemed like sometimes you had to play dumb. The coaches acted like anybody who was too interested in anything besides sports might be a potential troublemaker.

One time an assistant coach actually gave me a hard time on the team bus because I was reading a copy of Newsweek.

You were more less expected to hang out with just other athletes and follow what the coaches said without question.

I was starting to hate that mindset. Several times I found myself in situations where I stood by silently while some jock bullied some poor non-athlete. One time I just sat there while my athlete friends refused to let Larry Smith sit down at our lunch table. It wasn't right and it wasn't me.

Now I'm not saying I was any kind of rebel. But I was starting to feel like there was more to life than just high school sports and farm work. Music was starting to become a very important part of my life.

Mike Gramm was a new kid who had moved to town from Idaho. He knew my cousin Darrin, the wild kid who used to always get in trouble.

Mike seemed cool but at the same time maybe not the most trustworthy guy you'd ever meet. One minute he'd be friendly and generous and the next he'd be making you feel like a moron. I'm not sure why we put up with it, maybe we were a little intimidated. He was good at manipulating people.

He was always saying stuff like, “You Sunnyrock guys are so lame. The kids in my old town never put up with crap from teachers. They were scared of us.”

Of course, I never saw him stand up to a teacher either.

He played trumpet in the school marching and jazz bands and had a nice stereo system with a receiver, turntable, reel-to-reel and large speakers mounted on his bedroom walls.

He didn’t even play his vinyl albums… he recorded them on to his reel-to-reel tapes and listened to those. At the time that seemed like a very high-tech way of doing things. Most of the kids I knew just listened to their vinyl records until they wore out or bought eight-track tapes.

My buddy Jeff Argent and I went over to Mike’s house to hear “Quadrophenia” by the Who. We were blown away by Pete Townshend’s ability to blend music, voices and the sounds of the ocean.

I think it was the first time a recording took me away to a whole different place and time. It was almost like a movie but better because I could enjoy it pretty much anytime I wanted.

Jeff was someone I’d known since the first grade. We always had different teachers prior to Middle school because of that reading test business but we’d hung out from time to time over the past few years and played sports together.

He was a drummer in the school jazz band. Unlike Mike, he was a solidly good guy you could always count on. We discovered we liked a lot of the same music.

When he was a freshman he had a fling with a wild girl two years older than us. He definitely had more carnal knowledge than me and pretty much everybody else we hung out with. But he didn't talk about that stuff much.

Mark McShane was a friend who I lost and then rediscovered. He and I had been pals back in the first grade but then his family moved to another small, nearby town called Merna. He moved back in the spring of 1973.

Mark's family had been through some rough times. His dad had a drinking problem and sometimes their family had a hard time making ends meet. It's hard to support a family on the money you make working on somebody else's farm and playing music occasionally.

Mark was also a musician. His dad had played in country and western bands around the area over the years and Mark had inherited his talent. He played keyboards, the guitar, saxophone and even the drums in a pinch.

We reconnected quickly. It was so much fun hanging out with him and his three younger brothers. It almost felt like we'd never been apart all those years.

We'd hang out at each other's houses, listen to music and talk for hours and hours about our favorite bands, sports and which girls we were currently lusting after.

Mark reminded me of Elton John because he wore glasses and played the piano. I got inspired and tried writing some lyrics… I figured even if I didn't have musical talent maybe I could still be eastern Oregon's version of Bernie Taupin.

We (along with his brother Bart) snuck into the Christian church a couple times and used their microphones, piano and recording equipment. I had written the words for a maudlin Elton-style tune called "Smilin' Jack" which we put down on tape along with some other stuff.

She waves goodbye
She knows he won't be back
So many tears cried
She calls him Smilin' Jack.

I really liked doing stuff with Mark and thought it would be the coolest thing in the world if we could form a band and perform original material. I even started thinking about writing the lyrics for a rock opera.

But eventually I started to realize my rock 'n roll fantasies were way out of line with reality. I didn't know how to play an instrument and I was just an average singer.

Actually, I had played the trombone for a while when I was younger but that really hadn't been all that pleasant of an experience. I seemed to spend a lot of my time just emptying out the spit valve.

Mark had genuine talent and went on to play with several different groups. He not only had musical talent but ended up becoming a gifted singer-songwriter.

I made peace with the fact I wasn't going to be in a rock band. I still wrote lyrics from time to time over the years, mostly just preachy political rants. It was a good way to vent when I was aggravated about some issue or another.

Chapter 36: Real Man

I've had a lot of musical and artistic heroes over the years.

Harlan Ellison writes amazing short stories. Stephen King figured out how to connect horror and everyday life. The Coen brothers put together amazingly original movies. Chuck Klosterman does great interviews and pens wonderful pop culture essays. Joni Mitchell proved that love songs could be sophisticated and musically adventurous. Bill Maher cuts through political bullshit and makes me laugh.

But the guy who's inspired me the most is the musician/producer/visionary Todd Rundgren.

The first time I heard him was in 1970. He had just released "We Gotta Get You a Woman". I thought it was a pretty cool song… instead of some guy pining away for one particular girl it was about two buddies who are out trying to crack the general code of feminine mystique. It seemed refreshingly friendly and almost humble.

The next Todd tune I heard was “I Saw the Light”. It hit the airwaves in 1972 and came off the double album “Something/Anything?”. I thought it was a little piece of romantic pop perfection. Every time I heard it I thought of two lovers walking on a warm summer night.

He released the album “A Wizard, A True Star” in March of 1973. I don’t remember ever hearing any cuts on the radio but I was always intrigued by the album’s druggy looking cover.

I didn’t actually buy a Todd Rundgren record until the Summer of 1974. I purchased “Todd” (another ambitious double album). The cover featured his face and his hair is about seven or eight different colors. This was considered a pretty radical look back in the mid-Seventies, especially for a straight guy.

He was radical in other ways as well. For the most part, he was playing all the instruments and doing all the vocals on his records.

I thought the songs on “Todd” were amazing. “The Spark of Life” sounds like a recording of the world being born. “Drunken Blue Rooster” is a robot chicken who’s had one too many. “The Last Ride” is a dark drive through the cold shadows of depression and wasted love. “A Dream Goes On Forever” is a tribute to the idea that true love is not only glorious but downright transcendent.

A couple months later I picked up "Something/Anything?". Most critics consider this Rundgren's best album. In addition to the two hits I previously mentioned there were also songs about a wide range of subject matters: lovable Vikings, hangovers, prejudice, a carousel burning down and the value of sluts. It also included one of the all-time great power-pop tunes "Couldn't I Just Tell You".

I came to find out he'd actually been in the business for a few years. He was in a Philadelphia-based group called The Nazz in the late Sixties. They had a modestly successful single called "Open My Eyes". They were somewhat out of step with most of the popular American groups of that era… they dressed more like the Who than the Byrds or Buffalo Springfield.

Eventually Todd left the Nazz and went out on his own. He wasn't just creating his own music but also acting as a producer for a variety of other groups and performers. Over the years he worked with Fanny, the Band, Hall and Oates, Cheap Trick, Patti Smith, the Psychedelic Furs, Grand Funk, the Tubes, Meat Loaf, the New York Dolls and a host of other artists.

The collaborations didn't always go smoothly. He worked with the English group XTC in the Eighties on the remarkable album "Skylarking". The record ended up being a critical and commercial success despite the fact Rundgren and the band's main creative force, Andy Partridge, were reportedly ready to kill each other by the time it was finished.

He said the main reason he did so much production work was so he didn't have to worry about whether or not his own projects made money. He kept putting out great, adventurous albums through the decades and you just never knew what he might try next.

It could be a musical treatise on cosmic fire, punkish rock anthems with his band Utopia, a collection of high-tech a capella songs, a much beloved sports anthem (Bang On the Drum) or even an entire album of his most popular songs done in a bossa nova style.

He was also way ahead of the curve when it came to technology. He was among the first artists to have their video played on MTV, he developed a revolutionary computer graphics system and he even attempted to set up an online patronage system so he could distribute his music without having to depend on record companies.

I've always admired his independent spirit. He could have written a thousand gorgeous love songs and probably made a fortune but more often than not he instead chose to examine the moral and spiritual questions we all contend with every day.

And he seems to understand just how important art is and how the drive to freely create it should always take precedence over money and fleeting fame. He is a true renaissance man.

I've gone to see him perform seven times. The last time was in June of 2009, a few days before he would turn sixty-one. He still had crazy dyed hair and lots of attitude and he played his guitar really loud. The audience loved it.

Chapter 37: Can't Get It Out of My Head

Junior year was definitely my favorite year of high school. You're older than everybody except the seniors but you're not so old that you have to get really serious yet about what happens after you graduate. At least that was my attitude.

In other words, you're kind of like Art Carney in the Honeymooners… you make dumb jokes, you have a few laughs, you don't take life too seriously. You can be an idiot and nobody's going to come down too hard on you for it.

This was a good change of pace for me. I needed to goof off a little and not be such a good boy all the time.

I was starting to get really tired of the way things were run in Sunnyrock. It felt like we were living in a place that would be perpetually twenty years behind the rest of the country.

If you played sports, you had a 10pm curfew during the week. The group Chicago came to play a concert in Boise on a Tuesday night. Jeff Argent, Mark McShane, Mike Gramm and I went to the show and sure enough the football coaches got wind of it.

Jeff and I were on the football team when this happened. People in small towns love to gossip and word got to the coaching staff that we were out past our curfew. Our punishment was getting ten "hacks" for our little act of rebellion.

A hack was a swat on the back of your bare thighs with a large wooden paddle. The first two or three stung pretty good but I could tell the assistant coach kind of let up after that. The last seven hacks were mostly symbolic.

It's just so weird looking back on it now. It seems like a more appropriate punishment for a disobedient 17th century sailor than a dumb 20th century high school student who just wanted to hear "25 or 6 to 4" performed live.

Soon after the football season ended, we juniors had to endure the annual letterman's initiation day. If you played a certain number of minutes in a sport you were entitled to receive a varsity letter and purchase a letterman's jacket to put it on. But first you had to go through an entire day of hazing by the senior athletes.

It was a tradition that wouldn't be around too much longer. We were nearing the end of an era.

When you first got to school you had to strip down to your underwear and put on a burlap sack. Then the seniors put molasses in your hair.

During the morning, any time a senior saw you in the hallway they could order you do to do pushups or whatever else they wanted. Guys dressed in burlap were scrambling from classroom to classroom trying to avoid their tormentors. The teachers and kids who weren't involved thought it was hilarious.

Around eleven we all left to go to a restaurant. We had to push the senior's cars and any time they saw a mud puddle, they ordered us to go roll around in it. This was in November and we weren't allowed to wear coats over our sacks so it was pretty miserable.

Once we got to the restaurant we had to buy them steak dinners and we only got to eat whatever fat they cut off the meat and threw at us.

I have mixed feelings about it. On one hand, it was kind of stupid and demeaning. But it was also kind of a cool male bonding experience. Sort of like boot camp in the military.

A couple years after I went through it some kid and their parents finally said enough was enough and threatened legal action. They wanted to receive the varsity letter without going through the initiation ritual. The school decided to discontinue the initiation.

Mark and I were also getting sick of being told how to look. If a male student wanted to participate in any extracurricular activities, he had to keep his hair off his ears and above his collar in the back. We decided to see what we could do to get the rule changed so it wasn't quite so strict.

The first thing we did was to put together and distribute a little mimeographed newsletter we called "Chunga's Revenge". I'm not sure why we called it that… it was the name of a Frank Zappa song and I guess we thought it was funny.

We both wrote articles about the hair issue and I did a couple cartoons. It was fun, our school didn't have a newspaper and I'd always wanted to try something like that.

Then we wrote up a petition and walked around town getting signatures. Most people were reasonably nice.

There were a few elderly folks who seemed confused about what it was we were trying to achieve but they ended up signing it simply because they were so grateful to have young people stopping by for a visit.

"So you're raising money for the school?"

"No, Mrs. Eldridge. We're trying to get the rule about how long we can wear our hair changed".

“Will this mean we’ll have to pay higher taxes?”

“No, Mrs. Eldridge. Tell you what, if you sign our petition we’ll make sure your taxes don’t go up next year”.

I will admit, there were at least a couple older folks who didn’t completely understand what they were signing. But we really tried to be honest most of the time.

It’s sort of scary what older people will do to have company. It’s no wonder they lose their life savings to scam artists so often.

A middle-aged lady named Mrs. Barron got pretty upset. She was a very conservative Mormon lady and she screamed at us to get off her porch and quit stirring up trouble. As I walked away from her house I muttered that she should go have twenty more kids and get a few more wrinkles.

We ended up actually accomplishing something. We got the appropriate number of signatures (to be honest, I have no memory of what the number was or what made it appropriate) and turned the petition into the Sunnyrock School Board.

A couple weeks later the head football coach held a meeting with all the athletes and announced the rules had been relaxed somewhat.

It was still pretty strict. They would let us wear a style that most people would say was comparable to how the Beatles looked when they first came to

America. So now we were only about ten years behind the rest of the country.

I suppose it's possible this was something the school administration had been talking about changing anyway. But I like to think our petition helped move their decision over the finish line.

Another little drama we went through that year was Jeff Argent falling head over heels for a younger girl named Meagan Thomas. Poor Jeff fell for girls the same way he played the drums… hard and not always smartly.

He didn't seem all that tore up when the wild older girl broke up with him. I guess that relationship was pretty much all about lust.

But this thing with Meagan was different. She was only fifteen but already seemed somewhat damaged. I think Jeff thought he could save her, maybe help her become a happy person who liked herself.

They went out a couple times and she thought he was a sweet guy. But she didn't want a sweet guy. She wanted the very charismatic guy who would treat her like crap.

Meagan wasn't the cutest girl around but she was sexually generous. At least she was generous with Stan Larsen. He had a steady girlfriend but saw Meagan on the side sometimes.

It was definitely a complicated scenario. Jeff was crazy about Meagan, Meagan was crazy about Stan and Stan was all too willing to use Meagan for a sleazy good time.

One rainy night I was sitting in Emma's Café with a small group of friends. Jeff was deeply depressed that Meagan preferred Stan to him. Nothing we said seemed to help much.

He just stood at the jukebox playing ELO's "Can't Get It Out Of My Head" over and over, hour after hour. I'd never seen anybody in that kind of romantic pain before. It was downright cinematic.

Chapter 38: It's Different For Girls

Janet was starting to have food issues during our Junior year. She would sit at the dinner table with us but barely eat anything. Or she'd pretend to eat something but then spit it into her napkin.

Dad and Nona would keep on her about it and she might finally get something down but then would go throw it up later. There was a struggle of wills every time the four of us sat down to eat together.

Our parents were very frustrated. They'd go back and forth between gently trying to convince her to eat and threatening to ground her if she didn't. Her behavior seemed pretty odd to a couple of people who'd grown up during the Depression and sometimes wondered where their next meal was going to come from.

She'd put on a little extra weight during the months before this started and I think she was starting to get kind of down about her social life. One particular night was really rough for her.

She got asked to a dance by a guy named Ned Schopenhauer. She was happy somebody asked her to go but she ended up having a miserable time.

I wasn't surprised. I knew Ned from the football team… he was one of the student managers, the guys who ran errands for the coaches and handed out towels to the players.

Managers were generally looked down on by the athletes and none so more than Ned. He was loud and annoying and didn't seem to understand what a low position he held in the school's athletic hierarchy.

And to top it all off, he was physically and hygienically unattractive. He had abnormally large nostrils and he always smelled odd. People called him Ned Needsashower behind his back.

I tried talking to Janet about what was bothering her but she wouldn't open up. I felt really bad she was going though this rough time but I had no idea how to help her.

Things started to turn around for her during the summer of 1974. She got a job cleaning house for an elderly couple and started dating a guy named Rick Bedford. By this time she'd lost that extra twenty pounds and she seemed to be getting her old confidence back.

Rick had moved to town about a year earlier. He worked at the drug store in Sunnyrock and always seemed to have a lot of spending money. He had kind of a squeaky voice, seemed to spend an inordinate amount of money on clothes and had zero interest in sports of any kind.

He seemed gay to me and my friends. We didn't care… we weren't particularly homophobic. It just seemed strange that he and Janet were dating.

But she was happy and eating normally again, so I certainly wasn't going to bug her about her new boyfriend. I figured there was a good chance I was wrong about Rick. It's not like I was all that worldly, maybe there were lots of guys out there who gave off that vibe but were still totally into girls.

Chapter 39: Darkness, Darkness

Senior year finally arrived. I was starting to feel sort of grown up.

This was fifth year of playing football and I wasn't all that excited about it anymore. My attitude about the coaches had changed. They used to seem intimidating but now I was starting to see them as annoying old men who really, really enjoyed their time in high school so they found a job that would let them stay there the rest of their lives.

Evidently I wasn't the only senior who was having a problem maintaining their focus. As the season progressed, the coaches realized this team wasn't headed for the playoffs. They gradually began to move younger players into the starting line-up. In retrospect, this was smart... Sunnyrock ended up winning the state championship the year after I graduated.

Which was quite a comeback, considering our class had the first losing football season in 42 years.

But we weren't particularly upset about it. We whispered among ourselves that it was kind of fun aggravating the coaches, paying them back for all the times they'd made our lives miserable during the last four football seasons.

I think if my half-brother Roger had been on a losing team back in 1958, he would have committed suicide. But it just wasn't that important to me.

I was really glad when the season ended. I'd had enough. But instead of enjoying my freedom I started to feel kind of down.

I had always been a sensitive kid. When I was young I took teasing too seriously and got my feelings hurt way too easily.

When I was younger I cried when I felt bad. When I got older I had to hold it in…which would result in me re-hashing the event over and over in my head.

They say depression is anger turned inward. I can vouch for that concept.

I would get mad when somebody teased me. But on some level I always believed what they were saying. A few years of that and you pretty much start to consider yourself a loser. Nobody can deliver a crueler reprimand than the voices inside your own head.

I was never sure how I ended up like this. I wasn't a remarkable student but my teachers definitely encouraged me to take whatever college prep classes were offered. I wasn't a great athlete but I did okay. Over the years I'd been on the football, basketball, track and tennis teams.

I had a good group of friends. I got along well with my sister and my parents. It seemed like pretty much everybody liked me… except me.

My feelings of self-hatred greatly intensified during November of 1974. Most of it stemmed from the fact I didn't have a girlfriend. I really didn't know why it mattered so much to me… I had no plans to stay in the area after graduation so any relationship I fell into would only last until I left for college.

But for some reason, I began obsessing about my inability to hook up with anybody. It was the failure that represented every other insecurity and moment of self-doubt I'd ever experienced. It was the King of the Failures and it was kicking my ass on a daily basis.

If I had my way, every high school in America would be required to post large flashing signs that read "Your Life Won't Actually Start Until You Get Out of Here".

I'd dated a little bit here and there over the years, mostly just taking different girls to dances. When I was a junior, I did date a Mormon girl who was a year older than me. Her name was Susan.

We would usually go to a movie and then sit in a diner and talk for hours. I liked her pretty well but conversation wasn't what I needed. I needed just a little bit of physical contact.

On the fourth date I tried to take her parking and she kind of freaked out.

I never really understood why she'd been going out with me. Maybe she thought it would be safe to spend time with me until she left for Utah and started pushing out the babies. After all, I was a reputation as an official nice guy.

Later during my junior year I went on a double date with a buddy of mine, his girlfriend and a friend of hers named Terry I was interested in seeing. We went bowling over in Brisco and I drove.

The evening went okay but then on the drive home I passed a semi-truck at a dangerous point in the road and was barely able to get back over before we had a head-on collision with an oncoming car.

It was a pretty scary moment… I looked at my three passengers when it was over and they all looked like they'd been watching their lives pass before their eyes.

This was a confidence killer. I was pretty sure Terry had no interest in risking her life on another date with me.

I was not doing well with women… one girl thought I was a sexual psychopath and another assumed I was hoping to die in a fiery car crash.

I just couldn't believe it. Here I was at almost the halfway point in my senior year and I'd never been involved in a relationship worth talking about.

My friends knew I'd been feeling bad lately. I'd been keeping to myself and hardly talking to anybody at school. I'd just walk through the halls with a dour look on my face, hoping somebody would notice and ask me what was wrong.
I was seriously into self-pity.

In December, my friend Doreen asked me to go to the Christmas dance with her. I was surprised and pleased. I'd known all her all my life and she'd really turned into a very attractive young woman the past couple years.

We had a really nice time. I felt relaxed and funny. There was no pressure, I was just dancing with someone I'd known for years and years and she had actually invited me. The evening would be a success if I could get her home without first involving us in a catastrophic car accident of some kind.

I didn't know what we were going to do after the dance. Much to my surprise, we ended up driving out to a secluded spot with Mark McShane and his girlfriend Tammy and we made out for a couple hours.

Looking back, that concept seems kind of strange. Why would two couples want to be in the same car kissing and petting? Maybe the girls liked it because it gave them an out if things started getting too hot and heavy.

By the time I got home I had completely thrown logic out the window and decided Doreen and I were now a couple and I was crazy about her and who knows, maybe we could both enroll at the same college and this was maybe the best night of my life. I kept wondering if I should call her on Sunday but I decided that might seem too pushy.

On Monday I went back to school and clumsily tried to gauge what was going on between Doreen and myself. She was friendly but no more so than before the dance. I didn't want to push too hard but on the other hand I also didn't want this relationship to die on the vine.

After a couple of frustrating days, I asked her friend Tammy what was going on.

"What's up with Doreen? I thought she liked me".

"She does like you. She likes you a lot but only as a friend. She knows you've been feeling bad lately and she wanted to do something nice to cheer you up".

"What the hell… I can't believe this. You can't fuck with people's feelings that way. It's just not right".

Looking back, I know I should have appreciated the fact Doreen was such a great friend. But that's not how the mind of a teen-age boy works. Love, lust, pride and anger are the tools a seventeen year old male has to work with. Mature introspection comes later.

The words "friend" and "nice" burned in my brain. At this moment they seemed like the two worst obscenities in the English language.

First I flew into a rage. Then a black cloud of depression hit me, suffocating in it's intensity. I'd been sad before but this was something different… an emotional weight unlike any I'd ever felt before. It was like the sky was crushing me.

Tammy told me this at a basketball game right before the start of the Christmas break. There was a dance after the game but I knew I had to be alone. I quickly left the gymnasium and headed outside.

It was snowing. I walked through the quiet streets of my little town until I got to the city park. I looked around to make sure I was alone and then I broke down, great sobs of pain mixing with the cold steam of my breath.

I had never felt so alone. I remember thinking that if the darkness swallowed me that night, the world would feel no loss whatsoever.

Chapter 40: The Kids are Alright

Eventually I started feeling less depressed and decided to get on with my life. There were only a few months of high school left and I decided I might as well enjoy them.

I started looking forward to finishing high school and making a new start somewhere else. I started thinking about where I might want to go to college and what I should study.

At this point I was mostly hanging out with Mark, Ronnie Felson, Josh Leonard, Max Wilson and Jerry Wilson. We called ourselves Muck, Buck, Yuck, Suck, Duck and Tuck.

Ronnie had a couple pet rabbits that suddenly died. One was named Alice Cooper and the other was Clint Eastwood. They were named after Ronnie's two favorite celebrities.

He was pretty upset about losing them. He wanted to have a little burial service at his place and asked us all to come over.

It seemed kind of silly but Ronnie was a good friend and we were glad to accommodate him. Well, most of us were.

Josh Leonard hated how people treated their pets these days. He'd been taught to believe humans had the right to do whatever they wanted to their animals… if your dog disobeyed, you should kick him in the guts. That would straighten out his attitude.

Ronnie had dug a couple little graves and was using shoe boxes for coffins. He'd put both rabbits in their shoeboxes.

He asked Josh to hold Clint Eastwood's shoebox. Then he said a prayer.

Then he asked if anybody wanted to add anything. Josh said, "I do. This is absolute bullshit".

Josh reached in the shoebox, grabbed the dead bunny and slam-dunked him into the open grave.

Ronnie leapt at him with fury in his eyes. I managed to get between them and then dragged Josh back to his car, scolding him all the way about what he had done. He thought it was hilarious.

Ronnie was a cool friend. He and his family had a boat and taught me how to water ski. I wasn't great (and never got up on one) but it was still a wonderful experience. We spent a lot of Sunday afternoons up at Bully Creek reservoir.

I remember another Sunday afternoon when we had just started high school. It was absolutely beautiful out and we decided to spend the day passing a football back and forth all over town. It reminded me of that Burt Lancaster film “The Swimmer”.

He always had good reflexes and a quick mind. One time we were over in Weston in a tavern and a fight broke out. Somebody dropped a twenty dollar bill on the floor and he somehow managed to swoop in underneath the two guys fighting and pick it up.

A couple months after the rabbit burial debacle, I volunteered to help my friend Max come up with a campaign skit. He was two years younger than me and running for sergeant-at-arms in the student government.

Our student government (like nearly all student governments) was kind of silly and pretty much just symbolic but I thought it would be cool if he won this position. There weren’t a lot of other options at our school and chances looked slim he was going to end up being a sports star or the valedictorian.

The campaign pretty much consisted of two activities: putting up posters encouraging people to vote for your candidate for no apparent reason and giving some kind of presentation in front of the student body.

I was good at making posters and had actually done a lot to help Janet win a student government position a year earlier. I was feeling kind of cocky.

I encouraged Max to do a skit because the speeches always seemed so lame and in high school you always need to anticipate what the smartasses might do and try to head them off. I really preferred that the crowd be laughing with him and not at him.

School assemblies could be fun but they could also be really cruel. A perfect example was the cheerleader tryouts… there was always at least one overweight girl who decided to live the dream but couldn't make her chubby legs complete the splits. And there were always a few assholes sitting in the audience who went out of their way to make her feel bad.

I really liked Max and his older brother Jerry. Jerry was my same age. They'd moved to Sunnyrock around the same time as Mark. They lived in town so we spent a lot of time hanging out at their house.

Max was quite a bit smaller than me so we decided I should be a ventriloquist and he could be my dummy. He got dressed up in a funny costume and put makeup on his face so it looked like he had a hinged jaw.

I sat on a folding chair and Max sat on my knee. We did a little routine with me asking him questions about how student government works and him giving me funny answers. It went over okay but

I actually hadn't really thought of a big finish so it sort of fizzled out at the end.

We were followed by his opponent's presentation. Max was running against Ronnie Felson's younger brother, Randy.

It started out with the Alice Cooper song "Elected" booming out over the PA system for over two minutes. Then a couple guys dressed as reporters ran out on to the gymnasium floor, pretending to snap pictures. Finally, out walked Randy dressed in a suit and tie, waving to the crowd.

He never said a word. It was the most efficient piece of political marketing I've ever witnessed.

The crowd roared their approval. I felt sick to my stomach... how could I not have seen this coming? The song was perfect and I knew Lonnie was an Alice Cooper fanatic. I should have put two and two together.

Poor Max lost in a landslide.

A couple months later I took another stab at public performance. I was taking a speech class and the teacher asked if anybody wanted to participate in a competition being held at a college located three hours north of Sunnyrock. Several of us volunteered.

I thought this teacher was kind of a fun guy. His name was Ray Waters. He was an English teacher and also my tennis coach. I played for him during spring of my junior and senior years.

He lived across the street from the tennis courts and sometimes he would drink a beer and smoke a cigarette while he watched us practice. He set a poor example health-wise but he had a great dry wit. Actually, compared to the other coaches he was a veritable Cary Grant.

You could write something yourself and present it or pick a piece by another author. Some people performed poetry and others did pieces of prose.

I decided that rock song lyrics were my kind of poetry. That was sort of my thing at the time… play by the rules but tweak the situation a little so I ended up looking cool. Or at least that was my deluded teen-age belief.

I did readings of "Rocket Man" by Elton John, "Midnite Cruiser" by Steely Dan and "Desperado" by the Eagles.

I tried my best to make these "song poems" sound profound but I could tell by the looks on the judges' faces they weren't buying it. In retrospect, I think I probably ended up sounding a lot like a beatnik performing at a New York City coffeehouse circa 1961.

Of course, the audience at the 1961 coffeehouse would have been mostly stoned. When you perform in front of stoned people it's a hell of a lot easier to persuade them you just said something profound.

Not winning didn't bother me too much. I just figured the judges weren't hip enough to understand where I was coming from. As far as I was concerned, Don Henley was a helluva lot more relevant than Robert Frost.

The event was held at Eastern Oregon State College in a town called La Grande. My dad had gone there for one year back in the late 1930's.

La Grande had a population of about 11,000 at that time. It was a nice, quiet town located south of the Blue Mountains and west of the Wallowa-Whitman forest. There was a lot of great scenery in that area.

I had time to check out the campus and part of the town. I liked it... the school was a nice size. I really didn't think I was ready to go straight from a town of fifteen hundred people to Eugene or Portland. I decided to apply to EOSC for the coming fall term.

Chapter 41: No More Mr. Nice Guy

I did have a brief fling toward the end of my senior year. There was a cute freshman girl named Mary Jane Redding who started hanging out with me and Mark and our other friends.

The relationship was pretty infantile, mostly just giving each other a hard time. We teased each other, she slugged me in the arm a lot and there were a lot of double entendres thrown around. It was fun and good for my confidence.

We went out for a couple months but things never got all that serious. When summer came and we weren't seeing each other at school every day it became apparent neither one of us was willing to work very hard to keep the relationship going.

A week after we officially broke up, I found out she had started dating Mark. I was pissed for a couple days but quickly got over it.

After all, the last thing I wanted at this point in my life was a girlfriend who still had three more years of high school left to finish. Definitely not a situation worth losing my best friend over.

Now that I had graduated, I was desperate to find a job. Dad offered to pay for a third of my college costs and I was getting a Social Security check every month (due to my birth mother's death) but I still needed to make money to cover my third of the deal.

The economy wasn't great at that time and employment prospects in the Sunnyrock area were always pretty limited outside of agriculture.

During the past couple summers I had worked on and off for several different local farmers, mostly stacking hay bales. Mark and I usually worked together and I liked it because each job only lasted three or four days at the most and then you'd get a break until somebody else called offering work.

Dad tried to help me find a steady job with a reliable paycheck. I appreciated his efforts but I soon realized any employment he suggested was probably going to be kind of horrible. He didn't plan it that way, but that's the way it seemed to turn out nonetheless.

He found me a job working for a crop dusting company during the summer after my junior year but

I only lasted a couple days. They wanted me to be a flagger for the pilot when he flew at night.

Standing in a dark field trying to show a pilot where to drop his load of pesticides wasn't my idea of a healthy occupation. It was more like a death wish. Even if you were good at the job you would probably get some of the stuff on you… and I was definitely not good at the job.

The summer after I graduated he told me he'd heard they were hiring up at a big corporate farm called Ridgeline. The job was simple… mostly you just walked through the fields fixing clogged sprinklers. It paid minimum wage (2.25 per hour at that time).

We worked fourteen hours a day, six days a week. The days seemed endless and the worst part was nobody on the crew (besides the boss) spoke any English.

They were all from Mexico. I felt like they were always pointing at me and laughing. I could never tell if they were sharing a joke with me or talking about how they wanted to force me to be a drug mule.

I worked there a month. By the time I quit, my friends said I looked like I had radiation poisoning. My hair looked fried, my skin was burnt and my lips were cracked.

Of course, part of my problem was that I was trying to get up at 4am everyday but still hang out with my buddies at night. I was seriously sleep deprived.

Dad wasn't too pleased but I figured I'd make the finances work out somehow. Things would be tight but I felt like it was worth it if I could spend a little more time with my friends before we all went our separate ways.

My recently graduated friends and I decided to mess with the town of Sunnyrock a little bit. One night we vandalized the bleachers at the football field, spreading toilet paper and some feces. Then we left a note that made it look like it had been done by kids from Brisco.

Brisco is a larger town about 15 miles east of Sunnyrock. There's always been an intense football rivalry between the two schools. Sunnyrock usually won and it was always so sweet to beat a team that had a talent pool roughly six times larger than ours.

It was so much fun to watch our handiwork unfold during the next week. The Sunnyrock school administration demanded an apology from Brisco, Brisco kids were being interviewed by their own school officials, kids from Sunnyrock planned a counter-strike on the Brisco football stadium, etc. etc.

I wondered if this was what it felt like when CIA agents toppled uncooperative foreign governments.

Amazingly, we conspirators all managed to keep our mouths shut. At least until we'd gone off to college or jobs in other towns.

During late August, I went out on a double-date with Mark and Mary Jane and a girl named Beth. We went to the Idaho state fair over in Nampa.

We had a nice time and Beth and I were sitting in the backseat on the way home.

Beth and I started kissing and this lasted until we got back to Sunnyrock. Mark and I got our signals crossed and when I was walking Beth to her door, he drove off.

I had the worse case of blue balls ever and I ended up having to walk the three miles back to my house in the dark. I really thought I might die.

There was one big final party around the middle of September. It was a kegger out in the woods north of Sunnyrock. We had a huge, roaring bonfire and everybody was getting pretty wasted.

I was there with Mark, Jerry Wilson, a guy named Alan Barnett and a bunch of other kids.

After a while, I could sense things were starting to get a little weird. A really big guy named Steve rolled an old couch on to the bonfire and got it stoked up even more, sending sparks flying everywhere. There just seemed to be violence in the air. It kind of felt like the high school version of "Lord of the Flies".

We were all reaching the end of an era in our lives. I knew if scores were going to be settled it would have to be tonight.

We all started drinking beers and reminiscing about stuff that had happened to us the past few years.

Darrin Desmond and Dave Johnson showed up. I immediately got the feeling this wasn't going to be your usual friendly party.

After a while, Dave started giving me a bad time and egging Darrin on to fight me. I don't think Darrin ever really had anything against me but he always seemed to be following Dave's orders, especially when he was drunk. Dave was like Darrin's fight promoter.

Dave looked at me and said, "I'm surprised to see you here, Hawthorne. But I know Darrin is really happy you showed up. He's been wanting to kick your ass for years".

I replied, "Well, we all want things, Dave. I want a million dollars and a brand new Camaro. But more than anything, I want your mother to quit sending me those naked Polaroids. She is one skuzzy old broad".

I figured that would get Dave moving but Darrin lunged at me instead.

He took a swing at me and clipped my ear. I punched him in the face and tackled him to the ground. I was heavier so I held him down and put my hands around his throat.

To be honest, I wasn't entirely sure what I was doing. I'd never really been in a regular fight before. I figured maybe I could make him pass out before he was able to hit me in the face any more.

Dave jumped on my back but then my buddy Alan intervened and pulled him off. Then a couple other fights broke out.

It didn't last too long. Other guys pulled me off Darrin and broke up the other skirmishes before anybody get hurt too badly.

It was so great. It felt so good to get back at them after all this time. I'd stood up for myself and actually done some damage.

Mark and Jerry Wilson and I stayed up all night re-hashing every gory detail.

I'd never been in a real brawl before. It was really kind of a rush. It was something I'd always thought about but when it was happening it seemed like everything was going in slow motion. My brain couldn't quite believe what the rest of my body was doing.

The next day I proudly displayed my bruises to Dad. He smiled and said it sounded like a pretty darn exciting fight. I think he was happy to know I could take care of myself if necessary.

It was ironic, when I saw Dave and Darrin at the twenty year class reunion I really enjoyed talking to them. We had a good laugh about that night back in 1975.

Chapter 42: Break On Through

The summer of 1975 seemed to drag on forever. We'd graduated around the twentieth of May and college didn't start until the last week of September. My sense of ennui was exhausting.

I mostly just hung out at home the last month or so before school started. I was so bored and so ready to get on with my new life.

The big day finally arrived. Jeff Argent was also going to EOSC and had offered to give me a ride. He stopped by the house and we loaded my stuff into his blue 1969 Chevy Chevelle. It was pretty crowded in there with all our clothes, records, stereo equipment and whatever but we made it work.

I hugged my folks goodbye and promised I'd be good about keeping in touch. Dad seemed really proud... I knew this was a moment he'd been thinking about for a long time.

There were a few kids from my high school who ended up going to college in La Grande. I'd known Regina Fosse, Martin Rhodes, and Jeff Argent since the first grade. Rob Stiller had lived in Sunnyrock for the past couple years.

It just so happened they all got assigned to the same dorm. I ended up in a different one over on the other side of campus.

My roommate was a big native American guy named Ed. He was a bit older and seemed very reserved. His only hobby seemed to be lying on his bed and staring at the ceiling. I was never sure if he was a deep thinker or just high on something.

He appeared to own only one record... Johnny Winter Live. I guess he figured you only needed one if you really, really liked it.

I spent a couple days trying to make friends with him but wasn't successful. He wasn't rude or anything... just really, really stoic. It was kind of like rooming with one of those big heads on Easter Island. I decided to make other living arrangements.

I figured if I was going to change rooms I might as well see if there was space in the dorm where all my hometown friends were situated.

The other dormitory consisted of two buildings that were connected by a recreation/television room in the middle. One building was strictly for male students and the other was strictly for females.

Jeff Argent had ended up alone in a double occupancy room and was going to eventually end up with somebody moving in so I asked if it could be me. He said no problem.

We'd actually hung out together quite a bit during the last couple years of high school. I knew he was still pretty hung up on Meagan Thomas but I figured college would be a great chance for him to meet somebody new and get a fresh start. I was feeling pretty optimistic about both our futures, dating-wise.

Rob Stiller was a smart, athletic kid who had moved to Sunnyrock at the end of our sophomore year. His girlfriend was Dina Everly, the girl back home I had such a crush on during high school.

They ended up getting married a few years later and then divorced a few years after that. I never heard why they split up. I was always curious because they seemed like the perfect couple.

Martin Rhodes was the ultimate nice guy. He used to come out to our ranch and spend the day sometimes. The first time he came out to visit he was terrified of the cattle… which seemed weird to me because I so was used to being around them.

He'd just become a born-again Christian but he wasn't obnoxious about it. The best way to describe him is a cross between John Denver and Ned Flanders from the Simpsons.

Regina Fosse was very smart and had a good sense of humor. We'd gotten to know each other in a chemistry class during our senior year in Vale.

Jeff and I both loved music and had a pretty respectable combined record collection. I leaned more towards American artists like Todd Rundgren, Rick Derringer and Steely Dan. He loved English bands like the Moody Blues, Deep Purple, Emerson Lake and Palmer and Jethro Tull. We had a lot of people stopping by the room to check out our albums.

Jeff was very serious about putting together a whole image for his new college life.

He'd bought his Chevelle, started wearing his hair long and grew a droopy Fu Manchu mustache. He looked like he should be in a Foghat tribute band.

The mustache kind of bugged me sometimes. It seemed like he was always combing it or washing it or trying to get food out of it. It was just a nightmare when they served soft ice cream at the cafeteria.

The other guys in the dorm were a mix of types. Some were football players, some were nerds and some were pretty cool. As far as I could tell, nobody came from a particularly wealthy family. La Grande wasn't a place where rich kids would choose to spend four years prior to joining their daddy's company.

Bill was a really nice guy who had come to EOSC with his high school girlfriend. She lived over in the adjoining girls' dorm. He was always talking about how crazy it made him that she wouldn't have sex with him until they were married. The poor guy was practically climbing the walls.

Jamie was a football player who was cool when he was sober but pretty much a dick when he drank. He had this weird habit of passing out in one of the shower stalls when he'd had too much. I guess he figured if he had to throw up, that was the smart place to be.

One of the first to stop by our room was a guy named Sam Bliven. He liked to call himself Sam Oblivion. He was short, stocky, had greasy long hair and almost always wore Army surplus clothing. He looked like a cross between a Hobbit and a Vietnam war protestor.

Oblivion was a perfect nickname. It seemed like he was stoned almost every waking minute of the day. He was a nice enough guy but I got the sense the heavy marijuana use had done some damage. He often referred to himself in the third person and seemed really angry.

"Sam Oblivion is such an asshole sometimes. I'm not sure why anybody would like Sam. Girls don't like Sam. As a matter of fact, sometimes Sam doesn't like Sam all that much".

This was behavior I hadn't dealt with before. I didn't know whether to laugh or direct Sam to the nearest mental health counselor.

He also had a tendency to get easily distracted when he was in the middle of telling a long story and then forgetting what he was talking about. Of course, that was a pretty common trait among people who smoked a lot of dope.

The guy next door lived alone. His name was Gary Bays and supposedly he'd been a star athlete in Eugene.

This guy was scarily charismatic. He was about my height, slender, had green eyes and could grow a beard in about five minutes. Maybe girls didn't care about the beard part but I thought it was pretty cool.

I assumed he did really well with the girls. But it extended beyond that... I got the feeling he could convince anybody to do just about anything.

If charisma was a corporation, Stan Larsen would have definitely been in charge of the Sunnyrock branch. But Gary Bays would have been the regional manager.

There was almost something Satanic about him. Not in the evil sense but certainly in the manipulative sense. I don't think he'd ever hurt anybody but I got the feeling he could probably talk somebody into punching themselves in the nose. And they would probably send him a thank you note for doing it.

Jeff and I had a stereo system that you could hook four speakers up to. It was probably a bit much for a dorm room but we thought it would sound great.

Ten minutes after Jeff and I met Gary, he'd convinced us how great it would be if we extended speaker wire to his room and let him use two of the speakers so he could listen to our stereo over there. I think we ended up actually thanking him for suggesting the idea.

Two weeks later, he convinced Jeff to lend him the Chevelle so he could drive home to Eugene and see his girlfriend. I was pretty stunned. Jeff was really obsessive about that car and before this I would have been surprised if he had let somebody else drive it twenty miles, let alone across the state.

We all got invited to the girls' dorm for a "get to know you" party the Saturday night before classes started.

It was a good night. By the time the evening was over, I'd tried pot for the first time, drunk a bunch of tequila and made out with a girl I'd only known for an hour.

That was a relief. It appeared my problems with the opposite sex might finally be over. Nobody (except my friends from Sunnyrock) knew me here and I could re-invent myself any way I wanted.

It was kind of amazing how all the anti-drug commercials, good parenting, Sunday school lessons and health class advice went right out the window. When somebody handed me a lit joint I didn't think twice about trying some.

I was in college now and was eager to take advantage of the freedom I'd finally been given.

I was very happy. It appeared this next phase of my life was going to be a lot of fun.

Chapter 43: The Spirit of Radio

I wasn't sure what I wanted to do with my life. I guess that's not unusual for somebody just starting college.

Jeff and I both decided to major in journalism. We both liked talking about current events and history and this wasn't too long after the Watergate scandal so becoming a reporter was considered a reasonably cool career choice.

We figured it was only reasonable that if we had cool careers then women would think we were cool and be attracted to us.

Neither of us actually came out and said this was our reason for going into the journalism program but I always figured it was true on a subliminal level.

It was a silly way to plan our lives but that's what happens when almost every waking hour is spent primarily thinking about the opposite sex.

Park ranger was also a good choice at that time, especially if you happened to look like Jackson Browne or Dan Fogelberg or James Taylor. I loved their music but whenever I saw their records in a woman's room I knew my work was really cut out for me or really (to be quite honest) just impossible.

This was the post-hippie era and there was a new formula involved when you tried to describe the perfect man. I think girls my age had learned a thing or two from their older sisters and decided the specifications needed to be a bit more exact.

A lot of young women wanted a sensitive guy who happened to be gorgeous but somehow wasn't vain. And he had to have a job but couldn't be all caught up in the corporate thing and he had to appreciate the environment. And he couldn't be possessive but would love you so much he would never stray. And he might smoke a little dope but only with you and only in front of a blazing bonfire while he played love songs on the acoustic guitar.

Add this all up and you get park ranger/environmental scientist/singer-songwriter or some other variation.

Those lucky bastards back in the 60's had it made. All they had to do was let their hair grow long, buy a VW van and change their name to Freedog or Starman. If you irritated the girl's parents she slept with you out of gratitude.

At one point I'd actually considered going to a private college in Forest Grove, a small college town up in northwest Oregon. They apparently had a broadcasting program that included internships at Portland television stations. But then I found out how much more it cost to go to a private school.

We did want to eventually get on the staff at the college newspaper. I'd always wished we 'd had something like that back in high school.

However, our main focus initially wasn't about trying to be the next Woodward and Bernstein. What we were excited about was joining the staff of the college radio station.

It wasn't very powerful. In fact, it could only be picked up within the city limits (and the city was not very big). But we were still thrilled to get the opportunity to try our hand at broadcasting.

The first thing we had to do was take a class that prepared us for the FCC license test. Then we drove down to Boise on a Saturday in November and took it.

Once we were legal, the training began. The station manager was a really nice guy named Eric. He was a couple years older than us and very supportive.

Back then you had to work two turntables, a cart machine and a microphone. The cart machine was what played the pre-recorded station promos and other assorted announcements. The station didn't have a particular musical format so the disc jockeys were free to play whatever they wanted.

One guy always played classical stuff, another one favored jazz, somebody else went back and forth between comedy albums and old blues cuts. Jeff and I favored rock, soul, funk and pop music.

It was really nerve-racking at first. I discovered a lot of the stuff I took for granted when listening to the radio was actually the result of precise planning.

We didn't even play regular commercials but a strict on-air schedule had to be maintained if we were going to fit in songs, patter, public service announcements and the four required station IDs an hour. I started thinking about how much harder it would be at a commercial station where you had to make sure the ads for Crazy Ralph's Car Stereo Shack all got played at the right time.

The goal of a good DJ was to stay on top of things so he or she could get all this stuff done and yet sound like they didn't have a care in the world. It was kind of a Zen exercise.

Jeff and I had different styles. He wanted to be the classic FM DJ, the guy with the slow, deep voice who was all about the music.

He would play nine or ten cuts in a row and then list off the names of the songs, what album they were from and who performed them. If he'd had sponsors they would have been something like Good Dirt Granola or Sky High Rolling Papers.

I found this kind of annoying… there was no way for the audience to sync up the music with the info unless they were willing to write it all down like some old guy keeping the box score at a baseball game.

I wasn't exactly Casey Kasem but I did try to break things up a bit. I would play a couple songs and then talk about the artist or the album or maybe some other music-related news. I even threw in a few bad jokes here and there.

It was a lot of fun. We got free issues of Billboard magazine and lots of promotional copies of new music that was about to come out. We spent a lot of our free time hanging out in the studio.

I eventually started doing my own top 40 countdown show. I actually played all the songs we had on hand that were currently in the Billboard top 40 but I would alter the standings to reflect my likes and dislikes.

In my musical universe, "Slow Ride" and "Bohemian Rhapsody" ruled the chart for weeks while disco rarely got out of the bottom 20. Surprisingly, nobody ever asked me about this… either they liked what they were hearing or nobody was listening.

I was starting to get some confidence. I was even feeling okay about girls.

Sam Oblivion, Rob Stiller and I went to a dance about a month into the school year.

Rob was just hanging out but Sam and I were pumped up to meet some ladies. Sam even wore a non-military shirt.

It was kind of boring for a while but then I got asked to dance by a tall girl named Joanne. I think she lived in the female section of our dorm. She seemed very drunk.

After a few obligatory fast dances and a couple grope-filled slow ones, she kissed me on the neck and whispered "I shink we should go be alone somewhere… is your room available?".

I happily nodded yes… Jeff had gone home for the weekend so I knew we'd have some privacy.

When we got to my room we fumbled around and finally managed to get our clothes off. I didn't last too long but she was kind and said it had been great. I got the feeling most of her lovemaking sessions were like this… a minute and a half of grunting and then some undeserved praise.

Suddenly her face turned three shades of green. She jumped up and ran into the restroom to vomit.

I would venture to guess a surprising percentage of first-time sexual encounters end up with one or both of the participants puking. After all, since the beginning of history people have loved the ritual of getting drunk and making love.

My tryst with Joanne didn't lead to any kind of relationship and that was fine with me. It was just great to have finally done the deed.

Girls always say they want their first time to be special. Eighteen- year old virgin males just want their first time to be soon.

Mother Nature is constantly whispering in your ear, saying you need to get out there and replenish the species. Of course, I wasn't ready to create another human being yet but I was certainly eager to take some practice runs.

Girls were certainly more assertive about this stuff in college. A couple months later I got seduced by and slept with Lana, the program director of the college radio station. She was a year older than me. That also ended up being a one-time thing because she was just using me in an effort to make Eric jealous. It didn't work but I still enjoyed my night with her.

Chapter 44: White Punks on Dope

Neither Jeff or I had smoked pot before coming to college. We'd drunk our share of alcohol but drugs were still considered pretty exotic in Sunnyrock. Or at least I thought they were, maybe I was just naïve.

We really didn't party all that much in high school. One time when we were juniors a few of us went over to Jeff's when his parents were away and threw together some kind of toxic concoction made out of 7-Up and about ten different kinds of hard liquor. We didn't have much alcohol because we just brought small amounts we could swipe from our folks without being too obvious.

I'm pretty sure we acted a lot drunker than we actually were.

Another time a bunch of us drove up to a ranch Jeff's folks had up in the mountains. We spent the evening drinking some God awful cherry flavored vodka and then I fell asleep.

When I woke up I was still drunk and had shaving cream and pipe tobacco all over my face. It kind of freaked me out at first… I thought maybe I was having some kind of weird allergic reaction.

Now here we were getting stoned more or less every night of the week. Our neighbor Gary loved coming over and getting us high and he seemed to have an unlimited supply.

"What are you guys up to? I think this would be an excellent time to get stoned". Gary really liked using the word excellent.

"Geez, we got high last night. We thought maybe we should actually study for a while tonight".

"Oh, come on. You can study later. This will help you relax, open your mind up so you can absorb those facts and figures better".

"Oh, okay. I guess a couple hits wouldn't hurt".

Of course, once I got stoned I had no interest in school work. I barely had the necessary brain power to work the controls on the stereo… memorizing dates and names from the Industrial Revolution was totally out of the question.

I'm not sure why he enjoyed smoking with us so much. Maybe it was because we were new to it and he liked watching how we reacted to stuff.

Sometimes he would sneak up behind us and try to scare us or maybe play weird little mind games in an effort to make us freak out. Nothing all that bad but it still contributed to my perception that he was a master manipulator and we were his yokel pawns.

That was a major difference between drinking and getting high... very often (at least back in those days) you would meet guys who seemed to really enjoy getting other people stoned out of their minds. I guess it was some kind of weird control thing or an ego trip they were on. Or maybe they saw themselves as the captains of some kind of psychic cruise ship.

We'd sit and listen to music for hours on end. We especially loved long, extended cuts that featured sound effects. "Wish You Were Here" by Pink Floyd was definitely one of our favorite albums at the time.

I was also really into 10cc. Their art-rock was full of great effects like the amazing overdubbed voices on "I'm Not in Love". The dope definitely enhanced whatever we were listening to.

One night Gary introduced us to Thai Stick. It took us to a whole new level of messed up. I remember thinking, "Oh my God. I'm getting out of control, now he has me smoking shit from other countries!".

Thinking about that night always reminds me of the song “A Passage To Bangkok” by Rush. The lyrics describe the kinds of dope they smoked as they toured the world.

I started laughing about something Jeff said and then kept on laughing for the next twenty minutes. Five minutes into this seizure I couldn’t even remember what I was laughing about but I didn’t care because it felt so good.

Then my throat started making a weird clicking noise because I was laughing so hard and this caused Gary and Jeff to start their own uncontrollable laughing fits.

None of us could actually talk for the next ten minutes. It was like we had all contracted some strange laughing disease. I started to wonder if I’d ever be able to stop.

I lay down on my bed and stared at Jeff’s poster of a guy surfing. The curling wave started moving and then so did the surfer.

I was absolutely amazed. I didn’t know pot could make you hallucinate.

One thing I really liked about pot was that it made people mellow and silly instead of aggressive. During high school it seemed like at least one or two guys always wanted to fight somebody after drinking a few beers. And then they’d want to cry and tell all their friends how much they loved them. It was both exciting and really kind of pathetic.

Nobody wants to fight when they're stoned. I don't even think it's physically possible.

You get a bunch of guys together to smoke pot and generally all that happens is that people get hungry and constantly lose track of what they're talking about. It's really not all that different than what happens in a nursing home.

It started to catch up with me after a while. My grades weren't so good those first three months. I felt like I'd destroyed a lot of brain cells and I resolved to ease up on the partying during the second quarter of the school year.

I could also see what it was doing to Gary. Whatever collegiate ambition he had seemed to be drifting away like the smoke from his bong. He took five classes during the first quarter of the school year, two the second quarter and just a week-long first aid class in the Spring and I'm not even sure he finished that.

Things were starting to get a little tense between Jeff and I right before Christmas break. I think we'd just spent too much time together over the past three months… we took all the same classes, we both worked at the radio station, we shared that small dorm room and we even drove home to Vale together occasionally.

One night it just came to a head. We were talking about music and I mentioned how popular the Eagles were. He said, "I'm sick of hearing how great the Eagles are. Poco is a much better country rock band."

It was an amazingly unimportant topic to be arguing about that really didn't matter. It was a catalyst.

We finally ended up losing our tempers and started wrestling and knocked a bunch of stuff off our shelves.

It was a good catharsis for us. Nobody got hurt and it helped us understand why we'd both been so tense around each other lately. We made a point not to sign up for all the same classes the next quarter and that seemed to solve the problem.

We still loved talking about music. We'd both noticed it was changing a lot lately.

The popularity of Country and Southern rock had started to run it's course. Foghat even declared they were fools for the city. I guess you can only be laid back so long before you get bored and decide to head back downtown.

And the old English groups like Jethro Tull and ELP were starting to seem very disconnected from any spirit of rock 'n roll rebellion. It's hard to present yourself as anti-establishment and still bring a full orchestra and choir to every stop on the tour.

I could sense from the new music we were getting at the radio station that people were getting hungry for something new.

I've always been intrigued by the idea there are pivotal moments in history that jump start big shifts in the culture. Sometimes we're aware of them and sometimes they're nearly untraceable, just a subtle tug that pulls us in one direction or another.

Maybe it's the Beatles appearing on Ed Sullivan. Or the black American athletes raising their fists in Mexico City. Or Al Gore winning the Nobel Prize.

I've always had a theory that the Doobie Brothers song "Black Water" is what killed "country rock" in America. Oh, that genre of music continued on for a while after the song came out but I think on some level the seeds of pop culture destruction had been planted.

I always liked that group but there was just something so cheesy about that section of the song where they sing a capella and clap their hands. It almost feels like something you'd hear on the old Mitch Miller show back in the early Sixties.

I think it ended up sending a subliminal message into the American psyche that said we needed to get off our lazy musical asses and produce some real rock 'n roll before we forgot what it sounded like.

Mark McShane introduced me to "Born To Run" in September 1975. He started college in Idaho a couple weeks before I left for La Grande and so I was over at his new dorm visiting him.

It was truly one of the most amazing records I'd ever heard. Bruce Springsteen and his band had created a picture of modern America that was every bit as heroic and dramatic as any story from the Old West or Camelot. It was like West Side Story but with real people instead of dancing imaginary street gangs. I immediately ran out and bought my own copy and took it with me to La Grande.

And even though the songs were about the desperate lives of real people, there was still so much passion and art wrapped up in it. This was rock 'n roll that made your heart pump and inspired you want to turn up the volume and drive down the highway toward the future.

It was just so much fun playing that album for the guys in our dorm. It had an energy and a grandeur that made people's eyes light up the first time they heard it. Jeff would put on the headphones and listen to it over and over and over again.

Watching Saturday Night Live had definitely become one of the week's highlights. At first I wasn't too impressed because the skits seemed kind of juvenile. But as the weeks progressed the show seemed to find it's rhythm.

A quick side note regarding SNL: I've been watching it now for 35 years. Sometimes it's pretty funny and sometimes it's pretty lame. But one thing you have to admit is that it has helped launch or at least promote the careers of an amazing number of comic actors and actresses.

It absolutely drives me crazy when I hear somebody around my age say they really never cared for it after the first season.

Hey, don't get me wrong... I loved Dan Ackroyd, John Belushi, Chevy Chase, Garrett Morris, Jane Curtin, Gilda Radner and Laraine Newman. They were awesome.

But what about Bill Murray, Eddie Murphy, Al Franken, Joe Piscopo, Julia Louis-Dreyfus, Dennis Miller, Dana Carvey, Chris Farley, Mike Myers, Amy Poehler, Tina Fey, Tracy Morgan, Adam Sandler, Martin Short, Christopher Guest, Chris Rock, Harry Shearer, Molly Shannon, Will Ferrell, Billy Crystal, Janeane Garofolo, Jimmy Fallon and dozens of other very talented folks?

That's an amazing amount of talent to dismiss simply because you got old prematurely and couldn't stay up past midnight on Saturdays.

Even when the comedy wasn't great, the musical acts were nearly always worth checking out.

Sometime in March of 1976, the radio station received a promo copy of Patti Smith's debut album "Horses". I thought it was great. It had a raw, uncompromising sound coupled with the intelligence and passion of poetry.

About a month later I heard she was going to be on SNL. I was really excited.

The only place I could watch her was in the dorm TV room. I was alone at first but then a bunch of football players came in and sat down. They weren't really up on the current music trends… their idea of a good time was getting drunk and singing along with Doctor Hook and the Medicine Show.

When Patti Smith and her band came on, the football players started booing and making fun of her. She was different. She didn't fit their idea of what a woman entertainer on TV should look or act like.

This really fired me up. I felt like I'd been putting up with small minds like these for far too long. After Smith finished her song I looked at them and said, "You guys better wake up. You've just seen the future of rock 'n roll". Then I turned and left the room.

Looking back, I will admit my outburst was a little over the top. But damn, it felt good. That was something I would have never done back in Sunnyrock.

Chapter 45: Thin Line Between Love and Hate

Not too long after the “Patti Smith” incident I met a new student named Marcy Collins. She had transferred in from a community college over in the Salem area.

She lived in the women’s section of our building. We both happened to be hanging out in the TV room one day and struck up a conversation about tennis. We agreed it would be fun to get together and play sometime.

She seemed nice and was what I considered athletically attractive. Kind of like those female volleyball players you see in the Olympics… tall and fit and healthy with nice legs and cute freckles.

A couple days later I heard a knock our dorm room door. It was Easter morning.

When I opened the door I found a basket of goodies with a note from her attached to it… "Nice to meet you, thought you might like a treat. We should get together and play tennis sometime".

One thing led to another and we started seeing each other. She was a year older than me and definitely more worldly. She didn't have a roommate and it wasn't long before we were taking full advantage of that fact.

It was so different in college than back in Sunnyrock. Even if you had a girlfriend in high school you still had to go through the standard negotiations… a kiss on the first date, more kissing and a little outside the clothes touching the breast action on the second date, an unbuttoned shirt on the third date, a possible refusal on the fourth date when you try to take her bra off because things are moving too fast and she doesn't want you to think she's a slut but then bra off on the fifth date because she's worried you'll think she's a prude and you might break up with her.

Then you start going back and forth about the nether regions and things get really intense. It's like the Cuban missile crisis with panties and zippers.

Marcy cut right to the chase and immediately invited me into her bed. She was on the Pill and I was her boyfriend and she wanted to make love with me and sleep with me whenever I wanted. I was stunned by the simplicity of her request and only too happy to comply.

Sleeping was hard because the two of us had to fit on her twin bed. And then I had get up early enough in the morning to sneak out of her dorm before the other female students were up and about.

I started feeling a little delirious. I wasn't just enjoying the sex but also everything else that goes into an intimate relationship… seduction, passion, the hunger you feel for your partner's body. I started thinking of us as lovers and also began to understand the power of that word.

Lovers can make their own little world out of love and lust and laughter and be free at least temporarily from all the noise and pain and pettiness the real world rains down on us.

I probably could've been more suave. The first time she performed oral sex on me, I thanked her over and over and over again. I briefly considered getting her a trophy. Firemen who rescue babies probably receive less adulation. Intercourse was great but oral sex truly seemed like a gift from God.

One Saturday night we decided to play strip poker with a couple named Howard and Ellen. We were drinking White Russians and smoking pot.

Eventually, we were all naked. Much to my horror I began to get an erection. Marcy and the other couple teased me in a good-natured way. Ellen laughed and commented that I didn't seem to have any impotency problems.

Another night Marcy and I went out for Chinese food and then drank a bunch of red wine back in my room with Jeff and Gary and a bunch of other friends. After a few glasses, I was so drunk I must have gone on mental auto-pilot.

I was really hung over the next day. Everybody started teasing me about eating Chinese food the night before and when I asked them how they knew what I ate they showed me the red-colored rice I'd thrown up on the front lawn of the dorm. Jeff asked me if I was trying to spell my name out there.

My partying and lack of sleep gradually wore me down. One weekend in May I came down with an oral trifecta… cold sores, canker sores and strep throat. I quickly lost ten pounds because it was too painful to chew or swallow anything.

After a couple months I realized that even though I was having fun with Marcy, I really hadn't developed any strong feelings for her.

We had pretty different outlooks on life… I believed it was important to have some kind of comprehensive philosophy about life and how you interacted with people. She seemed to think all that mattered was making a decent amount of money and partying as much as possible.

I was also ready to leave La Grande and go to school in a more metropolitan area.

When I went home that summer, I took the coward's way out and sent her a Dear Marcy letter.

She wrote me back. She was very upset and shocked. She was hoping I would change my mind later after I'd had more time to think about it. I was kind of surprised that she cared about me this much but I still felt like it was time to move on.

We saw each other a few more times after she graduated from EOSC and moved back to Salem. We'd go out to dinner and I'd normally spend the night. It seemed like she was bit less pleasant each time we got together.

I will fully admit, I was a selfish jerk when it came to Marcy. I wanted to sleep with someone from time to time and I took advantage of her.

The last time I saw her was on New Year's Eve 1980. I was living in Eugene and she called and invited me to come up and spend the evening with her in Salem.

I had eaten a couple of hard boiled eggs that morning that were probably past their expiration date. My stomach rumbled throughout the day but I figured it would pass.

When I got to Salem, Marcy said we should go to a nearby tavern she liked. She suggested we take both our cars in case either of us wanted to leave early. It seemed kind of odd but I didn't make a fuss.

A male friend of hers joined us and we drank a couple of pitchers of beer. All of a sudden, I felt very queasy.

I ran into the bathroom but didn't make it to the toilet. I sprayed vomit all over the wall. Suddenly, I truly understood what they meant by the term "projectile vomiting".

A guy standing at the urinal looked over at me with horror on his face. He was just trying to drain his lizard and here I was re-enacting a scene from The Exorcist.

I apologized and staggered into the stall. I fell on my knees and hugged the toilet for next half hour or so. I vomited eggs and beer and everything except the lining of my stomach.

I finally recovered enough to stand up and walk back to where Marcy and her friend were sitting. I told her how sick I was and how I thought maybe I had gotten food poisoning from those hard-boiled eggs.

She smiled and said, "Maybe you should drive back to Eugene tonight".

I grimaced and asked her if there wasn't some way I could spend the night at her place.

"No, sorry, can't help you out. It's New Year's Eve and I plan on partying until the sun comes up".

I felt so miserable I didn't even have the strength to get mad. I went out to my car and drove the sixty four miles back to Eugene. The last twenty miles I felt so sick I started shaking.

I've always wondered if she put something in my beer or if she just took advantage of the fact I had food poisoning. I've heard a few drops of Visine in a drink will cause the kind of reaction I had.

I guess it really didn't matter… I had to admit I'd used her over the years and it was probably about time karma kicked me in the ass for it. The universe has a way of working these things out.

Chapter 46: Burnin' For You

It was nice being back in Sunnyrock again but still frustrating in terms of summer employment. I figured I'd work for Dad or whatever farmer might need help for a few days.

I wasn't even sure how much money I needed to make because I hadn't decided yet where I was going to go to school the next year.

Janet was home for the summer too. She had attended a community college in Bend, Oregon for a year and then came back to Sunnyrock. She was kind of in the same mindset as I was, not really sure what her next move would be. She and Rick had broken up and she had started dating Mark.

She and I talked about people we'd met and stuff we'd experienced during our time away from Sunnyrock. We had a good laugh about how much we'd both partied.

It was good to know we hadn't drifted apart.

It was right around this time that I discovered Warren Zevon. I had read a review of his new album in Time magazine and it sounded interesting.

I had to sneak the album in the house… Dad was a little aggravated at the time about how much money I was spending on music. It wasn't all that much but then again I didn't have that much either.

I loved it. He had that southern California sound (Jackson Browne produced it) but the lyrics were edgy. And he had a deeper voice that gave credibility to the song stories he wrote about outlaws and drunks and mercenaries and crazy baseball players.

He reminded me of a really good fiction writer, but instead of using the written page this was someone who could paint a picture within the confines of a three and a half minute song.

It always annoyed me that he only had one hit single, "Werewolves of London". It's a fun song but I think it gave a lot of people the impression he was a novelty act, someone you'd end up hearing on Doctor Demento right after they played that tune about the Purple People Eater.

Hell, the song isn't even really about werewolves!

I'm not surprised he died relatively young. He drank so much vodka in the late 70's he earned the nickname F. Scott Fitzevon.

He definitely had highs and lows in his personal life but I pretty much loved every album he put out between 1976 and his death in 2003. I always had a feeling he was one of those artists that produced their best work when they were feeling really miserable.

His view of life was usually sardonic but I always got the feeling when he wrote a love song it was probably far more sincere than the usual pabulum you hear on the radio.

It was nice being back home but also a little strange. Part of me wanted to go right back to doing the stuff we did before I went to college. Another part of me felt like I couldn't truly go home again.

Driving around was always one of our main activities, especially in the summer. This was when gas was still cheap.

The summer after our junior year a girl named Jackie Chambers was working at the Shell station on one of the main streets. She was a year younger than us and all of a sudden she had this amazing figure. It was hot and she would wear cutoffs and halter tops.

Mark, Josh Leonard and I were all infatuated with her. We would just drive around town again and again and again so we could stare at her. Then sometimes we would stop at the station, talk to her some while we were getting more gas and then go drive some more.

I got together with some old Sunnyrock buddies on the third of July. It was a hot Saturday night and after we drove around for a while we were going to stop by a dance being held at the town VFW hall. Mark McShane's band was playing.

We had the windows down and the music was loud and we were giving each other a hard time just like in the old days. I loved being in college but it still great being back temporarily with buddies I'd grown up with.

That's something I love about small towns... if you drive around long enough you'll eventually run into people you know. And they can tell you where to find other people you know.

It was great hanging out with my high school friends. We had a lot of catching up to do.

Jeff Argent had come down from the mountains for the weekend. He was going to be working as a logger for a couple months.

He looked like he'd put on a bunch of muscle and we'd only been out of school for three weeks. He was no longer the skinny dude I'd wrestled with back in December.

He was in a really good mood. He said, "Man, I have been working my ass off up there in the mountains. It's really nice to have a couple days off and come down and hang out with you guys." I put my arm around his shoulder and pretended to wrestle with him. I had missed my roommate since school let out.

He spotted Meagan Thomas at the dance. They started talking and it looked like they were having a really nice time. Jeff looked really happy.

Then Stan Larsen showed up. When Jeff left to go outside for a while, Stan walked over and started flirting with Meagan.

After a few minutes, Jeff came back and saw her with Stan. You could see a dark shadow pass over Jeff's face… it was like he had a wound that could never completely heal.

I walked over and patted Jeff on the shoulder. I said, "You doing okay there, buddy?".

He stared at her back and replied, "This is such bullshit. He walks into the place and she lights up like a fucking firecracker. I'm really just so sick of her and him and the whole goddamn thing".

He said he was going to go out to his car and listen to music for a while. I wondered if he had a tape of "Can't Get It Out of My Head". I hoped not.

Jeff's parents were out of town so he said we could party at their house. He took off by himself. After the dance ended, twenty or so of us went over there.

We were there a couple hours and we were starting to wonder where Jeff was. The phone rang and I answered it. It was Jeff's cousin Bill, a local cop.

He said Jeff had been killed in a car accident and we all needed to clear out of the house as soon as possible.

I hung up the phone and yelled for everybody to shut up and listen. Then I told them what had happened.

My friend Rick Dennison started laughing and said, "Hey, that's a good one. You almost had us there". Then one of the girls noticed all the blood had drained out of my face and said, "Oh my God, he's not kidding".

A pall settled over the room. We quickly cleaned the place up and left.

Later we figured out Jeff must have got drunk after seeing Stan with Meagan. Apparently there were six empty beer cans found in the car and the cops said he was doing over a hundred miles per hour when he flipped his Chevelle over on the road leading out to Bully Creek Reservoir.

Some people were mad at Meagan for a while because they felt like she'd led Jeff on and caused his death. I thought Jeff's sister might try to really hurt Meagan.

Others blamed Stan more. At first I felt that way too.

But ultimately I came to the conclusion it wasn't really anybody's fault. It was just one of those tragic situations where desire, alcohol and too much horsepower combined to wipe away the life of a really good person. It was just such a awful, pointless tragedy and a death that will always haunt me.

Chapter 47: Don't Let the Sun Go Down One Me

About six months ago I had a dream I was back in Sunnyrock. I was driving a silver Monte Carlo, the one my dad used to own. When he brought it home in 1972 I thought it was just the coolest car ever.

I was driving down the highway between Sunnyrock and Brisco. I turned off the highway into the driveway of the house we lived in during my high school years.

I walked up to the house and looked in the living room window. I could see Dad in there talking to Jeff Argent.

I knocked on the window and yelled their names but they ignored me. I started to get really frustrated.

"Stairway to Heaven" playing somewhere. That was one of Jeff's favorite songs. For some reason it seemed very odd to hear that song in my dream but not odd to see two dead people hanging out in our old house.

Then I felt a hand on my shoulder. I turned around and there stood the actor Bill Murray. "It's okay", he said. "Don't be mad at them. It's just not your time yet".

That really helped. Bill Murray just seems like such a decent guy.

My stepmother Nona passed away in 2000. She was 87 and had lived a good life. I know that's a cliché but it seems to fit her... she lived a long time and was healthy for most of it and got to do some pretty fun stuff.

They were living in Brisco when she died. When she got to a certain age they moved there because she had so many doctor appointments.

After her death, Dad moved back to the farm for a while. I went down to visit him during the summer of 2002. One day we went to a potluck lunch at the senior center in Sunnyrock.

It was held down in the basement of the building. They were all really nice folks but I got a weird feeling sitting among them. I felt like I was in a scene from the Diary of Anne Frank... they were quietly eating their lunch, hoping and praying that Death wouldn't find them down in this sanctuary.

A few months later he was having dinner at the Brisco Elk's club and was introduced to a widow named Mabel Archer. They hit it off and became friends. Not long after that she asked him if he wanted to move in with her.

It was purely platonic. They were just two lonely older people glad to have someone to spend time with.

She was really good to him. When he was diagnosed with a rare type of throat cancer, she drove him for treatment five days a week for eight weeks in a row.

I was really grateful she was helping him out. However, my wife and I found she could be a little exhausting at times.

If you asked her a question about herself she would get this faraway look in her eyes and then go rambling on for five or ten or fifteen minutes, jumping from subject to subject.

"When I was a kid we didn't get toys from the store. Somebody might make you one or maybe we'd just play with a stick and a rock. Boy, I hate rock music. When I was a kid we had good music. We'd go over to my uncle Joe's house and everybody would sing and laugh and then we'd have dinner. We'd have ham and potato salad. Speaking of potatoes, my son used to drive truck during the potato harvest around here. Never complained about working hard, not like these kids today. By the way, today your dad was feeling better…".

I wondered sometimes if she would even notice if I left the room while she was rummaging through her mental archives.

I really didn't mind the lengthy monologues so much. I just figured that's what some people do when they get to be 85 or so. Maybe I'll do it too.

What I did mind was her really negative attitude about the current state of the world and the people who live in this era. In her opinion, everything was better in the past. This was something that really got on our nerves.

My wife and I have always sworn we won't be like that when we get old. We believe change is a necessary part of life and every generation will have its positive and negative aspects. People don't react to things the same way now as they did in 1932 because the world is a very different place than it was in 1932.

Dad recovered from his cancer but then started having respiratory problems. The doctor told him he had the agricultural equivalent of black lung. He'd spent a lot of time over the years leveling land and had absorbed a great deal of dust into his lungs.

He was using an oxygen tank for a while but finally it got so bad he had to go to the hospital. I drove down to Brisco and the first thing he said was that he wanted to take advantage of Oregon's assisted suicide law. I told him we were in a

Catholic hospital and there was no way they were going to oblige him.

After a few days, we got him settled into a nursing home. He was very depressed. A lot of people stopped by to see him but that didn't seem to lift his spirits much.

I sat there thinking about the inevitability of certain events. I had pictured this scenario in my mind so many times over the years. And here we were… me sitting in a chair and him laying in a hospital bed, both of us knowing that he would never go home again.

He had a moment of panic at one point. He looked at me and said, "Son, I need to get out of here. I want you to go get me some clothes so I can go back to Mabel's. This place is no good for me".

I had to tell him she wasn't strong enough to take care of him anymore. I hated saying those words, it felt like my heart was being torn apart. He had done so much for me over the years and here I was being forced by the cruel facts of life to extinguish his last remaining hope.

I stayed for a week and then I had to get back home. I stayed in touch with Mabel and Uncle Mitch and other local folks and they gave me updates on how he was doing.

He pretty much stopped eating but the nurses and doctors in the facility took care of him the best they could. He finally passed away in the summer of 2004.

We had a nice memorial service. Dad had a lot of friends in the area and several people from my birth mother's side of the family showed up too. I gave a talk about what a wonderful father he had been and all the important lessons he taught me over the years.

I wanted to cry but the tears wouldn't come. I knew the pain would be stored and come out some other time. My half-brother Roger was very upset and I did my best to comfort him.

We all miss Dad a great deal.

Chapter 48: Over the Hills and Far Away

Jeff's death helped me make my mind up about changing schools. The event hung over me like a dark cloud all summer and I worried that La Grande would seem like a place full of holes he should be filling but never would.

I decided I wanted to do some kind of social work. Radio was fun but I was feeling a compulsion to do something that would make a difference in people's lives. Maybe work with kids, help them avoid making stupid decisions that could ruin or end their lives.

I knew it would take a while to save up much money. I decided to keep living at my folks' house and go to school at the local community college for a quarter.

I was hanging out with Ronnie Felson a lot at that time. We liked talking about current events. He was very conservative and very convincing and when we drove around we would solve the country's problems one by one. We were convinced that if the government listened to guys like us pretty soon there would be no more waste or welfare.

Ironically, I think there were a lot of folks at conservative think tanks having those same kinds of discussions around that time. We were just a few years away from the start of the Reagan era.

It's too bad we weren't getting paid to come up with our simple solutions. We probably could have started the Sunnyrock Institute or something.

I got tired of having to borrow my dad's car so I bought a used Mercury Capri. I put down a couple hundred bucks and was going make payments on the remainder. It was yellow with a black vinyl roof. I was really proud of it.

Unfortunately, within a week I got broadsided by a huge Plymouth Fury in an unmarked intersection. And it was my fault since the old geezer in the other car had the right of way.

There's a good reason the insurance rates for young, unmarried males are so high… generally speaking, they're idiots.

Luckily, I was just banged up a bit. I got the car fixed but the radiator always seemed to have a slow leak. After a few months I sold it and Dad gave me his Monte Carlo.

Ronnie got pretty mad at me. We had planned to drive my Capri back to Georgia during Christmas break. We were going to visit some relatives he had back there. He said stuff like this always happened to me.

In retrospect, it may have been a good thing I had the accident. Attempting to drive across the country and back in December might not have been the smartest thing. Getting hit in Brisco was probably preferable to breaking down on the side of the road during a blizzard in Kansas. Plus I hadn't really thought through how I was going to afford both this trip and moving out on my own.

I think he was also still kind of sore about the time we were warming up before a basketball game and we ran into each other and I cut his forehead with my braces.

Community college seemed pretty easy after my year at EOSC. It was the only time in my life I ever got straight A's. Of course, it helped that in one of the classes all we had to do was watch silent movies. I really liked that class.

I had received a perfect score in a World History class I took in La Grande. But I think I may have had an unfair advantage…it was taught by an elderly nun who seemed to be sweet on me for some reason. Maybe I reminded her of some boy she liked before she gave up the pleasures of the flesh.

I started thinking about where I might want to transfer to. Oregon College of Education had a good Corrections program. I didn't want to work in a prison but I liked the idea of being some kind of youth counselor or maybe a probation officer.

OCE was located in Monmouth, a little town west of Salem. My friend Tony Chavez was planning to go to a community college up in that area so we decided to get an apartment together in Salem.

This was the same Tony Chavez who had told me when we were little that I had to play backup utility outfield. We'd actually become pretty good friends the past few years.

He was a good athlete and had a razor wit. The only thing that seemed to bother him was when somebody said he was a Mexican-American… he claimed he was Spanish, not Mexican. I always chuckled when I heard him say that to people.

We loaded up our cars and headed north and west toward Salem. The wind was blowing so hard on I-84 the snow looked like a white dust storm.

When we first got to Salem we had very few furnishings. Just a little black and white TV, a couple folding chairs, a couple mattresses, some kitchen stuff, a stereo and my wooden crate filled with record albums. Our lifestyle was going to be pretty Spartan for a while.

I gradually started to understand that people on this side of the mountains had a somewhat different geographical perspective than I was used to.

The term “Pacific Northwest” can sometimes be confusing. Some people think it includes Washington, Oregon and Idaho. On the other hand, some folks think it’s just Washington and Oregon and that every square inch of both states is covered by Pine trees.

The truth of the matter is that Oregon and Washington are green on the west side of the Cascade mountain range and pretty dry on the east side. The reason it’s green on the west side is because it rains a lot between October and May.

So I would say western Oregon and Washington are definitely located in the Pacific Northwest, eastern Oregon and Washington are kind of located in the Pacific Northwest and Idaho is more or less just a PNW wannabee.

All that rain and the perpetually gray winter skies really got to me at first. I was used to the occasional eastern Oregon cloudburst or maybe a gentle June shower. Storms in Salem seemed to go on for days and days and there were times I thought my car was going to be washed right off the freeway.

But I really liked how fresh the air smelled and how green everything was. And best of all, there just seemed to be a lot more opportunities than back home.

Tony and I liked going to the movies. When we saw the first “Rocky” film we thought it was fantastic. We were both really moved.

Another Sunnyrock guy named Ron was going to school at Willamette University in Salem. Sometimes he came over and hung out with us.

One time Tony, Ron and I got stoned and I played the album “RA” for them. It was done by Todd Rundgren and his band Utopia. Most of one side of the record was dedicated to a cut called “Singring and the Glass Guitar”.

It’s a story song about some guys on a quest to find a glass guitar and vanquish evil. In other words, your basic Lord of the Rings rip-off. But it did feature some pretty cool audio effects that were supposed to convey earth, air, fire and water. When it came to the wind part I totally freaked out because I thought it sounded so amazing. Tony and Ron laughed hysterically at the way I was carrying on.

Josh Leonard (the bunny thrower) was also now living in Salem. He was going to school and working part-time, renting a house with his older sister. Tony and I spent a lot of time hanging out over there, enjoying the fact their furniture actually had padding.

We were all really poor but none of us were all that interested in cooking. We started going to an all-you-can-eat buffet place called Royal Fork. We would only eat one meal per day but we’d eat so much all we could do afterward was go back to the apartment and lay down on the floor.

One Saturday night Josh, Tony and I decided to play a drinking game. We had a case of Mickey's Malt Liquor. It was about eight percent alcohol.

After we played for a while and got sufficiently wasted, we decided to walk downtown and get something to eat. When we got to the diner we made a little too much noise and the manager told us we had to leave.

We were stumbling back to Josh's house and we stopped at a Dunkin' Donuts. I was getting the spins and the sight of all those baked goods sparked my vomit reflex. I lurched outside and dropped to my knees.

Right at that precise moment, a carload of teenage girls drove by and one yelled, "Hey, how are the donuts?".

Tony had an uncle who lived in Salem. He was in his late 30's and it seemed like he and his wife were perpetually fighting about this or that.

Tony was crazy about his uncle and only too happy to criticize the wife. The uncle had a mistress and Tony thought that was really cool. I never knew if it was some kind of Latino male macho thing or if he just really hated his uncle's wife that much.

One night Tony's uncle took us to a professional wrestling match downtown. I was surprised it was taking place in Salem, it seemed really out of place there.

It was kind of surreal... Andre the Giant was featured in the main match and it appeared that most of the audience was composed of Russian immigrants who had come down from a nearby town called Woodburn.

If I had known about David Lynch at that time it would felt like we were in a David Lynch movie. You know, that weird dreamlike feeling. There weren't any dwarves who spoke backwards but it still seemed pretty strange nonetheless.

The Portland Trailblazers won the NBA championship that spring. I had always been a Boston fan but I still enjoyed getting caught up in the excitement of our state's only pro sports team going all the way.

That summer I decided to stay and work in Monmouth. Tony was going back to Sunnyrock to work for the Bureau of Land Management for three months so I answered a roommate wanted ad in the college newspaper. I ended up moving into an apartment in Monmouth with a guy named Reed.

I soon discovered Reed was another more or less constant pot smoker. We got along okay at first but as the summer went on we ended up getting on each other's nerves.

Heavy pot smoking seemed to put me on an emotional rollercoaster... it was fun for a while but then my brain started to crave normal sensory input.

Reed always had the bong out and was always nagging me to get high with him and that started to really annoy me.

He was even worse than Gary back in La Grande... if you turned Reed down he would actually take it personally and pout about it. It got to the point where I would actively try to avoid being around him whenever possible.

One bright spot was that he introduced me to a cool couple named Bear and Cynthia. They were three years older than me and both of them worked at the college. Bear was a really big guy with long hair and a big brown beard. I never saw him wear anything except a sunglasses, a white t-shirt, blue bib overalls and sandals. I always thought of him as a responsible hippie.

I was working on a maintenance crew that painted dorm rooms at OCE. The highlight of the summer was meeting three slightly older guys who were competitive race walkers. Their names were Lance, Tom and Tim. Tom and Tim were brothers.

They were kind of goofy but I admired how passionate they were about their awkward looking sport. They were convinced that one day in the near future, millions of people would be walking heel-to-toe instead of jogging.

They encouraged me to try race walking. I decided after one trip around the track it wasn't something I wanted to pursue. I felt like a total geek and nobody was even watching me.

Lance also got me interested in the music of the group Rush. He was almost as fanatical about this hard rock power trio as he was about his chosen sport. I didn't really care for the vocals all that much but I admired the fact they seemed to combine hard rock and progressive music in a way I hadn't heard before. And I thought it was kind of cool they were from Canada.

A few years later they would become my favorite band. "The Spirit of Radio" was the song that really grabbed me. I began to recognize what an amazing group this was. Their lyrics were intelligent, their song structures were complex and even though there were only three guys playing, they were so talented it sounded like it could be six or seven.

The lyrics were especially important to me. I had really started liking harder rock the past few years but it seemed like most bands in the genre rarely wrote about anything other than bedding women, breaking up with women, missing the women and getting wasted.

But here were Geddy Lee, Alex Lifeson and Neil Peart doing songs about religion and class warfare and cultural conformity. I almost felt like I should get college credits for listening to them.

I always admired their self-discipline and camaraderie. They were rock stars but they weren't messes. They just kept touring and creating new music and supporting each other through the decades.

I was especially inspired by the way Neil managed to survive losing both his wife and daughter in the course of one year's time back in the late 90's.

They never got the critical praise they deserved but it didn't seem to bother them. They loved each other like brothers and they loved their fans and that's all that seemed to matter.

At the end of the summer, Reed decided to quit school and move back to his parents' house in Salem. Tony and another old Sunnyrock buddy named Steve moved into the apartment with me. Steve was studying Law Enforcement at OCE.

Chapter 49: Art For Art's Sake

I enrolled in a Spanish class that Fall term. I ended up sitting next to a tall guy with glasses named Dave Dawson.

It's strange how these things occur. Two guys decide to take the same class and happen to strike up a conversation. The next thing you know, it's 33 years later and you've been through so much together it's hard to imagine what life would be like if you didn't communicate with the other person on an almost daily basis.

Actually, I need to give Dave the credit. He started the conversation, tapping me on the shoulder and pointing out some especially good looking girl in the classroom.

I would venture to say at least a solid quarter of the conversations we've had over the past thirty plus years have started with one of us directing the other to check out some hot female. We love and appreciate the ladies. I'm sure when we're old we'll still be nudging each other and appraising attractive women.

And the nice thing is, the older we get the more women we can appreciate. When we're ninety even seventy year olds will seem like sweet young things.

He claims I was hesitant to talk to him but I don't remember. Maybe I was feeling shy that day or maybe I thought it was weird that a guy I'd never met before was telling me to look at a girl

I was also kind of lazy about making new friends because I had my three Sunnyrock pals living in the area.

I was amazed how quickly Dave and I hit it off. It almost felt like we'd been living parallel lives all these years.

As we got to know each other, we realized we had a lot of common interests... sports, movies, books, music, women. We both liked "The Waltons" and we had similar senses of humor.

While I enjoyed talking to Dave, I hated the class. I especially hated the idea you were never supposed to talk the teacher in English. I knew it made sense intellectually but it still drove me crazy. I dropped it after the first couple weeks.

Dave and I kept hanging out in our free time. He told me he'd grown up on a farm in the McMinnville area and now his folks lived in Salem. He'd gone to the University of Oregon in Eugene his freshman year but due to a lack of funds was now back living with his parents and going to school in Monmouth for a year.

We were both farm boys who had grown up knowing we wanted do something different than what our fathers did.

He was an aspiring writer. He'd already written several short stories and when we met he was working on an outline for a book.

I thought that was really exciting. Here was an eighteen-year old kid who had the drive and ambition to take on the challenge of writing a novel. While most people I knew were simply trying to get decent grades and keep their heads above water financially, this guy had the chutzpah to think he could create plots and characters and art.

Dave was very outgoing and eager to meet new people, partly just because he was a friendly guy and partly because as a writer he liked to study them and imagine how they might fit into one of his stories.

I always found it interesting when he would tell me about somebody he had just met and then later explain how he had built a story around a character based on that person.

I started to see that life and literature aren't really that far apart... the time each person spends on Earth can be seen as an amazing collection of stories, tragic and comic and inspiring and romantic and more often than not, very unpredictable.

I started hanging out sometimes at Dave's house in Salem. His parents were named Art and Vivian. His dad was a retired dairy farmer and his mother was a housewife with the sweetest Southern accent I'd ever heard.

They really made me feel at home. After living in college poverty for a while it was nice occasionally spending time in a house where you could get a home-made meal.

He also had two older brothers named Dan and Dirk and a sister named Dorothy. She was just a year older than me.

Dave and I took another class together at OCE that year. It was called Comparative Religions and it was taught by an East Indian professor who tended to get very excited when he talked about people using religion to transcend the limits of their banal human existence.

As he explained this concept, his voice would go higher and higher until it was basically a hoarse little squeak.

"When you really focus, your spirit connects with something bigger and you can actually feel it rising up out of this fragile shell you call a body. You chant or say a prayer or repeat a mantra and your essence soars out into space, searching the cosmos for that eternal place of beginning and ending, all time and no time, matter and anti-matter…".

There were a couple times I was worried he might end up having some kind of spiritual seizure. His intensity was quite impressive.

At first I was a little put off but I eventually ended up really liking the guy. I think he was just trying to make a fairly dry subject a bit more entertaining. Or maybe he was able to connect to the cosmos in some way and we happened to be the lucky folks who got to witness it happening.

Dave and I both loved going to the movies so we volunteered to write film reviews for the OCE college newspaper. I'd done record reviews for the EOSC paper and had found it to be pretty fun.

We made arrangements with the manager of one multiplex in Salem and actually got to see some films for free. But then somebody explained to him that his generosity didn't necessarily guarantee positive reviews and we had to start paying for our own tickets.

We were amazed someone could be managing a movie theatre and not know films sometimes get bad reviews. Salem may not be Manhattan but it's still located in the United States.

By the spring of 1978, I really felt like I needed to get out of Monmouth. In my opinion, it had to be one of the dreariest college towns in America.

The buildings were boring, most of the teachers seemed grouchy and there was a serious shortage of even moderately attractive women.

They didn't even allow stores to sell alcohol within the city limits. Of course, this was largely just symbolic since Monmouth was located right next to another town where you could buy it.

I couldn't stand the thought of being stuck there the rest of my time in college.

Of course, it probably didn't help that I was working part-time at a nursing home in town. My main job was driving a group of mildly retarded adults to their school every morning and picking them up in the afternoon. Sometimes I also helped the nurses when they needed to transfer an elderly patient to a different bed or clean up a mess.

It wasn't a great choice considering my depressive tendencies. I would have been much better off at the Sunny Day ice cream parlor or the Fun Puppies pet store.

I really admire the people who work in nursing homes. It takes a lot of patience and inner strength to go in there every day and work with elderly and infirmed people.

There were two residents that particularly affected me. One was an elderly gentleman who could still walk and always seemed relatively positive when he was dealing with the staff. One night he got angry about something and decided to walk out into the heavy traffic on the road in front of the nursing home. He was killed.

The other was a woman in her 40's who had very bad Multiple Sclerosis. She wasn't able to talk or move anymore and she always had a look on her face that said "please help me, I'm still young and I don't belong here".

I was also thinking about switching my major back to journalism. Corrections hadn't proven to be a very appealing course of study. The people in the profession who came to speak to our classes seemed really burnt out and not all that enthused about what they did for a living.

One speaker told our class "Look, I'm not going to lie to you. It's gonna be rough for the first few years. Most of your clients are almost what you would call professional liars. You do your best to help them stay on the straight and narrow and sometimes it works out but more often than not they find an excuse to go out and screw up their lives again. But if you hang in there you can eventually get an administrative job. The benefits are good and the pay is somewhat decent after you've been there a while".

He had bags under his eyes and stubble on his face. He looked like the kind of guy who might doctor his morning coffee with a little Old Crow just to make it through the day. Not what you'd call an inspiring presentation.

He kind of reminded of a History teacher I'd had back in high school. This guy was in his thirties, had a drinking problem and was going through a rough divorce. He would sometimes just tell us to read a chapter or two, turn on a Grateful Dead tape and lay his head down on his desk and go to sleep.

Dave suggested I transfer down to Eugene with him. At first I was reluctant to consider the idea because I only had about about a year more to go on the Corrections degree.

But gradually I started to consider the merits of the idea. It was a bigger town, they had a good Journalism program and I already knew people living down there.

Janet and Rick were living together in Springfield and Mark McShane was going to school at U of O. I'd been down to visit everybody a couple times.

One of those times Mark and I had gone to see Elvis Costello perform at an old church that had been converted into a community center. This was when E.C. was still viewed as sort of an angry young punk.

It was kind of odd... the opening act was a local guy who had long hair, wore a kimono shirt and played the kind of stuff you might hear at a Styx concert.

Maybe the other people in the audience didn't seem to really notice the irony of this pairing. To me, it was like going to a comedy club and watching Bob Hope open for Lenny Bruce.

Janet and Rick seemed to be doing well. She was going to a local community college part-time and working at a Dairy Queen near campus. He was working at a little grocery store.

I still had kind of a hard time relating to Rick. He didn't seem to have much of a soul.

When I was around him I felt like we were characters in a Woody Allen film. I was Woody and Rick was Tony Roberts, Woody's shallow buddy in "Annie Hall" who loved living in L.A. and wore a special suit to keep the gamma rays off his skin.

I always figured if you went to see a documentary about the Holocaust with Rick he'd just walk out of the theatre, yawn and ask if anybody was up for a pizza. Maybe go to that place with the really big ovens...

I eventually made up my mind and decided to take Dave up on his offer. I would start my new collegiate life in Eugene at the end of September. But first I needed to make some more money so I packed up my car and headed to Sunnyrock for the summer.

Chapter 50: Breakdown

I'd heard the Bureau of Land Management was hiring people to fight fires. I applied for a job there, hoping I could make a decent amount of money before I headed to Eugene.

Dad had never really liked the BLM much. He felt like it was just another bunch of government yahoos interfering where they didn't belong. He didn't mind the fire fighting part but he hated it when they tried to tell farmers or ranchers what they could or couldn't do with their own land

But he also understood how tough it was to find decent paying work in the Sunnyrock area. If there was a big fire season I could potentially rake in regular pay, overtime, double time and hazard pay. Maybe we'd even get to go to other states to fight fires. He didn't give me any grief about applying to work there.

I had to pass some basic mental and physical tests and then got hired. We spent the first couple of weeks getting in shape and getting our pumper trucks in order.

It had been an unusually wet spring, so it looked like we might not actually be called out to any fires for a while. We spent most of our days building fences or just driving around in the trucks.

Our main job seemed to be making sure nobody from the district office ever caught us loafing during one of their surprise visits. At times I felt like a character out of an old Sgt. Bilko episode, constantly pretending to work on something in case there was a surprise inspection of some sort.

I really didn't like the job much. I kind of felt like I was back in high school. There was a lot of macho bullshit and messing around and a couple of the Sunnyrock athletic coaches worked there during the summers. They were okay but their presence just made me feel like I'd never left town.

One bright spot was meeting a crew chief named Joe. He helped me break some bad work habits I'd been carrying around for a long time.

I'd always been a little hesitant about volunteering to do stuff I hadn't done before. He taught me it was always better to pro-actively jump in and help even if you screwed up a little bit at first. He said most bosses really appreciated people who were willing to at least try.

After you put a fire out, your crew would have to stay and monitor it for at least twenty-four hours to make sure none of the "hot spots" started up again. So we had a lot of time to sit around and talk about whatever.

I even started bumming cigarettes off Joe. I'd always hated smoking when I was younger but it's surprising what you'll do when you get brutally bored.

Janet and Rick got married in Sunnyrock that summer. I was one of the groomsmen. We wore these godawful peach colored tuxedos and had a party afterwards at Tony Chavez's house. We were drinking and sweating profusely while we danced to "Brick House" and other songs that were popular that year. The newlyweds seemed very happy.

The newlyweds seemed very happy. After their honeymoon they were heading back to Eugene.

I started feeling funny about being back in Sunnyrock. I didn't feel like I belonged there anymore but on the other hand I didn't know where else I would fit in.

I was amazed how quickly I'd become disconnected from the place I grew up. It looked so different to me now… small and lonely and sad.

I guess part of me always thought I could leave and grow up and yet somehow the town of Sunnyrock would always stay the same. Nobody I cared about would die or leave or grow old. Nothing really important would change.

I had always seen myself as a pretty clearheaded individual. But I have to admit, when it came to my hometown I was looking through the eyes of a wistful little kid.

It's funny, there were a lot of things I disliked about that town when I was growing up but there was also a lot of stuff that was good. The sunny days and clear skies, football games, working on a ranch, the nice people, always feeling safe…

I was discovering I couldn't go home again. It might be a cliché but that doesn't make it any less the feelings any less painful or powerful.

I'd been having some problems with depression on and off since I'd been in college. It was easy for me to see the dark side of life but it took real effort to feel good about anything, especially myself.

I was really pretty happy that first year in La Grande but I felt like Jeff's accident had caused my mood to short-circuit somehow. And I also wondered if I was carrying around some unresolved emotional pain related to losing my mother.

Basically, I was just trying to figure out why I was feeling so bad and hoping that if I did, maybe I could also figure out a way to make it stop. I was self-diagnosing and self-medicating. It was like I was on fire and trying to put it out with gasoline.

As the summer dragged on, I slowly grew more and more depressed. I spent a lot of time hanging out at a house Tony Chavez was renting. I was drinking way too much and starting to have a hard time sleeping at night.

One hot night in August I woke up with heart palpitations. My anxiety was getting out of control… there were dark shadows in my bedroom and they were whispering that I was a failure. I had been a failure in Sunnyrock and now it looked like there was a strong possibility I'd fail to settle on a degree and finish college.

I was all too ready to believe the voices in my head that had always told me I was a loser. I was the kid in the third grade who started crying in front of the whole class because he couldn't figure out how to do the long division problem on the blackboard. I was the kid who couldn't get his football uniform on right the first day of practice in the seventh grade. I was the kid who couldn't get the girl he wanted in high school and the kid who thought reading rock song lyrics at a speech contest was a good idea.

I resigned from the BLM a couple days after that. I'd been having trouble staying awake at work because of all the sleepless nights. I was starting to feel really self-conscious around the people I worked with. I imagine some of them probably thought I was taking drugs.

I went out one evening to help my dad irrigate. I was feeling like I'd hit bottom. It was hot and overcast and the sky was a strange copper color. Or maybe that's just the way it looked to me that evening.

I just couldn't contain my emotions any longer. I broke down sobbing and kept telling Dad how sorry I was I had failed him.

He was very understanding. He said "You haven't failed me. Everything's going to work out okay. I still want you to finish college and I'll do whatever it takes to help you make that happen".

Dad was always a good listener. And that's what I needed more than anything else at that moment.

Chapter 51: Fell on Black Days

Classes started in Eugene at the end of September. I was going to be sharing a house with Dave and a couple other guys.

I was still feeling pretty shaky emotionally. I did my best to act like nothing was wrong but it wasn't easy.

That's one of the worst things about depression… you have all this turmoil going on inside and yet it seems like every other human on the planet is happily going about their business. Occasionally it would get so bad I started to feel paranoid, wondering if maybe other people did know how bad I was feeling and were choosing to pretend they didn't care.

I usually just smiled and acted like everything was just hunky-dory. You get to be a pretty good actor after a while.

It was so different back then. It was really hard to tell people you had a mental health issue. It was like there were just two categories… either you were normal or you were nuts. There wasn't this huge gray area like now where half the population is taking medication every day for their depression, anxiety or OCD and able to function more or less okay.

The previous Spring I had broached the subject with Dave and told him I occasionally went through phases where I felt sadder than normal. But I didn't want him to think I was weird so I downplayed the seriousness of the problem.

I'd also talked to Mark about it during the Summer and he was very supportive but he wasn't really sure how to help me.

He did take me to see "Animal House" in Boise and that cheered me up for one evening. Plus it was cool since it was filmed in the town where I would soon be attending college.

The biggest mistake I made when I got to Eugene was smoking pot on a more or less daily basis. I wanted to fit in and didn't have the strength to deal with even the smallest amount of peer pressure.

It was just kind of standard college operating procedure at that time… it's what you did to unwind, it's what you did when you wanted to celebrate something, it's what you did because it was Saturday. I always felt good when I got stoned but really fragile the next day.

Our two other roommates were named Marty and Sam. They were both easygoing guys Dave had met in the dorm during his freshman year. Marty was from the Portland area and Sam grew up in Montana.

We all got along fine for the first week but then Marty and I had a misunderstanding about who was allowed take what out of the refrigerator. It was a completely normal roommate conflict but I was feeling so low at the time I figured I'd be kicked out of the house and then I had no idea where I would live.

I started to crack. This little conflict was the icing on my depressive cake. I'd just hit town and already I'd revealed what a loser I was.

I felt like every moment of weakness and mistake I'd ever made was visible on me.

I was walking around wearing a coat made out of failure…there it all was, getting on the wrong float in the parade, not making the top Little League team, standing up at the blackboard in the Fourth grade crying because I couldn't do the long division problem, weeping in the cold darkness of a December night back home.

I'd reached a point emotionally where the depression was like an eclipse. I tried and tried to think about my good traits and all the stuff I had accomplished so far in my life but it didn't seem to register.

The dark voices inside me said that positive stuff belonged to somebody else or didn't really matter in the big picture. They told me I was one of the world's losers and what was happening to me in Eugene should come as no surprise. I'd tried to be a success in the world outside of Sunnyrock and had done okay for a while but now I'd hit a wall I'd never be able to climb over.

The voices said that for people like me the downward spiral and ultimate surrender was a foregone conclusion.

I'd been so wound up the past few days I'd already skipped some classes. I was beginning to wonder if coming to Eugene had been a good idea. I felt like my living situation was already in jeopardy and what little confidence I had left when I came to this new town was nearly gone.

Thoughts of suicide started to drift into my head more and more often each day. I couldn't stay in Eugene if I wasn't going to school and I couldn't face the embarrassment of giving up and going back to Sunnyrock.

I got into this weird habit of planning my funeral. I was like a young woman who spends her time fantasizing about her wedding day but my dreams were much, much darker. The best I could hope for at this point was that the people in my life would say a few nice things and miss me for a while.

Sometimes I like thinking about making a mix tape of songs I wanted played. I guess you could say I was Death's D.J.

Maybe my life had been a waste of time but at least I could make sure my going away party was cool.

It's funny, for some reason I always felt like there were all these people back home who spent their time waiting for me to screw up so they could point their fingers and laugh at me. Of course it wasn't true… the only people in Sunnyrock who ever thought about me were ones who just wanted me to be happy. I was just so damn insecure at this point in my life.

I remember going for a long walk, trying desperately to figure out what my next move should be. I'd reached a point where dealing with college seemed beyond the limits of my emotional strength. For that matter, just getting up and existing every day was starting to seem like a real struggle.

I walked for miles and miles through the pouring Eugene rain. To comfort myself, I made up a punk rock song called "Mad At the World" and yelled it out as I marched down the sidewalk.

Look at me now
I'm nutty as a squirrel
I'm mad as a hatter
And I'm mad at the world.

Later that night, I called my dad and let him know what was going on with me.

"Hi Dad. I'm not doing too good. Been feeling pretty bad since I got here".

"I'm sorry to hear that, son. Have you been thinking positive thoughts?"

"I'm trying, Dad. But there just seems to be so much pressure. I feel like I'm gonna crack up or jump off a bridge or something. I'm getting kind of scared".

"Well, hang on. Don't do anything rash. I'm gonna get over there and help you straighten this out".

And just like that, he told my stepmom what was going on, got in the car and drove all night to come see me.

When he got to Eugene, we had a long talk. He wasn't exactly sure what to do. Truly effective antidepressant medications weren't available yet and even doctors had trouble figuring out how to help people like me.

I wasn't so bad off I needed to be institutionalized but on the other hand it was clear I needed help of some kind.

Dad said "I think we need to find a church and take this problem to the Lord". I was kind of surprised when he said this and normally I would have resisted the idea but I felt like I had hit rock bottom and was fresh out of any alternative solutions.

It was a Sunday night so we figured we'd just drive around and find a service to attend.

We stopped at a little church on the outskirts of town. At first it seemed to calm me down some. It was kind of nice just sitting there listening to the lady play the organ.

Then the minister came out. He was kind of a scary looking old guy wearing a black suit, a white shirt and a old-fashioned bolo tie. He had this intense stare and I wondered if you looked up close into his eyes if you might see a lightning storm or something. I wouldn't have been surprised to see he had the words "GOOD" and "EVIL" tattooed on his knuckles.

"I believe in an angry God", he began. "I believe in a God who doesn't suffer whining and disobedience and changing things around just so life is a little easier in the short run. I believe in the God who turned Lot's wife into a pillar of salt and who will burn all the sinners who have stepped away from the straight and narrow path!"

A few minutes later, the woman sitting next to me began speaking rapidly and loudly in some kind of Asian sounding language. I was shocked because she was a middle-aged white woman who definitely looked like she lived in a trailer park.

Then people all over the church began speaking in tongues. I'd never seen this before and it only made me feel worse.

This was not a good time for me to be witnessing some kind of strange supernatural phenomena… now I was not only depressed but also starting to question my sanity.

We stayed through the service but then didn't really hang around to visit with anybody. I was really anxious to get away from these people.

I think Dad felt bad about the way this little excursion had turned out. He was religious in his own way but this definitely wasn't the kind of church he'd been hoping to find.

The next day I told Dad I didn't know if I could stay in Eugene. It was hard for me to talk because I kept breaking down and weeping uncontrollably. He finally decided to call some friends who lived in a small town located about a half hour east of town. They said I could come stay with them until I was feeling better.

I think Dad was worried if I left Eugene, I'd never finish college. He had never told me what to study or where to go to school but he definitely wanted me to get a college degree at some point. I was just worried about getting through each day without doing something really bad to myself.

I withdrew from all my classes and moved out to Greg and Linda's. I was so grateful for their kindness.

Dad had a complicated family tree but Linda was essentially his niece. She and her husband Greg had been coming over to our farm the past few autumns to hunt pheasants and spend time with Dad and Nona. When I was younger they would let me borrow their ATV and ride it around on the property.

Greg was one of the head guys at the electrical utility that provided power for the Eugene-Springfield area.

Greg and I played pool a lot of nights after he got home from work. I actually got pretty good at it. During the day I would just hang around the house and read or watch television or nap or talk to Linda. They also had a couple of married daughters and son-in-laws who stopped by to visit from time to time. I was just trying to rest and get my emotions under control.

Greg and I also argued about politics from time to time. He had some strange foreign policy concerns.

"You know, Jim", he said, "You don't hear this a lot these days but I think we need to worry more about the Japanese. I don't trust them in the least. I wouldn't be surprised if they're planning another Pearl Harbor for us".

I grinned and replied "Geez, Greg, I think that one is kind of a long shot. Half their economy depends on selling us cars and stereos. I don't think you can simultaneously conquer us and ask us to purchase a Toyota".

He laughed as he chalked up his pool cue. "Well, I'm keeping my eyes on those bastards just the same".

They treated me very well. It felt so good just to take a little time off and not worry about anything. Maybe that's why a lot of kids have trouble like this at some point in their late teens and early twenties... they've gone through grade school, junior high, high school and then some college and finally their brains just want to stop and rest for a little bit.

Mark drove out to see me a couple times. Dave didn't have a car but we talked on the phone on a regular basis.

Staying in touch with them helped me a lot. Their visits and calls kept me from feeling like I'd completely lost my place in the world. They encouraged me and reminded me about all the good times we'd had in the past and all the great stuff we'd do in the future.

For some reason, the concept of friendship has always been very important to me. I've known lots of people who could pretty much just get by only spending time with their families. I'm not like that.

Family is great but I also need to be around people I've chosen to be with. Humans are humans and I don't always prioritize based on sharing DNA with somebody.

I didn't go into Eugene much for a couple months. I knew if I was going to climb out of this pit I needed to stay away from craziness for a while.

I did go in one Saturday night to hang out with Dave and his roommates. They had some other people over and there was a guy there named Duke who kept shoving the bong in my face. I finally passed out and when I woke up I saw the Rolling Stones were performing on Saturday Night Live.

I was really messed up. I remember lifting my head up off the carpet and mumbling "Hey, look, it's the Rolling Stones on a live TV show. How cool is that?". Then I passed out again.

Dad and Nona were also good about calling and checking on how I was doing. They just kept telling me to take it easy and not to worry about anything.

I gradually started feeling better but I knew it would take a while to fully climb out of the emotional pit I'd fallen into. I was so badly depressed there were times it took all my strength just to put one foot in front of the other and do the simplest tasks. Nothing seemed easy because every last bit of my confidence was gone. I began to realize that confidence is for the body what lubrication is for a machine… without it you seize up and cease to function.

I did go see a psychiatrist a couple times and he gave me some kind of medication but it didn't seem to help much.

I finally started to get a bit restless around the middle of December. I knew it was time to leave Greg and Linda's. I was scared but I knew I needed to get my life moving forward in some direction again.

I decided to take another stab at school. This time I signed up to live in a dorm.

Chapter 52: Head Games

I was assigned to a dorm and then I got to pick what floor I'd be on. I chose one where there were two wings for female students and two for the guys.

Initially, I was stuck in an extra large room with two guys named James and Harold. I was kind of surprised, I didn't even know there was such a thing as a three person dorm room. I guess maybe it was just the result of an imperfect architectural plan.

Fortunately, they weren't pot smokers as far as I could tell. I really needed to get back into the swing of things with a clear head and it would help if I could avoid marijuana for a while.

Unfortunately, that didn't mean they were drug-free.

I happened to meet James first. He seemed abnormally chipper, shaking my hand and telling me "hey, how's it going, I'm doing great, I took my vitamin A this morning and I feel like I should go climb a mountain or something. Wow, you have a lot of records, I'll have to check those out".

James and Harold loved taking acid. They thought they were being hilarious when they referred to it as vitamin A.

In my experience, very few people get funnier when they take drugs. Humor about people who take drugs can be hilarious but very few folks can get high and then make their non-stoned friends laugh. They don't have any timing and a good deal of the time they forget to finish the story.

Stoned people can make other stoned people laugh but it's almost more of a group exercise, like a group of dogs howling in unison when they hear an ambulance siren.

It was hard to relax around them. I'd be laying on my bed reading a textbook and then suddenly the two of them would come rushing into the room wearing ski masks and shooting at each other with water pistols. The first time this happened I about had a heart attack… I wasn't sure if it was my roommates or Palestinian terrorists.

Or maybe they'd take acid and attempt to invent their own version of Pig Latin. That got old really fast.

James and Harold also spent a lot of time planning elaborate practical jokes to pull on each other. I was constantly being told about their separate schemes and then sworn to secrecy. I started to feel like I was living in the middle of a game show. Or a really bad Marx Brothers movie.

I wondered how they managed to live like this and still get good enough grades to stay in school. I guess they must have been really smart.

Needless to say, this living situation got old pretty fast. I was trying to relax and re-engage with the world and these two freaks weren't making it easy. I asked at the housing office if there were any double occupancy rooms on the floor that had an opening.

I was able to move in with a guy named Rod. He lived in an extra large corner room and sort of looked like William Shakespeare.

He was a brilliant graduate student but I guess he chose to live in the dorm because he was too busy to deal with an apartment. When he wasn't studying, he was involved in four or five different role-playing games.

I'm pretty sure Dungeons and Dragons was his main passion but I think he also participated in games that replayed historical war campaigns. Luckily for me, he didn't feel the need to spend a lot of time bragging about his recent imaginary victory over Napoleon or trying to persuade me to get involved in D&D. I guess there were plenty of smart yet socially awkward folks on campus he could roll the dice with.

He was a reasonably friendly guy and was hardly ever in the room so I definitely felt like living with him was a big improvement over life with James and Harold.

Chapter 53: Court and Spark

It was fun living on a floor with both men and women. There was an interesting mix of types… a few extremely bright but introverted people who seemed to rarely leave their rooms when they were in the dorm, a few friendly low-key folks and a contingent of standard fun seekers who held a party more or less every Friday night in one guy's room. The drink of choice was a toxic punch they made with 7-Up, fruit juice and Everclear.

I took it easy on the alcohol but it was fun to be meeting some new people.

There was a relaxing area in the middle of the floor where people hung out and read. I noticed a particularly cute girl sitting there one day and struck up a conversation with her.

Her name was Maureen and she was from Boring, Oregon. It's a small town located near Portland.

She was petite with really pretty auburn colored hair and big blue eyes. She seemed to have a very sweet personality and I immediately developed a huge crush on her. She reminded me a lot of a girl I'd known at church camp when I was younger.

I saw her in the cafeteria a couple days later. She was sitting with another woman who appeared to be around our same age. I said hello and asked if I could join them.

Maureen was friendly but it was obvious her friend was annoyed I'd interrupted their conversation. The look on her face said, "why is this boringly average dorm rat bothering us?".

She was attractive but in a much less obvious way than Maureen. I thought she looked somewhat French with long, dark brown hair and delicate features. She wore glasses and a strangely purple shade of lipstick I'd never seen before.

Later I asked a couple guys what Maureen's status was and they said she was involved with a Pakistani student who drove a black Trans Am and seemed to have a lot of money. Somehow I didn't think she'd leave him for an eastern Oregon farm boy who recently purchased a used Datsun for four hundred bucks.

Her friend's name was Eve Badeau. She had transferred to Oregon the term I had dropped out. Her dad was an executive for Kimberly Clark.

He'd been transferred from the east coast to northern California. Eve decided to change schools and attend the U of O so she could take advantage of their well-respected Asian Studies program.

I kept running into her over the next couple weeks. At first she was a bit cool to me but as we got to know each other, her attitude shifted from bitchy to teasing. She'd see me sitting in the lounge area and say "Oh look, it's the cowboy. Did you round up your herd today? Smells like you may have brought in a souvenir on the bottom of your shoe".

I enjoyed giving her a bad time too. I asked her if the daily check from Daddy had arrived yet and how could she stand to live with the rest of us middle-class riffraff.

I got the feeling this might be a different kind of relationship for her. Maybe a bit more natural and less predicated on who was from what family or who made what amount of money. I liked her for her and she liked me for me.

I found myself being attracted to her confidence and sophistication. Well, at least she seemed sophisticated compared to most of the women I'd known over the years. And I thought it was cool we both had French last names… who knows, maybe we were fated to meet.

She could be very funny. She loved talking like Edith Ann, the little girl character created by Lily Tomlin. She was also very passionate about art and I liked that a lot.

The reason her lips were purple was because she was born with an enlarged heart. She struggled mightily to get through each school day. She was majoring in both Asian Studies and Statistics.

She eventually opened up and told me she was involved with one of her professors.

She said, “It’s not like I’m madly in love with him or anything. But he’s smart and nice most of the time and best of all he has his own apartment and furniture. It’s just so nice to be able to get out of this daycare and spend some time in a place suitable for an adult”.

Normally an attitude like that would have really put me off. But I got the impression maybe this girl didn’t know any other way to think. She came from a world where status and earning potential were located way up high on the prospective mate checklist.

She tried to come off as a jaded East coast ingénue but deep down I sensed she was really just a vulnerable twenty-year old who was scared to really give her heart away to anyone.

She seemed to let her guard down as we spent more and more time together. After a while I started to think of it as a case of opposites attracting.

I admired her intelligence and actually got a kick out of her pretentiousness. She liked the fact I'd grown up on a cattle ranch but also knew quite a bit about books, music and movies.

It was a bit like Annie Hall getting involved with Gary Cooper. Or maybe a modern version of Gary Cooper who liked to read Rolling Stone.

I started to think maybe I had a real shot with her.

One Friday night a bunch of us were going to drive out to a natural hot springs located about twenty miles outside of Eugene. But plans changed and it ended up just being Eve and myself.

The rain was gently coming down on us as we sat in the hot water. We both had on bathing suits and that was okay by me. I wanted this night to be about romance and not just a fling. We talked for a while and then kissed and then I held her in the misty darkness.

It was very romantic in an old-fashioned way. For some reason I kept thinking about Lancelot and Guinevere while we sat there in the gloomy mist.

The next morning I tried not to get too worked up about our evening together. I knew from past experience that just because two people share a nice moment of intimacy, it doesn't necessarily mean anybody can assume anything.

And Eve seemed like somebody who liked to have a good time without necessarily committing herself to anything more substantial. I kept telling myself "be cool, be calm, she's just another chick". I still had emotional scars from what happened with Doreen after the dance back in Sunnyrock.

But this time I wasn't disappointed. I ran into Eve in the cafeteria and she seemed genuinely happy to see me.

"Where have you been keeping yourself?" she said with a smile. "I wanted to tell you how much I enjoyed our little adventure out in the woods last night".

I noticed a couple overweight girls from our floor nearby doing their best to eavesdrop. I was sure before the day was over lots of tongues would be wagging about Eve and Jim and the crazy aquatic sex we had out in the boonies. Who knows, maybe we even invited some of the forest creatures to participate.

Each day after that we grew a little closer both emotionally and physically. I started hanging out in her dorm room quite a bit and we started playing a game where I would slowly remove all her clothes but none of my own.

"I am Doctor Hawthorne", I would whisper in her ear. "It's imperative we do a complete gynecological exam at once". She would laugh hysterically up to a point and then begin shuddering in pleasure when I slowly slid my hand between her thighs.

I had to be very gentle. Because her heart was larger than normal, everything else was a little further south than normal. This made her almost painfully sensitive to stimulation.

She taught me about the clitoris and how she liked to be touched. I began to realize what a lousy lover I have must been for Marcy… I had all the best intentions but had displayed the finesse of a guy working a jackhammer.

Eve finally broke things off with the professor and we became a bonafide couple. I have to admit this gave me a smug sense of satisfaction. Honest feelings and attraction had won out over a steady income and Scandavian furniture.

Though, ironically that ended being the kind of furniture I always bought once I had some real money.

I introduced her to my friends. She and Dave hit it off okay but Mark didn't seem to be too taken with her. I think he found her kind of exhausting.

She was romantic and artistic and overly dramatic about nearly everything. One minute she could be laughing and on top of the world and the next she'd be weeping and telling me she felt like she might only have days left to live.

But I could tell it wasn't a mental issue like manic depression. It was the heightened emotions of a human being who had spent her whole life looking over her shoulder, wondering if this was the day Death might come to take her away. She was like a soldier with PTSD. I figured that had to affect the way a person reacted to things.

I appreciated how much energy she put into our relationship. She was always giving me sexy cards or leaving me notes that put me in the mood.

One Saturday night I was in my room smoking pot with a couple guys from the floor. Eve had told me she had plans with some girl friends that night.

There was a knock on the door. When I opened it, there stood Maureen. She looked at my two friends with a very serious expression on her face and said, "You guys have to leave".

By this time I was pretty high and very puzzled about what was going on. I suddenly grew concerned there was something wrong with Eve. But then Maureen left the room and Eve walked in wearing a trench coat.

I asked her what was going on and she said, "I hope some sex." Then she untied the belt on the coat and revealed the sheer black teddy she was wearing, complete with garter belt and stockings.

I gasped with pleasure. Nobody had ever dressed up like that for me before. But my head was also spinning because I had smoked so much pot. I told

Eve, "Wow, you look amazing. I can't believe you did this for me".

Then I lay back on the bed and passed out for the night. All her efforts had been wasted on a silly college boy who spent the night in a cannabis-induced coma.

Unfortunately, it didn't take long before I started to feel like I was running interference between her and the rest of the world.

One night a mutual friend of ours was goofing around in the dorm. He had just seen the first "Halloween" movie the night before and he started chasing Eve down the hall while clutching a fake rubber knife. For some reason she instantly believed this completely normal twenty-year old she'd known all year had suddenly turned into a serial killer.

She screamed "Oh my God, he's trying to kill me!". She ran into my room and fell to the floor, gasping and sobbing and doing her best to warn me there was a mad killer on the loose and that I needed to save her. It took an hour for us to get her calmed down.

Now I will admit, it probably wasn't wise for that guy to be trying to scare someone who has a heart condition. But her reaction was pretty over the top.

One night Dave and I went to see "A Clockwork Orange" on campus and then met her afterwards for a drink. She and I had a disagreement about something and she began berating us, saying "we had no business going to a film like that. It's that kind of art that warps men's minds and taps into your latent misogyny! I wouldn't be surprised if some poor woman gets raped by some schmuck who saw that flick tonight".

He was a good sport about it but I could tell he thought she was being pretty hysterical.

She could be moody and high strung and hard to please. Her medical problems were a big factor and so was the fact she came from a wealthy family and was used to getting whatever she wanted pretty much when she wanted it.

Sometimes we were good for each other and sometimes bad. We both had bouts of depression… she often became despondent about her health and I was still on shaky ground emotionally. Occasionally I would find myself plunging back into the pit of self-hatred I'd struggled with for so many years.

I had to be careful about how much I drank, especially hard liquor. Sometimes her fussiness would wear me down and alcohol seemed to shorten my fuse. There just seemed to be so much drama attached to everything in her life.

Every so often I would end up snapping at her and then feel terrible about it.

But for the most part, we kept each other afloat. This was a new level of intimacy for both of us… a safe place where we could share not only our passions and dreams but also our fears and insecurities. Sometimes I pictured us in my mind as two little kids holding hands, trying to find our way in the dark hallway of adulthood.

During the summer of 1979, Eve went home for a couple months and I got a job at a cannery in Salem. Dave's folks were kind enough to let me stay at their house and just chip in on the food bill.

I spent my first week at the cannery working on the line, picking out the stuff that didn't belong in a can of green beans or corn. Usually it was just little sticks or rocks but occasionally a dead mouse or bird would come through.

Then I got promoted to a much better job where I just had to go to various spots in the factory at certain times and clean up any spillage. I was partnered with a very nice Samoan guy who spoke very little but smiled a lot.

Dave had a summer job working at a public library. We'd spend our free time going to the movies or playing tennis.

In September I took a bus down to visit Eve and her family. They lived in Redding, California. I was feeling pretty nervous. I'd always imagined her dad being the stereotypical rich guy who didn't want his daughter messing around with anybody who wasn't pre-Med or pre-Law and at this point in my life I was worried I might be pre-Unemployment.

But he turned out to be a really nice guy. He asked me a lot of questions about my life growing up and what studying journalism was like. He didn't seem the least bit judgmental. I think he just appreciated the fact I seemed to really care about his daughter.

Eve's mom was nice but neurotic. It was obvious she was in the habit of getting loaded during the cocktail hour and making speeches.

"You kids are such a great match even though you're from completely different backgrounds. Hey, maybe it was Fate. Hey, will somebody get me a refill, this martini glass isn't going to fill itself…".

Eve had a younger brother and two much younger sisters. The brother was nice to me but seemed to be a bit on the troubled side. Maybe not like Christopher Walken in "Annie Hall" but you could tell he had some issues.

Chapter 54.: Show Biz Kids

At this point, Mark had dropped out of school and was living with his brother Bret. They were living at a cheap motel and paying rent by the month.

I thought it was pretty cool in a seedy rock ‘n roll sort of way. You know, the kind of place where you might go next door and bum some cigarettes off Iggy Pop or check if Lou Reed has any Methadone he can spare.

That’s one of the great things about being young. You can live in squalor and get through tough times because you still have hope that you’re headed toward something better.

I always admired the fact Mark and Bret never seemed to need a lot of stuff. Just a place to sleep and store their musical equipment. It was almost like they were permanently living in a motel room they'd use if their band was on tour.

We still spent a lot of time hanging out and talking about music. It was our biggest passion.

They were both in a group called Attack and the Fun Boys. The name was supposed to symbolize the group's desire to play pop music with punk attitude and energy.

It seemed like they had a good read on the kind of music people wanted to go out and hear live at that time.

American kids were generally too happy to buy into the Johnny Rotten safety-pin-in-your-nose culture but on the other hand there seemed to be an appetite for bands that fell into the New Wave category… stuff like the Cars, Blondie, the Ramones and the Talking Heads.

Those groups all seem very tame now but at the time they were cutting edge. I remember being shocked by the lyrics of "Just What I Needed" when Rick Ocasek says he needs someone to feed and someone to bleed.

The name Attack and the Fun Boys was a little awkward sounding but still light years better than some of the other monikers they had discussed using, such as the Cow People. That one always made me think of a tribe of prehistoric dairy farmers. Of course, Mark might have been joking when he suggested that one.

Mark played rhythm guitar, sax, the bass and sang the lead vocals. Bret was on the keyboards and shared bass duties with Mark and the other two members handled the lead guitar and drums. They performed a mix of originals and cover versions. One of my favorites was a powerful cover version of Neil Diamond's "Solitary Man".

Mark wrote most of their original tunes. My favorite was "Sex Police". The title makes it sound like something you'd hear on a Rick James album but it was actually a social commentary. Mark was actually one of the more conservative people I knew when it came to any kind of decadence.

They didn't make much money playing music but they seemed to have a lot of fun. There were just too many bands and not enough venues in the Eugene area at that time.

I went to see them play as much as possible. I wasn't just Mark's friend but also a big fan. I thought he wrote great songs and I loved how passionately he performed. He was like a young Springsteen.

A few years earlier he and Bret had been in a band back home. When they did "Won't Get Fooled Again", Mark's scream would make the audience go crazy.

I would usually go watch Attack and the Fun Boys with a guy named Tom Prince. He was a friend Mark had met back when he was still enrolled at the U of O and living in a dorm.

Tom was really smart and a lot of fun to hang out with. We spent a lot of time talking about music but also politics, philosophy and other topics. He would later earn a law degree and work for the government.

He was an amazing dancer. And when I say that, I don't necessarily mean he was what most people consider a "good" dancer... he just sort of went into a trance and started jumping around like he was performing some kind of punk ballet. If the Ramones were the definition of basic rock 'n roll, Tom was their dancing equivalent.

I used to think a good t-shirt design would be a photo showing Tom in mid-air at a dance. Sort of like Pete Townsend without the guitar.

Mark had been having a long-distance relationship for a while with a woman named Nancy Harmon. She was three years younger than us and still lived in Sunnyrock. They'd met during the summer of 1978, right around the time I quit the BLM. I was briefly involved with her friend Jenny during that same period.

I finally got to see Patti Smith perform live around this time. She was at a little club in downtown Eugene and they'd set up folding chairs in nice, neat rows. After three or four songs, she couldn't stand it anymore and yelled "These fucking chairs are driving me crazy. Get rid of 'em right now if you want me to play any rock 'n roll".

It was kind of funny… like obedient rebellion or something. Everybody folded their chairs and set them off to the side, then proceeded to cluster in front of the stage and dance.

She certainly didn't disappoint. She was sincere and funny and angry and spontaneous and not the least bit worried about the way she looked.

This wasn't a "rocker chick" like Pat Benatar, wearing black spandex and basically standing up in front of her musician pals serving as eye candy. This was an honest-to-God poetess and songwriter who howled and sweated and poured her life into every performance.

It was great. I wanted to tell her about that night I defended her in La Grande but I settled for jumping up and down and shouting out the lyrics along with her and the rest of the crowd.

Chapter 55: Everyday People

When Eve and I got back from visiting her family in California, I moved into a house a couple miles away from the U of O campus. I was sharing it with a woman named Paula and couple named Frank and Carrie. I had met Frank and Carrie when I was living in the dorm.

Bonnie was really nice. She had grown up in the Eugene area and was currently working as a waitress at one of the nicest restaurants in town.

She and Carrie were friends and back in the Spring I was looking for a subject to interview for a Journalism class assignment. The professor wanted us to talk to a non-student if possible and Carrie had suggested Bonnie.

The subject of the interview was the death penalty and Carrie knew Bonnie had some strong opinions on the subject and would be happy to share them with me.

There was certainly nothing wrong with Bonnie being a waitress but after I talked to her for a bit, I was kind of surprised that's how she was choosing to spend her time.

Her family had money and she definitely came across more like somebody who would be in school earning a Sociology degree, getting prepared to go out and save the world.

Who knows, maybe she figured the world had enough paid do-gooders and they didn't seem to be accomplishing all that much. She did some volunteer work in her spare time and maybe that took care of her humanitarian side.

The interview went well and Bonnie and I immediately hit it off. She just seemed like a really nice person I would enjoy hanging out with.

She just seemed so grounded and mature compared to a lot of kids I'd met the past few years. This was someone who spent 40 hours a week dealing with adults in the real world, not the protective womb of academia.

When I heard she was going to get a house with Frank and Carrie in the Fall, I asked if they would consider letting me be a roommate as well. After she checked with them, it was agreed we'd all get a house together.

Carrie was from the Boston area and had that unmistakable accent. I remember her saying “I told Frank it would be wicked smart to pick you up as a roommate. You seem like a really good guy”.

She was majoring in Archaeology and seemed wicked serious about her studies. She and Eve had also met in the dorm the previous year and were friends.

Her boyfriend Frank was a handsome, carefree guy from Hawaii. He had this annoying habit of walking around with no shirt on and looking totally excellent.

He was really nice but I always got the impression he resented the amount of self-discipline college required.

He was majoring in Art and always seemed angry about being forced to produce work within the confines of a particular style or theme. “Why do these professors think they need to tell us what to do, put us in a creative box? That’s not what art is about. As far as I’m concerned these should be called freedom classes. I should be getting an MFA… master of freedom arts”.

I remember thinking if he resented the demands put on Art students in extremely liberal Eugene, then using his talents to make a living later would totally drive him over the edge. Wait until he had to deal with deadlines and budgets and asshole clients. It would make his college years seem like Paradise.

I wondered if Frank had gone to some kind of hang loose progressive high school back home. Or maybe had just smoked too much good dope growing up.

He seemed like the kind of guy who would always find the world disappointing. I imagined him trying to change the system from within and constantly running into walls. Walls he had painted.

I ran into him in Portland in the mid 80's. He was working at a television station and when I asked him how it was going he immediately started grousing about how all they seemed to think about there was profits.

Eve decided just to keep her dorm room. Of course, she spent most nights over at the house with us.

Dave had moved into a bigger house. He now had four roommates... Marty and Sam from the previous place and the two Johns, Wellhaven and Erickson.

John Wellhaven had come out to Oregon from the east coast. He was an interesting guy... he always struck me as a very strict hippie.

He had a beard and always wore a baseball cap, faded Levis, old t-shirts and black hightop Chuck Taylor tennis shoes. It seemed like he only listened to Dylan and Hendrix and a few other artists from the Sixties he considered "pure".

I always got the impression he looked down on anybody who dressed differently than him or who dared to like any music recorded after 1971. I thought it was strange that people of our generation had already started to calcify.

I had always thought one of the main differences separating us from our parents' generation was that we embraced the philosophy other people could live pretty much how they wanted as long as they did no harm to others.

But humans are humans and we have a natural tendency to get pretty judgmental once we reach a certain age. That age arrives sooner for some than others.

I did hear through the grapevine that he loosened up some later in life. Maybe the stern college persona was just his way of standing out a little from the rest of us.

Sometimes Dave, John Erickson and I would go to the beer garden held on campus on Friday afternoons. They usually had a live band. One of our favorite groups was called the Nads. I think the only reason they called themselves that was so the crowd would yell "Go, Nads, Go!".

One time two guys named Bob Rennert and Keith Whidbey came down from a private college up by Salem. We took them to the beer garden.

Keith was one of Dave's best friends growing up. I thought he was nice but really kind of boring. It seemed like everything he said, wore, listened to and enjoyed followed a very predictable upper middle-class script.

Bob seemed like a spoiled rich kid who felt entitled to do pretty much whatever he pleased to whomever he pleased. I never really cared much for him. He lit a paper airplane on fire at the beer garden and threw it at some people at another table.

I got along well with Marty and Sam now. Marty had a big record collection and was always happy to let me listen to his stuff. He and I liked a lot of the same hard rock groups and one time I stayed up all night at their house with the headphones on listening to his records.

Like a lot of people that age, I was a little contrary when it came to my musical tastes... I didn't usually gravitate to stuff that was universally popular and I made a point to tell people I thought the Beatles were vastly overrated. I grew to appreciate them both as a group and individuals a lot more later on in life.

It just seemed like a lot more fun rooting for and promoting the underdogs. And it gave me one thing I could be snobby about. Everybody knew about the Beatles and Boston but I was busy talking to Mark and Dave about Television or Jules and the Polar Bears.

I always borrowing records or lending records and I spent a lot of my free time hanging out in Eugene's many record stores. And when I was in the stores I would talk to the people who worked there about music.

I noticed that the clerks who liked progressive rock like Genesis or ELP or King Crimson were often a bit ripe smelling. I guess it wasn't music you sat around listening to with your girlfriend.

I met a guy from Chicago named Robert who was into progressive rock. He was a sweet person but socially awkward because he was so smart he had a hard time relating to what most people liked to talk about.

For some reason, my emotions always seemed amplified when I went into a record store. Back when I first came back to school and was feeling very fragile, I happened to hear Alice Cooper's "From the Inside" in a store and it really shook me up.

It was a concept album he'd done about his struggle to overcome alcoholism. I didn't have that exact same problem but I could still relate to Alice's fear of losing control.

More often I would hear something new that filled me with joy. The first time I heard "Once in a Lifetime" by Talking Heads was in a place called Everybody's Records. I had never heard anything like it before… by the end of the song I was practically dancing through the aisles. It was just that powerful.

We were all pretty poor so we got good at finding cheap entertainment. There were places around town you could get cheap pitchers of beer and food. Or maybe we'd drive over to Springfield and see a double feature for two bucks.

One night I told Dave and another guy about the hot springs where Eve and I had gone. They thought it sounded cool so we drove up there.

After we'd been sitting in the water for about half an hour, we heard the roar of a bunch of motorcycles arriving nearby. Before we knew it, there were five naked guys and five naked women sharing the hot springs with us.

We were all stoned and feeling extremely paranoid. I was sincerely hoping we could manage to get through this experience with a minimum of knife wounds.

I kept thinking about how embarrassing it would be if we were found dead up here the next morning. People back in Sunnyrock would probably think I got myself involved in a pot smoking gay hot tub murder-suicide over there on the coast.

Well, I definitely wasn't feeling gay.

The hard part was not looking at the naked biker chicks. Three of the five were very attractive and I was concerned my libido was working at cross purposes with my survival instincts. I was praying I wouldn't have a repeat of what happened at the strip poker game back in La Grande.

One of the guys noticed us gawking at a good-looking redhead and conspiratorially whispered "Zeus doesn't like anybody looking at his woman". He introduced himself as Red Dog. It appeared he was going to try to spare us from some horrible fate possibly suffered by an earlier group of horny college boys.

I leaned over and whispered to Dave, "Do you think this would be a good time to leave?". He whispered back, "Yes, I do. Because we're still alive".

We gingerly got out of the steaming water, grabbed our clothes, took one last gawk at the women and then headed back to the safety of civilization.

Chapter 56: I Dream of Wires

John Erickson was a lot of fun and had a mind that seemed to be going a hundred miles an hour all the time. He has obsessive-compulsive disorder coupled with a zany sense of humor and a passion for books, music, sports, cartoons and current events.

And it turned out we had more than just all those interests in common. He grew up in La Grande and was going to college there the same year I was. He even worked at the college radio station the year after I was in town.

One of the ways his particular OCD seems to present itself is statistics. John has an amazing mind for numbers, especially anything to do with sports. Sometimes he's involved in multiple sports fantasy leagues simultaneously.

His strongest asset is just being a really nice guy. I've met few people who are more consistent about treating everyone they meet fairly and decently.

One important thing we've always shared was a love/hate relationship with the eastern Oregon area. While we appreciated it's natural beauty and slower lifestyle, we both struggled with the conservative politics that often seem to dominate there.

Eventually he moved back to La Grande and got a job as a speech therapist. I often stop and visit him and his family on my way back from Sunnyrock. We keep in touch via e-mail nearly every day and are always mailing each other books and copies of cds.

He plays the keyboards and guitar. Sometimes I write lyrics and he sets them to music and records them.

The lyrics I write these days are almost always about politics or social issues of some kind. For me, writing a love song is a lot like drawing a cartoon of a female… it just doesn't come naturally. Plus the fact I feel like the world has more than enough love songs already.

John and I've had an interesting relationship in the sense that we're very close but have actually spent very little time together in the same physical space over the past thirty something odd years. But we communicate at least four or five times a week on average via the computer.

It started with e-mails and that seemed wonderful after years of writing letters and mailing them. Now we could almost have conversations, respond to each other's questions, send each other articles, you name it.

In August of 2004 Dave showed us both how to set up blogs. I was hooked on the concept immediately. There were just a few months left until the 2004 presidential election and this new kind of website provided me with a much needed outlet for my visceral hatred for Bush and Cheney.

I was so agitated about the Bush administration I got up at 4am on election day in 2004 and put up some homemade signs at different points next to I-5 between where we lived and Seattle. Then later that day I stood on a freeway overpass and held up my anti-Bush sign. A lot of people honked their approval and a few flipped me off.

John started out doing a lot of political posts but now has shifted to a friendlier theme, mostly stuff about music and his family and lots and lots of pictures of his cats.

I mostly posted stuff about politics but sometimes also talked about music, movies, books and sports. I met a conservative blogger from Philadelphia who sometimes puts my articles on her site. I love sparring with her regular readers… they hate me and I hate them. One even told me he hoped the terrorists would kill me.

I've also met a guy from Missouri who has a blog dedicated mostly to providing obituaries for recently deceased celebrities, an Englishman who's as obsessed with Todd Rundgren as I am, a woman from Chicago who dreams of being a nightclub singer and lots of liberal political analysts.

And now social networking sites like Facebook have expanded the technology even more.

I think it's interesting how humans use technology to solve their own individual problems or pursue their own pleasures but what we're doing in the larger sense is evolving technologically. I can see a day when we will actually be able to use computers to go beyond just sharing opinions and videos and recipes and spreadsheets and literally feel what someone across town or on the other side of the globe is feeling. Maybe that's when we'll stop wanting to kill each other so badly.

Chapter 57: We Don't Talk Anymore

Fall term of 1979 started out okay for Eve and myself. We were both busy with classes and having a good time hanging out together.

She was sort of superstitious in her own way. She was always talking about soul mates and destiny and quoting me song lyrics she felt applied to us more specifically than any other couple in the world. For a few days I felt like I was involved in a ménage a trios with Eve and Kenny Loggins.

One evening in early October there was a party at the dorm where she was living. I happened to go upstairs to visit a friend who lived on the fourth floor and when I looked out the window I saw her down in the courtyard flirting with one of the wealthy Pakistani guys.

When I confronted her about it later, she was apologetic but also excited. She said “Oh my God, this is so amazing. We are so strongly attached to each other now you could sense I was down there with that guy. It’s like Fate tapped you on the shoulder and made you look out the window”.

I never knew if she honestly felt that way or was just trying to head off my anger. If it was the second option, I have to give her props for quick thinking.

I really didn’t see it as a magical event… I told her the fact I’d seen her flirting with the Pakistani simply meant she was still somewhat obsessed with guys who had a lot of money and it had never better happen again.

We got away one weekend to the Oregon coast. We drove over on a Friday night in the middle of a howling rainstorm. We had rented a cabin and the wind was blowing so hard the place filled up with smoke when I tried to start a fire.

But we finally got things under control and had a romantic evening. Eve didn’t seem to mind all tht much when I screwed up, usually it just made her laugh.

The next day it was sunny and cold and we walked down the beach.

It was fun. We were both in a good mood and I said “Wow, this is really nice. It’s kind of like we’re on our honeymoon”.

She had a startled look on her face. She took my arm and as we walked along she said "Yeah, I know what you mean. I've never had a relationship get to this phase before". We both got kind of quiet and mulled over the enormity of this conversation.

It was like we both had thought balloons over our heads filled with little pictures of us telling everybody we were engaged, the wedding and us moving into our first place. I had never even come close to fantasizing about marriage with someone I was dating.

About a month later, she joined me when I went home to spend Thanksgiving with my parents. They were very nice to her and she returned the favor. My dad asked her a lot of questions about the courses she was taking.

Dad seemed to like her a lot but for some reason referred to her later as "that little hippie girl". I guess she must have been wearing one scarf too many or something.

I took her out and showed her the ranch and the cattle. She found them very intimidating… she was terrified when we were just sitting in the pickup slowly driving through the herd. But I guess if I'd never been around a herd of cattle
I might feel the same way.

Things started to turn sour on the trip back to Eugene. We were riding with Mark and it was snowing. Eve was getting hysterical about the road conditions and criticizing Mark's driving. At one point I thought he was going to make her get out of the car and I can't say I would have blamed him.

We finally made it back. Over the next few days, it seemed like we were having lots of little fights. She was stressed out because of her heavy course load and I was getting tired of dealing with her mood swings and general inability to get along with other people. There just seemed to be way too much drama in my life and it was pretty much all being generated by her.

A couple days before the beginning of Christmas vacation, I decided I'd had enough and I was going to break up with her.

I thought it was a good time to do it… she was flying home to spend the holidays with her family and I was headed to Sunnyrock. I calmly said I thought the breakup would be easier on both of us if we were physically apart for the first two or three weeks.

She didn't appreciate my logic. She screamed "You idiot, you've ruined Christmas and you will never find another woman who cares about you the way I do. You're gonna regret this for a long, long time".

She was pretty hysterical and of course that behavior only made me more certain I'd made the right decision.

To make matters worse, I ended up having to give her a ride to the airport in Portland. There was a lot of quiet tension in the car. Ironically, the Cliff Richard song "We Don't Talk Anymore" came on the radio and added a whole lot of extra poignancy to our sad situation.

Mark and Nancy's relationship had gradually grown more serious. He wasn't sure he was ready to take the next step but she gave him the classic romantic ultimatum... either they were getting married or they were breaking up.

So they got engaged and the wedding was set for late December. It was going to be held in Sunnyrock.

Mark asked me to be his best man. To be honest, I wasn't totally confident about them getting married but I was still very pleased he asked me to stand by his side during the wedding. We'd come a long way together over the past few years.

The ceremony was fine but during the reception Nancy's dad, Ed, had a few belts of Jack Daniels and suddenly remembered how pissed he was his daughter was marrying a non-Mormon.

Nancy's dad was what you call a "Jack Mormon". He was religious enough to get upset about her marrying outside the faith but not so strict he would deny himself the occasional whiskey binge.

He got up out of his chair and started yelling at Mark. He yelled "You sonofabitch, you have no business taking my little girl away from here. This was a big mistake and I'm gonna make you pay".

Then he drunkenly started swinging but three of us managed to break it up before anybody got seriously hurt. We hurriedly got the happy couple out the door and on their way to their honeymoon destination.

Tom Prince had come down with us for the wedding. I assured him fighting wasn't standard fare at Sunnyrock weddings. At least it hadn't been at the few I'd attended.

Tom and I decided to get a drink somewhere else before heading to my parents' house. We went to a tavern called The Cowboy. After we were there for half an hour, a couple guys started arguing about some old grievance and once again the fists started flying.

People who live in small towns really know how to nurse a grievance. You just sort of keep it your back pocket most of the time and only take it out once in a while when you feel like getting drunk and mixing it up with somebody.

The grievance being fought about at the The Cowboy was a classic cross-generational grudge… they were fighting about something somebody's uncle had done to somebody else's father. I don't know how long ago the original conflict occurred. Some of these resentments really had long life spans.

We got out of there unwounded. Poor Tom had a stunned look on his face. He had come to Sunnyrock to attend a nice, peaceful wedding and had ended up in what appeared to be a training camp for Hollywood stuntmen.

Chapter 58: I've Seen That Movie Too

The Christmas break of 1979 was really lonely. Eve and I were broken up and I couldn't even get much comfort from my folks because they went to Vancouver, Washington to visit relatives. Dad asked if I would come home and feed the cattle while they were gone.

I appreciated the fact he thought I was mature enough to take care of things for him and I was also eager to pay him back in some small way for how supportive he'd been all these years.

I went to a couple movies during the week just for something to do. I drove over to a theatre near Boise to see "1941". I loved it. I think it's about the most underrated comedy ever made.

Movies continued to be a big part of my life. Even with a busy school schedule I still managed to see quite a few in Eugene and a neighboring town called Springfield.

I sometimes went with Mark and Bret and Tom. And Dave and I still went as often as time and finances allowed.

Dave and I were even involved later in a thing called “Secret Cinema”. We would get together with three other friends once a month on a Saturday night to have dinner and watch a video. This was in the late 80’s.

But it wouldn’t be just any random video… it would have to fit a certain pre-assigned category such as “documentary” or “so bad it’s good”. Then we would rate the film.

After everybody had taken their turn showing one in that category, we would tabulate the results and the winner would be taken out to dinner.

It started out as kind of a lark but soon we were getting really competitive. Often there were tense discussions about whether certain films actually fit the category or if others were simply too universally admired to be allowed.

I won the first round with “To Kill a Mockingbird”. I justified my choice by telling everyone I had never seen it. There was a fair amount of residual bitterness but they did pay for my dinner.

The great thing was we ended up exposing ourselves to films we probably wouldn't have watched otherwise. "The Umbrellas of Cherbourg" was a good example... I had never even considered renting a French musical before. I didn't exactly love it but it was an interesting experience.

Dave brought an amazing 1957 film called "A Face in the Crowd". It starred Andy Griffith and Patricia Neal. Griffith played a rural sociopath who becomes a media sensation when he goes on TV and rails against his own sponsors.

In my opinion, it was a chilling preview of the kind of stuff you would hear coming out of the mouths of right-wing shockmeisters like Ann Coulter and Michael Savage four decades later.

We watched several fine documentaries over the years. My personal favorite was "Visions of Light", a film about the history of cinematography. Somebody else brought a fun one about Soviet propaganda films. It was fascinating to see the East Bloc version of a swingin' teen movie.

Some of them were just funny (even though they often didn't mean to be). During "The Fountainhead" we howled about the fact they constantly showed the front page of the city newspaper displaying a giant banner headline about some architectural controversy or another. I started to wonder if the story was set in a parallel world where Frank Lloyd Wright had been elected president.

Ironically, one of the "so bad it's good" selections was a film called "The Oscar" starring Stephen Boyd. It was about an actor who uses and abuses people right and left as he struggles to win an Academy award. The acting was wonderfully awful.

Secret Cinema lasted roughly ten years. I felt like that was a pretty good run, especially considering what a feisty group we could be at times.

Chapter 59: Wish You Were Here

When I got back to Eugene I began to realize it was going to be really tough not being with Eve anymore. This was the first time I'd broken up with someone and actually felt a real sense of loss.

There was also geography to consider. When I broke up with Marcy we were on opposite sides of the state. There was a good chance I'd run into Eve on campus sometime. I knew that moment was going to be horribly uncomfortable.

I felt like the radio in my car was conspiring to get us back together. Every time I started the engine, some maudlin ballad would be coming out of the speakers either telling me I couldn't live without her or she couldn't live without me.

What I needed to hear were songs that reminded me why I had ended the relationship. I imagined something by Hall and Oates:

Remember she always drives you batty
She really goes on and on
Won't let you watch A Clockwork Orange
You should be glad she's gone, gone, gone

I drove around a lot when I wasn't in class. Sometimes I just laid on my bed and stared at the ceiling (which wasn't all that far away because my room was an attic space the owner of the house had converted into a small bedroom). I did a lot of thinking and struggled to stay strong and not drift back to Eve.

We caved around the first of February. She and Carrie were still friends and one night at dinner Carrie asked me if there was any chance I'd be willing to get together and talk things over. "She misses you wicked bad", she told me.

We met at our favorite dark bar and immediately apologized to each other and promised to work on our issues.

"I promise to work on staying calm", she said. "I know I can be a handful sometimes. But I shouldn't take it on you. I should just trust you and have faith everything's going to work out okay. Thanks for being my port in the storm".

I told her I would try to be more patient. I knew she had a lot on her plate and that she was carrying a load that would exhaust a lot of perfectly healthy people.

This was on a Friday night. We celebrated our reunion by staying in bed naked together for the next 24 hours (with occasional bathroom and sustenance breaks). It was cool, it was like we were John and Yoko and our war was over.

Over the next five months we just enjoyed each other's company and tried hard not to think about the fact she would most likely be leaving the area soon. I just wanted to stay in Eugene for the time being but the economy was really bad and we had no idea what we wanted to do after we graduated.

I was hoping I could get things wrapped up and graduate in June. Taking a quarter off for my "mental health break" and changing majors a couple times put me behind schedule but Dad was patient and still willing to help me financially.

The worst thing was that I kept having nightmares about finding out none of the work I'd done over the past four years counted and I had to start all over again. I suppose that's not all that unusual.

I was finally getting to take some Journalism classes. I wasn't very well prepared for them… I had never used a computer and I didn't have all that much newspaper experience. Just record and movie reviews for the most part, not exactly the kind of stuff you'd yell "stop the presses" about.

I did have one sort of exciting reporting experience back in La Grande. The college was having financial problems at that time and was considering discontinuing their football program.

I did an interview with one of the school administrators on the subject and when it got published on the front page of the college newspaper, a bunch of irate, not-too-bright football players cornered me and accused me of trying to sabotage their scholarships.

Apparently they thought the act of writing about a decision was the same as making that decision. I think it was the same crowd that was mocking Patti Smith that one night.

The class I probably enjoyed the most was advertising. We got to pretend we were in charge of coming up with a full-scale media campaign for Hershey's candy bars. We wrote copy for radio, print and TV ads and did storyboards for TV commercials.

I got to do some cartooning when we did the storyboards. It was fun, I kind of missed it.

One sorority girl rapped during her presentation. It was kind of fun but that kind of music was still pretty much considered a novelty. I remember thinking "that stuff won't be around long". Of course, I thought the same thing about reality T.V. when it first started.

The big thing at that time was for the sorority girls to go south on Spring break, get really, really tan and then wear about twenty gold necklaces. I thought they looked ridiculous. And I knew if they kept tanning like this they were going to look like lizards some day.

I'd never liked the fraternity and sorority people much. I was proud to be a GDI (Goddamn Independent). In my opinion, the whole Greek system just seemed like a way for wealthy kids to institutionalize their elitism.

One time Mark, Tom and I got invited to a function at a frat house and we were going to leave some limburger cheese in an air duct.

But the guys in this particular house turned out to be kind of sad and pretty nice so we didn't have the heart to complete our mission. Plus I met a cute drunk girl there who tried making out with me five minutes after we met. And I was only too happy to oblige her.

Even though Mark was against decadence philosophically, he was still impressed with how attractive that drunk girl found me. He started calling me the King of Rock 'n Roll that night.

Chapter 60: Summertime Blues

Unfortunately, I wasn't able to finish up when Eve did. My advisor screwed up and when Spring quarter ended I found out I was still four credits short.

Eve's family had moved to Wisconsin by this time so she decided to move back there and live with them until I finished college and had a better idea what my future plans were.

I was so frustrated. I really didn't want to have to come back and take classes in the fall. However, there weren't many Journalism classes being offered during Summer term.

My advisor found me a one-day seminar on putting together high school yearbooks (worth one credit) and an unpaid internship at a local radio station that would take care of the other three. It was a small AM station and they needed a traffic reporter.

The station didn't have a lot of money. That's why their traffic reports were done from a car instead of a helicopter hovering over the city. My job was to drive around Eugene and Springfield during the morning rush hour and call in updates.

I made the most of my on-air time. I cracked little jokes and tried to make my reports not only informative but entertaining. "Hey guys", I said. "This is kind of a weird concept, trying to report about traffic when you're in the middle of it. Kind of like a cow reporter trying to describe a stampede". I could hear the guys in the station laughing through my headphones.

It was a pretty relaxed operation and the morning DJs were good about playing along with me.

Occasionally I would make the mistake of saying my next report would be made from a certain location but then I'd get stuck in traffic myself and not be able to get there in time. I never felt bad when this occurred... I was making the best of a patently absurd situation.

One Saturday morning they let me read the news at the station. Bonnie recorded the broadcast and when I heard it later I realized I had read it way too slow. I sounded like someone who wasn't completely comfortable speaking English.

About a month after I started at the radio station, we got bought out and immediately switched to a new format. Everybody got laid off. I felt bad for the DJs but they were old pros and took it in stride. Changing jobs and cities fairly often was just part of job.

They actually felt sorry for me. I thought that was really big-hearted considering I was just an unpaid intern and my advisor said I was still going to get my three college credits. It's not like I was going to have to pack up and start looking for a new job in a new town during a nasty economic downturn.

I still had my part-time job at the college printing shop. And I'd always liked running and now I had plenty of time for it. Eugene had miles and miles of well-kept sawdust trails you could train on. I was getting in great shape... I actually weighed less than I did when I was a senior in high school.

Any kind of exercise is good for depression but the amount of endorphins derived from running six miles or more is truly wonderful. I was getting in really good shape running the equivalent of a 10k every day.

I had kind of a strange training routine. Normally I finished my run around the same time Bonnie got home from work. We liked to sit around and talk about our days while enjoying a cigarette and a glass of Chardonnay. I'd get an amazingly good buzz doing this right after exercising.

Bonnie started dating an older guy named Randall. He kind of reminded me of my half-brother Roger. He was always giving me unwanted career advice or telling me about his latest get-rich-quick scheme.

"Hey, Jim… have I got an opportunity for you. I met this guy who knows a guy who's almost got the financing together for a business that's going to revolutionize how cars are washed…". And of course, just like with all of Roger's schemes, it never actually got past the bullshit stage.

And he had these huge, rough hands I hated shaking. It was like shaking hands with a tree.

I couldn't understand why Bonnie settled for him. He was always saying or doing stuff that embarrassed her. I guess maybe she had poor self-esteem and thought she didn't deserve to be with someone better.

On the other hand, maybe she wondered why I was with a woman who often seemed a little bit crazy. So I guess we just have to accept the choices other people make and hope it turns out for the best.

When the hours at print shop got cut back, I really had to struggle to make ends meet. It was getting to the point where just going out for a cheeseburger was kind of a big deal. One night I had a can of green beans for dinner.

I started signing up to do psychological and medical testing on campus for money. It wasn't anything all that radical, mostly just answering survey questions or sitting in a dark room and telling a graduate student when I could see a light projected or what color the light was. A chimp could have done these tests if they knew how to hold a pencil or verbally describe what they had just seen.

I also donated plasma a few times at a place downtown but finally had to quit because they were starting to have a problem finding new spots to put the needle in.

I was keeping in touch with Eve on a fairly constant basis and thinking a lot about our possible future together. However, I did stray one time that Summer.

An artist I knew had invited a friend of hers from North Dakota to come out and stay in Eugene for a bit. The friend's name was Stephanie and she was a cute blonde a couple years younger than me. She looked kind of Swedish.

As chance would have it, one Saturday night we ended up hanging out at my house by ourselves. I happened to have a couple of bottles of cheap wine on hand and eventually she made a move on me. Pretty soon we were in my bed.

The next morning I woke up with a guilty smile on my face. I watched her sleep and when she opened her eyes she was smiling at first and then a look of horror crossed her face.

She sat up and started grabbing her things in a panic. I looked at her and asked what was wrong. She replied "Oh my God, I can't believe we did this. I have a fiancée back in North Dakota. This was a terrible mistake!".

She put on her top and cut-offs and ran out the front door. I never saw her again. Hopefully everything worked out okay for her back home.

I finally graduated in August of 1980. I was so sick of school but glad I'd stuck with it. Dave had enough credits to graduate in June but held off and went through the ceremony with me. I really appreciated that.

Dad and Nona came over to Eugene to see me get my degree. They were so proud of me.

He had said many times he regretted never finishing college. And he had been so patient and great about encouraging me to keep going these past few years. I definitely felt like graduating from the University of Oregon was something I'd done for both of us.

We were driving around town the evening after the graduation ceremony and he asked me to drive by the fraternity house he had stayed in when he'd gone to school in the late 1930's.

He said, "I think I'd like to go in and say hello to any of the fellas that happen to be there today.

Tell 'em I lived there for a while, see what kind of stuff they do now".

I loved my dad dearly but I have to say there were times he seemed to have trouble remembering what decade he was currently living in. He often tipped waitresses like it was still 1936 and here he was wanting to go into a frat house in 1980 and see what innocent pranks the guys were pulling on each other.

Somehow I managed to talk him out of it. While he was thinking about secret handshakes and his memories of yesteryear I was very concerned we'd walk in on some frat boy sucking on a bong while undressing a cheerleader.

Chapter 61: The Rover

I lived briefly during the late Summer of 1980 with Robin Sykes, my old friend from Sunnyrock.. She was the one who had bought my "Pistol Pete and His Sister" comics back in grade school. She'd been going to school at the U of O the past couple of years.

Robin was renting a small house in Eugene. It was fun hanging out with her and, she knew a bunch of other poverty-stricken students who lived nearby. We would stretch our food dollars by getting together and having a potluck every few days.

It was kind of like living in a commune but you didn't have to worry about people not doing their share of the chores or hitting on your old lady.

I was living with Robin because the lease on the house I'd been sharing with Paula, Carrie and Frank had expired. Carrie had finished school in June and moved back to Massachusetts to attend graduate school. She and Frank had gone through a pretty nasty breakup right before she left.

Bonnie and I were really concerned for a while that Frank might commit suicide. One day in May I was on campus and heard an ambulance siren. Somebody said some guy had jumped out of a high window to his death.

I rushed over to where I saw the crowd and the cops gathered. There was a covered body laying on the ground. It turned out to be someone else. I felt sorry for the poor bastard but also relieved it wasn't Frank.

I didn't commit to continue living with Bonnie and Frank because I was going to be taking a trip back east with Dave and his folks beginning in October. We were going to drive their RV across the country. And I really had no idea what my plans were once I got back to Oregon.

I was really excited. I hadn't traveled much and it was nice to have an opportunity to do so before I got a regular full-time job. I knew a lot of them only offered two weeks of total vacation the first few years.

Our ultimate destination was Alexandria, Virginia. Dave's grandmother had passed away earlier in the year and his folks needed to take care of some things before they put her house on the market.

Our first stop was to see some of Dave's relatives in Wenatchee, Washington. His brother Don and his family lived there.

After that we cut across the top of Idaho and headed into Montana. We stopped in Miles City because Dave and I wanted to visit with Sam Jones, one of the guys Dave had lived with in Eugene.

Sam took the two of us out on the town. When we were walking around I commented "This is amazing. It looks like there are at least two or three bars on every block. If I was an alcoholic this would be my idea of paradise".

That was the first time I went to a strip club. We were snickering as a dancer contorted herself to the Diana Ross song "Upside Down". It almost seemed like a play-by-play description of what was happening on the stage. The three of us were cracking up.

It felt kind of strange after spending the last two years in politically correct Eugene.

I was thinking Eve and Carrie and Bonnie would have all been pretty put out if they knew Dave and I were in a Montana cowboy bar watching naked women gyrate for money. But we figured even liberals need to go out and get a little wild once in a while.

Our third night was spent in the Badlands of South Dakota. It was so amazing… I had been to some remote places but this was like camping on the surface of Mars. The next day we saw Mount Rushmore.

Not long after that, we drove across Minnesota and then they dropped me off in Neenah, Wisconsin. I was going to spend a few days visiting Eve and her family while Dave and his folks continued on to Virginia.

I was really excited to see her. I didn't know what I was going to say and the only plan I had was to just try and relax and wait and see what happened. We'd been writing each other since she left Eugene but hadn't really discussed any ideas about what might happen in the near future.

Her brother really liked Wisconsin. "Man, this place is awesome, Jim. They drink beer here like it's water. I get so blitzed every weekend". I guess it was good he was getting out of the house at least.

The first couple days I just goofed off while Eve was at work. I got to try out the health club her folks belonged to and another day I borrowed a car and drove up to Green Bay so I could see what Packer Stadium looked like.

It was fun having cocktails with Eve and her folks. Her mom and I had a good discussion about religion after dinner one night. It started when we were talking about people who believed in the Anti-Christ and the second coming of Jesus.

She said, “I just believe God is basically the personification of love. If I love my children, that’s God. If I help my neighbor, that’s God.” I tended to think that was a bit simplistic but on the other hand I couldn’t really argue with her since I wasn’t sure what I believed yet.

She also let me smoke one of her unfiltered Pall Mall cigarettes and I thought I might meet God right there and then.

I began feeling a lot of internal pressure to hurry up and decide what I was going to do about my relationship with Eve. The clock was ticking but both of us were scared to be the first one to address the subject.

I knew I was experiencing an emotional blind spot…I was scared of losing her and so happy to be with her again. These emotions were making me forget just how nuts she made me sometimes.

The last night I was there, I decided to go for it. I told Eve, “Look, I know I don’t have a job right now and the economy is tough but I really think we should be together. Will you marry me?”

Her eyes filled with tears and she said, “Yes, I will. I love you and I want to be your wife”.

When I woke up the next morning I was in a full panic. I bet I looked like Stephanie did the morning she ran out of my bedroom in Eugene.

I did a quick mental review: I had no job, my car was a piece of crap and economy was in the throes of a recession. I didn't even know if I wanted to stay in Eugene when I got back. I pictured the two of us trying to deal with all this as a young married couple and it scared the crap out of me.

I briefly flirted with the idea of calling it off once I was safely back in Oregon but my guilt got the best of me. This wasn't a Marcy situation, this was someone who I'd really loved off and on. She deserved the courtesy of at least being told the news in person.

I told her I'd changed my mind. I started to explain why but she suddenly said "you fucking bastard" and hauled off and slapped me in the face as hard as she could and that pretty much ended the conversation.

I got on the Greyhound bus that morning and felt a mixture of sadness and relief. I loved her but there was no way I could take care of her at this point in my life. I could hardly take care of myself.

I rode the bus from Wisconsin to Chicago and then Cleveland. The bus station restroom there was full of either Amish or Mennonite guys. It seemed a bit surreal for some reason. I was surprised to see them, I had always thought they had strict rules about using motorized vehicles.

On the way to Pittsburgh, I struck up a conversation with a friendly Arab guy who ended up buying me a sandwich. I guess he just had a lot of money to spend and was grateful to have someone to talk to for a while.

I finally made it to Alexandria. Dave and I had a great time in the DC area. We went to the Smithsonian, the White House, Georgetown and the Washington Monument. We saw Menachem Begin getting out of a limo.

We paced ourselves. Some days we just went to the movies.

We discovered a bar in Georgetown we really liked and arranged to meet an old school friend of Dave's there for a drink.

When he got there he had a grin on his face. He said "Hey, nice place you guys picked out to meet up at. Have you noticed you never see any women in here?".

We looked around and it slowly began to dawn on us our new favorite watering hole was a gay bar. The two farm boys from Oregon felt quite foolish.

We discovered the best way to get a bus to come was for me to light a cigarette. Or for us to start singing "You've Lost That Lovin' Feeling".

Dave's parents took us to an authentic Japanese restaurant where you were supposed to take your shoes off. There was an overbearing blowhard sitting behind us who practically ruined our meal with his loud pontificating. We took his shoes with us when we left.

When we told Dave's parents what we had done, his mom was kind of upset at first. But then she started giggling and said , "Oh, it's all right. The guy totally deserved it".

After about three weeks, Dave and I realized our funds were getting low. We decided to take a bus back home. His folks weren't planning on bringing the RV back until the first of the year.

The trip back was brutal, especially for six-foot-six Dave. We tried to sleep but it wasn't easy and every time I woke up I seemed to have a new crick in my neck. We never had a chance to shower so our hair just kept getting greasier and greasier and our body odor ever more pungent.

And this was back when people could sit in the last few rows of seats and smoke. There wasn't any kind of divider, so that lovely aroma just got mixed in with all the other scents.

We finally stumbled off the bus in Salem. It felt really good to be back in our home state.

We found out a few days later that Dave's folks had been the victims of a home invasion. Right about the time we were getting to Pittsburgh, a guy had come to the door asking if he could use their phone and then pulled a gun. He tied them up and robbed the house. Fortunately. neither of them was hurt.

Chapter 62: Bohemian Like You

So now I was back in Eugene and not sure what my next step would be.

Luckily, I was still able to live with Bonnie and Frank. Their new place only had two bedrooms but they said I could sleep on the couch or use Frank's room when he was gone. Not a bad deal for fifty bucks a month.

Frank had a new girlfriend. It was the artist who had introduced me to Stephanie. He seemed really happy for the first time since I'd known him.

The new girlfriend was kind of plain but had a good heart and really knew how to handle Frank and his many moods.

Personally, I never found Carrie all that attractive either. She always seemed to have a runny nose and greasy hair and was constantly wiping snot on her sleeve like a five-year old. And while I found the Boston accent entertaining, I would never classify it as sexy.

I had a little money left in the bank so I decided to wait until after Christmas to look for work. I spent some time writing a short story.

I was really into Stephen King at the time so I thought I'd take a shot a doing something in the horror vein. I wrote a story about a guy who goes through a near-death experience and discovers how wonderful the afterlife will be.

After he's revived, he decides he's been sent back to kill as many people as possible and expedite their journey to paradise. The rest of the story is basically just one big shoot-em-up sequence.

It was a fun exercise. Kind of a twisted story but it felt good to let the creative juices flow.

I had an interesting experience when I happened to become friends with a law student who was five or six years older than me. His name was Alex. I think he eventually wanted to work for the ACLU or an environmental organization.

We were out having beers one night and I made a snide comment about the political climate in Eugene, saying I thought the whole Sixties thing was mostly an excuse people used to cover up the fact they wanted to get high and fuck whoever they wanted whenever they wanted

I didn't totally feel that way but I was young and wanted to show off. This was an era when a lot of people my age were trying to distance themselves from the liberal mantra of our Baby Boom elders. We wanted to be liberal but not passive resistance, longhair, back-to-the-land hippie liberal.

My making that statement was a bit like Johnny Rotten wearing a "I Hate Pink Floyd" t-shirt.

He got an angry look on his face and replied, "That is utter bullshit. We were marching and putting our asses on the line so guys like you wouldn't end up in Vietnam or some other hellhole. We changed this whole goddamn country for the better and I won't sit here and tolerate you badmouthing us just because you're too stupid to know better".

Then he added, "So finish your beer. I want to head over to that Mexican place by the mall and see if we can pick up some women."

I didn't argue with him. I was really pretty stunned by the ferocity of his response and eager to see if he had any skills with the ladies.

It was weird. I'd never been chewed out by a older liberal before. It was kind of hard to wrap my mind around the concept.

The job market in Eugene was terrible. The country was suffering from both rampant inflation and a stagnant economy. The Eugene area was particularly bad off because so many people had been laid off from timber-related jobs.

Even menial jobs were hard to find. There were just too many college kids competing for whatever paychecks were available.

I was desperate for cash. I didn't know if I was going to stay in Eugene but I figured I needed to build up a little nest egg before I could even consider where else I might go.

Everybody seemed to be having a hard time. Mark McShane was actually dressing up in costumes and delivering singing telegrams to help make ends meet.

We were so poor we couldn't even hang out much in bars. Mark, Tom, Bret and I started buying quarts of this super cheap beer called Bohemian. Then we started referring to ourselves as the Bohemian Club.

At first I checked out the want ads in the paper every day and applied for those jobs. Then I just started walking from business to business, asking if they had any openings. Still no luck… I was beginning to feel like somebody had declared an official Jim Hawthorne Hiring Freeze.

I finally got a job working at a cannery warehouse on the outskirts of town. Since I was new, I had to settle for the graveyard shift. This was really hard work… loading 30 pound boxes on to conveyor belts constantly for eight hours straight. I actually didn't mind the exercise but I was just so exhausted all the time.

I just couldn't seem to adapt to sleeping during the day. Eventually, my life became very simple… eating, putting boxes on a conveyor belt and trying to get enough quality sleep so I could then get up and do it all over again.

I started to think of myself as a warehouse zombie, a pitiful creature only being kept alive to help insure people in the Northwest had plenty of canned beets and green beans on their local grocery shelves.

Then I got the ultimate punch in the gut. Things got slow and I got laid off with a bunch of other guys. I was starting to feel cursed… apparently now God didn't even think I was fit to be a warehouse zombie.

I went out and applied at more places but couldn't find anything. Even the job placement businesses were going out of business.

A couple of sympathetic interviewers told me I should cut my losses and go check out the job market in Portland, or better yet Seattle or San Francisco.

I finally decided they were right. I really liked Eugene but it was basically just a college town and opportunities were somewhat limited there even in the best of economic times. And the current times sucked badly.

I asked my folks if I could come home for the Summer and hang out there for a while before I made my next move. They said that would be great.

I ran in a 10k with Tom Prince on the day before I left Eugene. That night Tom, Mark, Bret and I went down to a local dive called the Vet's Club and enjoyed dollar well drinks while we listened to a great old combo called the Mellow Men. There was a good deal of toasting and talk about no matter what happened, we'd remain steadfast friends. It was a good day.

Chapter 63: Before the Deluge

I began to realize I was really ready for a change. There were lots of things I liked about Eugene but I was also beginning to feel like a lot of the people there (especially the gray ponytail folks) had a remarkably unrealistic perspective regarding the town's place in the universe.

Holding a bake sale every Thursday on campus to support the Sandinistas probably wasn't going to be a major factor in how that conflict turned out.

Years later, people from Eugene would play a role in one of the biggest events I would ever be a part of.

I moved to Seattle in late October of 1981 and over the course of that decade and the 90's it became a dynamic, confident city. Real estate values had jumped, unemployment was at a minimum and the area was no longer held hostage by the fortunes of Boeing.

Seattle was chosen to hold the WTO conference in 1999. There had been trouble at some of the previous WTO meetings held in other countries but I guess the Seattle city government was naïve enough to think Americans could care less one way or another about globalization.

And to be fair, I'm not sure the people in the Seattle area did feel all that strongly about the new global economy and the international corporations that seemed to be taking over everywhere. But there were thousands of protestors who were willing to make the trip to Seattle and make their voices heard.

It didn't take long for the mayor and the conference planners to realize their mistake. Not all the protestors were willing to passively carry signs and chant slogans. Some were actively taking steps to shut down the conference if possible.

There was also a large contingent of self-described anarchists roaming around the city breaking plate glass windows and doing their best to torment the police. Supposedly the majority of these kids had come up from the Eugene area but nobody knew for sure.

Rumors started flying about all kinds of stuff, especially wild theories about how well the anarchists were organized and what they were planning. People were getting a bit hysterical… after all, these were teen-agers in black hoodie sweatshirts, not terrorists.

I was working downtown and the management started to worry about our safety. They closed our office around 11am the second day of the conference. Most everybody went home but my friend Greg and I decided to venture downtown and check out the action.

We walked down Stewart street and checked out the damage. Somebody had thrown a trash container through the front window of the Starbuck's I went to every day.

When we got to the Niketown store, there were black-clad anarchists jumping up and down on top of the glass awning. It was obvious to Greg and myself that they were more focused on having a good time than pushing any particular socio-political agenda.

The streets were packed with a strange assortment of people… unionists, hippies, young kids just looking for excitement, troublemakers. There were even people dressed as sea turtles, protesting some trade agreement they felt was hurting the environment.

The cops were trying to keep people in certain parts of town but they were overwhelmed by the size of the crowds surging everywhere. The city government was desperately trying to maintain some kind of order without calling in the National Guard.

It was interesting… the Seattle city government was largely composed of people who'd been activists of one sort or another back in the 60's and 70's. You could tell by the way things were playing out that we were seeing a situation where older liberals felt guilty about coming down too hard on young people but meanwhile the city was being wrecked block by block.

It was kind of like the political equivalent of a Baby Boomer who smoked a lot of dope in college having to tell his teen-ager why it wasn't a good thing.

I also think we'd misplaced the memory of how quickly a peaceful protest could turn into nasty violence. We remembered Woodstock and the Summer of Love but had forgotten about Kent State and Altamont.

I wasn't happy about the damage but I was excited to be participating in this historical event. I suddenly wished I had become a reporter.

Greg decided to go home but I hung around downtown for a while longer. I felt like a little kid out looking for adventure. I even went out of my way to go somewhere I could get a little whiff of the tear gas. It was so strange… one of America's "nice" cities had turned overnight into Apocalypse Town, USA.

Maybe the fact we were only days away from the start of the new millennium was a factor in all this strangeness. The world seemed both gravely apprehensive and surprisingly hopeful about the arrival of the year 2000.

Many people with a conservative religious bent wondered if this new thousand year stretch might be an age filled with spiritual wonders and horrible catastrophes. They said the signs were everywhere if you were wise enough to see them.

Pessimists wondered if we were headed into a new dark age. Maybe life would get much tougher and every day would bring another battle for survival. Too many people, too much pollution, not enough resources to sustain us all.

Optimists rejoiced, confident in their belief we were on the verge of a golden age fueled by scientific knowledge accumulating at an unbelievable rate. We would leave superstition behind and build a new, clean world powered by unlimited power from the sun, wind and oceans.

Most of us just wondered if all the machines would go on strike once the clock struck midnight.

It was amazing. I had thought about the 21st century for so long and now we were finally going to begin living in it.

It's funny, when I was a kid I would read sci-fi novels set in 1980 or 1995. Now here we were living in the year 2000. We didn't have world peace or jetpacks but there were still awesome discoveries on the horizon.

The Internet was radically changing how people communicated and interacted, stem cell research promised to rescue us from a host of diseases, new alternative energy ideas were being put forward every day… the list went on and on. I guess (despite my depressive tendencies) you could put me down as an optimist. I always said if humanity could avoid blowing itself up we might end up doing some amazing things.

One guy I worked with got so freaked out about Y2K that he started sending hysterical e-mails to our company's CEO warning about the impending catastrophe. It finally got to the point where he was advised that he would be fired if he didn't knock it off.

Dad and Nona and Uncle Mitch were also very concerned about the computers failing. They put in a supply of food, bottled water and candles. Nona was pretty much convinced civilization would begin tearing itself to pieces immediately.

I wasn't sure if she dreaded that possibility or welcomed it… I got the feeling she felt like the sooner things went to shit, the sooner Jesus would come and set things right for good.

My wife and I stayed up and watched a TV program that showed the millennium celebrations being held around the globe as each country greeted the dawn. It was glorious.

I felt for a couple hours like the people of the world were ready to make a new start and maybe work together instead of continually coming up with new ways to make each other bleed.

Chapter 64: Losing My Religion

When I got to Sunnyrock I was a little rattled by how religious my folks had become. I got there on a Saturday afternoon and the next morning I was advised they were taking me to their new church.

They weren't demanding I go. It was more like an assumption… oh boy, Jim's home and we're sure he'll love our new church and everybody in it because we do!!

The whole thing had kind of snuck up on me. I guess I'd been so involved with my own little dramas I'd somehow missed the fact they'd turned into red-blooded, hand-waving Evangelicals.

Nona had grown up in a Pentecostal church but hadn't attended regularly for the past twenty years. Dad went to an Episcopal church as a youngster but never really seemed all that interested in religion when I was growing up.

When they got married, they had lots of fights about his gambling problem. She basically laid down the law one day and told him if he didn't quit playing cards for money, she was leaving.

She'd recently started going to a nondenominational church in Brisco. He started attending services with her. I guess he figured he might have a better chance of beating the gambling bug if he got right with God. Or at least got re-acquainted with God.

The church was located in an old shopping center. The place was pretty bare decoration-wise but there were plenty of people there. Dad told me the congregation was mostly made up of folks who'd become dissatisfied with the churches they'd grown up in.

There were formerly angry ex-Episcopalians, formerly disgruntled ex-Methodists, formerly moody ex-Presbyterians, and a even a few previously grouchy ex-Catholics. They weren't angry, disgruntled, moody or grouchy now, however… they all seemed to be happy, happy, happy.

He said, "The crowd seems to be mostly folks who felt like their old church was starting to get way too liberal". Then he grinned and said "Plus there are a few old coots like me who aren't allowed to gamble anymore and needed some other way to spend our time".

I started to imagine the series of events that might cause somebody to leave their mainstream denomination… maybe it started with a young person getting up in front of the congregation and singing some kind of religious folk song. Then the youth pastor decided to grow a beard so the kids could relate to him better. And before you know it, you've got somebody publicly declaring they think it's possible non-Christians might not go to Hell. This last one is what really set a lot of people off.

After all, what's the point of belonging to a group that doesn't believe it's better than everybody else?

They were actually very nice. Almost too nice… I had become somewhat paranoid about religion during my time in college. I kept looking at their peaceful, smiling faces and wondering if they'd be serving Jim Jones Kool-Aid after the service.

I was looking at religion differently now than I had before I went off on my own. When I was a kid, I lived in a small town and almost everybody was a Christian of some sort. If you weren't a Christian nobody bothered you about it (at least as far as I know).

When I went to college, I met people who actually had different takes on God, humanity and the universe. I disagreed strongly with some of them, sort of agreed with some and agreed very much with others.

The most important thing I learned from the experience was that each human is entitled to form and express their own opinions about these issues. I mean, if you can't make up your own mind about issues regarding life, death, good, evil and God, how much freedom do we really have?

I no longer felt like people I disagreed with on religion were bad or wrong… they just had different beliefs than I did. My mind had been opened and it was going to be really hard to ever really seal it up again.

The novel "Stranger in a Strange Land" had a big effect on me. It illustrated what it would be like to stand back and understand unemotionally how a religion is created when a charismatic leader arrives somewhere or a seemingly divine incident comes to pass.

I also had a more personal reason to be paranoid about religion. A few months earlier I'd had an unsettling experience when my old friend Josh Leonard had given Mark McShane and I a ride from Salem to Sunnyrock.

I'd gone to the same church with Josh from early childhood up through the end of high school. The first three years he was out on his own, he sowed his wild oats like the rest of us.

When he was twenty-two, he decided to renounce his worldly ways and become a hard-core Christian. He threw out all his rock record albums and called every woman he'd ever dated to apologize for the lust he'd previously had in his heart. Then he quit his job, moved to Boise and enrolled at a Bible college.

When we were driving over the Cascades, the three of us started talking about his newfound religious zeal. He decided it would be a good time to try some power evangelizing, driving faster and faster on the swerving mountain highway.

He was yelling "Who's afraid to die? I'm not afraid to die because I've accepted Jesus as my lord and I know I'm going to Heaven!". Mark and I both got really pissed and eventually he settled down and started driving normal again.

I was amazed that someone I'd known almost twenty years was so arrogantly blind with religious certainty they were willing to risk our lives that way. He could drive off a cliff if he wanted but he didn't have the right to take Mark and I with him.

It's funny, you often hear preachers and priests tell stories about how an individual's singular act of kindness brought another person to Christ. I would venture to guess that the hurtful or reckless actions of zealots push away just as many folks from the religion (or any other religion for that matter).

The late 70's and early 80's was when the Religious Right really started gaining power. I remember seeing a lot of "I Found It" bumper stickers on cars and wondering what that was about.

It was kind of weird... I almost felt like I was starring in a made-for-TV movie where I was the concerned parent and my folks were the impressionable young cult members.

It seemed like they were constantly going to church services or study groups or potlucks and the people in the church were always crying or holding their hands up in the air or spouting the newest religious catchphrase I'd never heard before.

It was interesting because in a couple years I would be working for a large corporation and see a lot of the same kind of behavior. Not the crying or hand waving but plenty of other rah-rah tactics.

Apparently we were entering an era when it wasn't good enough just to attend church or be a good worker… now you needed to approach everything in your life like it was a HUGE FUCKING DEAL. You couldn't just feel a certain way, you needed to express it and make sure everybody understood what team you were on.

The minister was slick and I got the impression he wanted the church to get a lot bigger and a lot wealthier fast… sometimes it felt more like venture capitalism than a group of people following an individual who taught that you should always treat others as you would have them treat you.

Being around all this heart-on-your-sleeve holiness made me want to go sit in a dark bar, order a drink and light a cigarette. I guess it was just too much of a culture shock.

I didn't mind if they went to church but I was getting more and more aggravated when Nona tried to rope me into joining their activities.

Everything started to take on religious overtones. I felt like if I asked her to pass the salt at dinner she might point out that was what Lot's wife was turned into and if we didn't all change our wicked ways God would punish us just as badly. I would just sit and listen and nod my head.

I didn't want to argue with her because I didn't really know what I believed. Plus the fact I was only going to be living with them temporarily and I really didn't want there to be any bad feelings floating around in the house.

There was a small scandal while I was living with them because Nona had left a small Buddha statue sitting out on the patio. I think she might have picked it up on a trip she had taken to Asia one time.

Somebody driving by on the highway saw it and started a rumor my folks had converted. I thought it was pretty funny in an ironic sense.

My dad wasn't so pushy but I could definitely see why this new blend of religion and politics appealed to a lot of white men his age.

They felt like the country had gone crazy over the past twenty years. Everybody was talking about rights and equality and leveling the playing field. You had to be careful what you said around people, always having to worry if some woman or gay or racial minority took offense somehow.

But maybe now the ship could be put back on course. Ronald Reagan was president and the white alpha males were back in charge.

The GOP had a great new plan. They could use the churches as their ideological training centers and not even have to pay taxes. And if a candidate ran on a family values platform it was damn hard to criticize them. They could use God as their shield.

The country needed to be reminded... gays were sick, women were helpmates, non-whites needed to keep their mouths shut and God was a fervent free-market capitalist.

I'm not saying the church Dad and Nona attended was overtly political. But it was representative of conservative organizations located all over the country that the Republicans were eager to utilize in one way or another.

I was never quite sure how Jesus fit in to this new GOP version of Christianity. After all, he had long hair and a beard and seemed very concerned about people taking care of each other. He even taught that we should turn the other cheek when someone attacks us.

In other words, he was your basic hippie longhair socialist pacifist.

It was strange. One of the reasons I was glad to be leaving Eugene was because it had started to feel like everybody there was liberal and totally unwilling to even listen to a moderate or conservative opinion. Now I was on the other side of the state having to hear everybody rant and rave about socialism and secular humanists and tree huggers.

But we got through the Summer with a minimum of tension. Dad paid me to paint our two houses and a barn. I enjoyed the nice, mindless work and the hot eastern Oregon climate.

Chapter 65: Papa Was a Rolling Stone

Dave had moved to Corvallis and had a job with the phone company. He called me and said they needed temporary help for a few weeks while students were getting settled in for Fall term at Oregon State University.

I had decided to give Seattle a try. I remembered reading it had been named America's most livable city just a few years ago. And my stepbrother Russ and his family lived up in that area.

I figured it would be a good idea to take Dave up on his offer and build up my cash reserves a bit before heading to Washington state. He said I could stay at his place in Corvallis.

He and John Wellhaven were living in the bottom of an old house. We referred to it as The Bunker.

It was pretty primitive… it had lights and running water but no heat other than a woodstove. Fortunately, it was still early September.

The guy who lived upstairs in Dave's house was named Vaughn. He was a very kindly older gay man who sometimes came down and shared his dope with us.

We always cracked up because Vaughn would basically fellate the plastic bong tube when he was taking a hit. I don't even think he realized he was doing it.

I drove up to Portland, took the standard Pacific Northwest Bell employment test and interview. I passed it and they assigned me to be a greeter. My job was to ask OSU students questions when they first came in to the Phone Center store and put them in the appropriate line.

While I was working there, I met a couple of single mothers who were with the company.

Dave introduced me to a tall redhead named Barb. The first day we knew each other we played a game of dirty hangman and ended up in my bed at the Bunker later that night.

The other woman was a short, stocky blonde named Victoria. She had a very pretty face. She invited me over to her place for dinner and did her best to seduce me. I got out of there with my pants still zipped, mostly because I felt weird about fooling around with her little boy asleep in the next room.

I got the impression both these women desperately wanted a step-daddy for their little boys. While I considered myself a reasonably handsome fellow, this was the first time I'd encountered women who seemed eager to get me drunk and bed me mere hours after making my acquaintance.

I almost felt like there was some kind of weird pagan harvest festival being held in Corvallis and I was caught in the middle of it. Meeting women had never been close to this easy before… maybe I'd been named Lord of the Potential Stepdads or something.

I felt sorry for them. I knew it had to be tough trying to raise a kid by themselves and I hoped they would eventually end up with the right guy. But I was committed to starting a new life in Seattle once my six weeks at the Phone Center was over.

While I was living in Corvallis, Janet and Rick split up. They'd been married a little over three years. She gave birth to a daughter named Angela in August of 1980.

Rick had finally come out of the closet. Janet thought he was having an affair with an attractive female co-worker but gradually the real truth came out.

I drove down to Eugene the night he told her. When I got to their house, all his clothes were spread out on the lawn. Janet was devastated.

She looked at me with tears in her eyes and said "I have no idea how to deal with this. If it was another woman maybe we could sit down and talk about how to fix things. But he wants to be with other men! How in the hell am I am suppose to compete with that? Do I get a sex change and grow a fucking mustache?".

I imagine after he told her, she probably took a few minutes and thought about hundreds of little telltale moments during their years together that should have tipped her off. Like his wearing skintight faded 501 Levi's with no underwear. Or the fact he used a larger variety of skin and hair products than she did. Or the fact he loved to look at magazines that primarily featured handsome male models.

My folks thought the situation could be fixed if everybody prayed enough. Well, actually Nona thought that and I think Dad went along with it to keep her happy.

I was dubious… I didn't know that much about homosexuality at that point but I was pretty confident it wasn't something Rick had much control over.

You could tell he was born gay. Deep down, I think we had all known it since the first time we met him.

And one some level, I believe Janet had always known it too. But denial can be a very powerful tool if you want to believe something bad enough.

I knew Rick wasn't going to get much emotional support from his family. They were a bunch of loggers who had moved to Oregon from Georgia. They probably had the reddest necks in Sunnyrock.

Chapter 66: New Kid in Town

I packed my possessions into my mildew-infested Dodge Dart and headed north to Seattle.

I didn't have a lot... just clothes, some paperback books and a crate full of record albums. My philosophy was you should never have more than one car load's worth of stuff. That way you could pack fast and move anywhere in one trip.

Somehow I'd managed to pick up very few practical household items during my college years. I'd lived in dorms, eaten out and relied on the kindness of women I'd met along the way. But I knew now I would need to be more responsible and start living like an adult.

Initially I was going to be staying with my stepbrother Russ and his family. Russ was probably 30 years older than me and worked as an engineer for the city of Des Moines. The name always struck me as odd, I kept thinking I should see some cornfields.

Russ and his Sheila said I was welcome to stay with them until I got enough money together to get my own place. I really appreciated their generosity.

I knew it was going to be pretty lonely for a while. I didn't have any old buddies to rely on in Seattle. I would need to go out and meet new people and create my new life pretty much from scratch.

But that was okay. I felt good about the fact I was brave enough to strike out on my own this way.

Russ was very nice but he'd recently got caught up in religion much the same way my folks had. One day we were talking about current events and we got on the subject of how much influence Christian leaders should have on foreign policy.

Russ said, "Hey, this is a Christian nation, pure and simple. As far as I'm concerned, if the president receives a vision from the Lord telling him to do something, he needs to just go ahead and do it".

I said, "What if the Lord tells him to nuke China and kill millions of people?".

He replied, "Well, we need to follow God's will. Most of them aren't Christians so I would say the Lord knows what He's doing even if it seems harsh to us".

That was bad enough but then he started messing with football, one of my favorite things in life. When we'd watch Seahawk games together, he'd always point out which players were Christians.

I guess he thought since I loved football and some of the players on the screen made a big deal about going to church, I would then complete the equation and decide it was all connected somehow. That would have probably worked if I was eight years old.

It actually had the opposite effect on me... I started to resent players like Steve Largent a little bit. I started thinking he should just catch the damn ball and let me worry about my own spiritual needs.

I hated that kind of sneaky evangelizing. My stepsister Doris had tried something similar a few years earlier when she gave me a Christian comedy album for Christmas. It was so lame.

I got to Des Moines on a Saturday, took it easy on Sunday and then Monday took a bus to downtown Seattle and put in an application at Pacific Northwest Bell. My having worked at the Phone Center didn't guarantee I would get hired in Seattle but I definitely felt like it would help. The interviewer suggested I apply for the Service Representative position.

I had to take a couple tests. One involved taking an exam while listening to instructions telling me to do something else. I guess that was a way to see how well I could multi-task. Kind of like the office version of juggling while riding a unicycle.

They said I passed the tests and would contact me when a position opened up.

I was okay with that. I had figured I probably wouldn't be offered a job immediately. I opened up the want ads to see what else I might do in the meantime.

I didn't have a lot of experience and the economy was still lousy so I set the bar pretty low for myself. I put in an application to be a telemarketer selling storm windows. Their office was located in a business park south of Des Moines.

I got hired. I was feeling pretty darn efficient... I had moved to Washington on Saturday and here I was filling out my W-2 form on Monday afternoon.

My elation didn't last long. It was really a gross job. You would call a couple hundred numbers a day and try to get people interested so they would consent to have a salesman come out.

I developed a thick skin pretty quickly. A lot of people hung up on me or swore at me but I just kept dialing. The girl who started the same day as me quit after four hours.

A lot of elderly shut-ins just seemed to be happy getting a call from anybody. I tried to at least make sure they understood I was calling to sell them something and not just because I was a nice young man. I didn't want to be a total sleazeball.

I wasn't especially good at it but I hung in there. After six weeks, I had more seniority than anybody except the owner of the company. He thought that was pretty funny.

I worked four hours in the morning and four hours in the evening. I spent the afternoons going to the movies or hanging out at a nearby mall.

There was a store that sold big screen TVs and I spent countless hours watching whatever laser discs happen to be playing. It seemed like it was nearly always a REO Speedwagon concert.

I finally got a call from the phone company. They said I could start in a week.

I immediately quit the phone soliciting job and drove down to Eugene for a couple days. I wanted to hang out with Mark, Tom and Bret a bit before starting my serious new business career. I also checked in on Janet to see how she was holding up.

I was really nervous about starting my new job. So nervous I woke up on my first day at 2:30 am, assumed it was time to get up and got ready for work.

I was assigned to work in Small Business accounts. This was considered a better gig than being an operator or working in Residential Services.

I was never sure why they let me start in Small Business… maybe it was because I had a college degree. Perhaps those five years of college had paid off in some small way after all. Or maybe the interviewer liked me for some reason or maybe it was just total dumb luck.

We spent the first day in Orientation. I found out a lot of phone company people had degrees in fields not specifically related to telecommunications.

That made me feel better about the path my life had taken. Apparently I was part of a large group of bright yet indecisive individuals.

I'd never really had a burning passion to become a journalist. I loved talking about current events and politics and enjoyed writing but I was just as happy to make my living some other way. The last thing I wanted to do after college was moving to some small town and starving to death while trying to get the scoop on whether or not the local school levy was going to pass.

I was going to be in class for the first eight weeks. There was a lot of information to learn. This was in late 1981, still two years before Pacific Northwest Bell and the other Baby Bells would be stripped away from AT&T.

We (AT&T) provided service to the vast majority of the country. The company was so big it almost seemed like a separate government entity. Once you got your foot in the door it was easy to transfer any place else AT&T had offices.

My initial training class consisted of me and five women. Ellen was a very sweet woman three years older than me, Laura was a saucy Latina a couple years younger than me, Star was a punk rocker

Union steward, Astrid was a horsey looking but nice middle-aged woman and Jenny was a woman in her Sixties who had to start working because her husband had left her for someone younger.

When we'd been in class for about a month, we got news that our instructor's home had burnt down and two of her three young daughters were killed. We were all devastated. The instructor ended up taking a personal leave for a few months and we finished our training with someone else.

Chapter 67: Gimme Shelter

Janet called me and said she was thinking of moving to Seattle. She wondered if I wanted to get a place with she and her daughter Angela.

She couldn't afford to keep her house in the Eugene area and she also felt like a change of scenery would do her good.

I said that would be fine. I figured we both needed moral support at this point in our lives. She was still trying to make sense of what had happened to her seemingly happy life and I wasn't terribly excited about the prospect of living alone.

They drove up and after a few days we started hunting for an apartment. We found a decent one in Woodinville, a suburb not too far east of Seattle. It was decently priced and located close to a spot where I could catch the bus to work.

Not long after we got moved in to our new place, my Dodge Dart finally died for good. I called a junkyard and had them haul it away. Janet had a Firebird I could use if necessary.

I wasn't too upset, it had only cost me four hundred bucks and it had ran long enough to deliver me to Seattle and my new life. Besides, it was starting to smell like a terrarium.

Work was going okay. I would get stressed out sometimes because there was so much to remember about the different products and regulations. But most of the folks in the office were nice and willing to answer my questions.

One thing that helped was being a young straight male. A lot of the older (age 30 and above) women seemed to enjoy mothering me. I loved joking around and gradually getting to know everybody.

There were also quite a few gay men in the office. It took a while for me to figure out which guys were and which guys weren't but eventually I developed a pretty good gaydar.

At first I was a little paranoid about them. I didn't really know what the rules were in an environment where gay people were free to just be themselves and do whatever.

I kept thinking about the people in Dad and Nona's church and how hysterical they would be about this situation. What if some guy tries to ask you out? What will you do if they try to recruit you and force you to help advance their Godless sodomite agenda?

It turned out I had no cause to worry. Gay guys were only interested in other gay guys. A couple were kind of bitchy and unapproachable but all the others were nice and very funny.

After I was in class two months, the instructor had us go out and take calls in the office for a week. I met an attractive woman named Joan Prescott. She was about nine months older than me and seemed really nice.

We flirted at work for a couple weeks, leaving each other little notes (this was way before texting or even e-mail). She invited me over for dinner on a Saturday night. I was pretty pleased, I loved it when women took the first step.

I was feeling pretty good. I did a review in my head: I'd moved to Seattle, been hired by two different companies, moved into my own place and now had a date with a very desirable woman. Things were really looking up.

Joan was average height and had a pretty face. She had a nice figure and it was kind of amazing when we first met because she'd been dieting for a couple months. Her best feature was her naturally curly blondish brown hair.

She fixed Chicken Cordon Bleu for dinner. We began drinking Chardonnay, making small talk about people at work and our families and where we grew up.

It's been my experience that it generally takes four glasses of wine on a first date to get a couple from the stiff getting-to-know-you stage to the really fun part. This is how it went with Joan…

First and second glasses: I'm talking about how I grew up on a ranch, where I went to college, how I lost my mom when I was thirteen. She's talking about her family, where she went to college, what her ambitions are. We're both earnest and somewhat serious and putting on our mature faces. There are little jokes here and there for seasoning.

I admit I sometimes used the mom story to make myself seem vulnerable and damaged. I don't feel good about it but dating forces you to pull out your entire bag of tricks.

Third glass: I'm telling her how pleased and surprised I am she invited me over. She teases me about not giving myself enough credit and says she's surprised I don't already have a girlfriend. I tell her a bit about my time with Eve but I conveniently leave out the part about proposing and then losing my nerve.

We're sitting very close and the air around us is thick with pheromones. We're both doing mental gymnastics, trying to figure out how fast things should happen at this point. We finally kiss.

Fourth glass: She tells me I'm a good kisser. I tell her maybe that's because she's the most attractive woman I've ever kissed. And up to that point in my life that was actually true.

At this point we're all over each other. We've passed each other's initial compatibility check lists and now physical testing can begin.

Liquor is liquid love lubrication. Pure and simple.

Of course, if you're both raging alcoholics my theory may not hold up. You might jump into bed together after the first glass or you might both pass out before you even hold hands. Who knows, you might even decide to go for a drive and cause an eight-car pileup.

Neither of us were alcoholics so things went well. We drank and made out off and on for a couple hours. Eventually, I was so wasted she suggested I spend the night. We crawled into bed and instantly fell asleep.

We made love for the first time the next morning but it wasn't exactly my best work. I had a really bad hangover and she had a waterbed. The water sloshing underneath us made it hard for me to get into any kind of dependable rhythm and seemed to amplify my headache.

But I was still very happy. When I left her apartment a couple hours later, I contemplated how amazing my luck had been lately.

The next few weeks we continued to see each other. My not having a car complicated matters somewhat. I found myself spending more and more nights at her place.

Things moved along pretty fast. After a month or so, Joan said I should just go ahead and move in with her. She said she'd even keep paying the rent by herself so I could save up for a down payment on a car and continue to help Janet with the rent on the Woodinville apartment.

I was both surprised and very pleased when she made the offer. But I was also a little worried Janet might feel like I was abandoning her.

She didn't seem to mind as long as I could still pay half the rent. She had met a guy named Jason there at the apartment complex and they were spending a lot of time together. She'd gotten a job working as a claims processor at an insurance company.

Chapter 68: Pacific Ocean Blues

My period of loneliness was ending but unfortunately, Mark McShane was single once again.

He and Nancy's marriage hadn't lasted long. I guess the fact their wedding reception had turned into a brawl might have been a sign their union wasn't meant to be.

He'd left Eugene and eventually ended up down in Orange County, south of LA. He was living with his brother Bret and another guy named Fred. Mark and Bret were working day jobs and trying to break into the music business.

They had a band but it was tough to get noticed. There was just so much competition. To play at a reputable club like Madame Wong's, you had to pay a "door deposit" up front and hope you drew a big enough audience to earn it back.

Plus they were kind of in the Springsteen/Graham Parker/Elvis Costello mode and the hot trend at the time was hair metal. Style was definitely winning out over substance in the LA area.

I flew down to see them. We had a blast just driving around checking out all the sights and soaking up the sunshine. Randy Newman's song "I Love LA" was popular at the time and whenever it came on the radio we cranked it up loud and sang along.

I even finally made it to Disneyland.

On the second to last day of the trip, we decided to go to Venice Beach. When we got there we ran out into the waves and started body surfing.

At some point, I noticed I was getting pretty far from shore and wasn't having much luck getting back

I suddenly realized if I didn't get some help I'd soon be too far out for anybody to hear me.

I began yelling as loud as I could. Luckily, I have the kind of voice that carries.

I saw a lifeguard run into the surf and come swimming towards me. He was able to calm me down and help me dog paddle in place. Then another one came out and helped us both back to the shore.

I don't think I'd ever been that tired before. I lay on the sand gasping for air. Fortunately, I hadn't swallowed a lot of water.

So that was how I learned about rip tides. I was really scared of the water for a couple years after that. Even going for a walk on the beach seemed like a spooky proposition… I always felt like the ocean was talking to me, tempting me to come in for a swim so she could carry me away again. I gradually got over it for the most part but I never went body surfing again.

Chapter 69: Lovers in a Dangerous Time

Joan and I were fine for the first six months. I was just happy to have a decent income and a pretty girlfriend. But things gradually started to unravel.

Looking back, I would say we probably moved in together way too soon. We probably should have gotten to know each other much better before taking such a big step. I began to discover our relationship had some fairly serious problems.

When Joan would drink at parties, she would act very cool toward me. She'd get a funny look on her face and barely acknowledge my presence. She was like the most selective amnesiac in the world… the only person she didn't remember was me. She never acted this way when just the two of us went out drinking.

I started to wonder if she had a separate evil personality that only emerged at parties. Well, not evil exactly… just one that seemed to have zero interest in her current boyfriend.

I will say I never caught her flirting with anybody else. She would get a buzz and then spend most of the party joking around with our gay male friends. Maybe she was channeling Liza Minnelli… she needed me for sex and them for witty cocktail chatter.

She also had no interest in current events. I had never really required this in a relationship before but I guess now I was getting a little older and starting to think about what kind of person I might realistically be able to spend my life with.

One time I complained about this issue. She said, "Maybe you could tell me about the news and then we could discuss it".

I told her that arrangement probably wouldn't be terribly stimulating for me. At that particular moment I felt like I was dealing with a younger version of Edith Bunker.

I also think some of my artistic likes and dislikes may have put her off a bit. We went to see "The Road Warrior" with our friend Jessica. When we came out of the theatre my brain was buzzing… I raved that this film the greatest jolt of adrenaline ever put on celluloid.

Both of them looked at me like I'd lost my mind. They had not enjoyed themselves one bit.

So I'm not going to pin that one on Joan. I suppose you could say that particular example may have been one of your basic man vs. woman entertainment differences.

We also had a bit of a sexual problem. She could never seem to achieve a real honest-to-God-scream-at-the-ceiling orgasm. Whenever she got close, she started laughing and that stopped everything. It was like there was a part of her brain that refused to let her become a fully satisfied sexual being.

I found this to be extremely frustrating. No matter how skillful or passionate I was during our lovemaking, it always ended with her reacting like she'd just heard a good dirty limerick.

She got a book about sex advice and decided it might be fun for us to try anal sex. We got really stoned and applied some lubricant. When I just barely put myself into her she screamed and jumped up like I had poked her with an electric cattle prod.

I felt really bad I caused her pain. But on the other hand, thinking about that moment always made me giggle a bit because it reminded me so much of a Tom and Jerry cartoon where the cat gets shocked and ends up hanging upside down from the ceiling.

We were smoking a lot of pot. Her brother was an occasional dealer and was always giving her big bags of cheap dope. If you could buy marijuana at

Costco this is probably what it would have looked like.

We also had some friends named Bill and Cindy who lived out in the country and grew their own. We went out there one weekend with Dave. He was living in central Washington but would periodically come over and spend the weekend with us.

There were a bunch of folks from the office there. Cindy had made some really powerful pot brownies and everyone was trying them. It's possible she should have advised people not to eat a whole piece.

One guy got really high and started freaking out. He was pleading "Please, please you have to take me to the hospital. This stuff is too strong, I think I'm gonna have a heart attack". Bill was trying to calm him down, obviously worried that a doctor's visit might prompt questions from the local authorities.

They were very potent. About an hour after I ate mine, I ended up laying down on the carpet in one of the spare bedrooms and passing out for the night.

Bill and Cindy were interesting. I got the impression he was an ex-hippie who didn't mind working 40 hours a week in an office so he and his wife could have this place out in the country where they could grow their dope and at least get away from it all on the weekends.

Another weekend a few months later, Joan and I drove out to their place and spent the day cross-country skiing with them.

That night we partied and Bill kept dropping hints that they wanted to swap partners. It didn't happen but Joan was mad at me the whole way home the next day because she felt like I had been sort of open to the idea. Which, I have to admit, I kind of had been ... Cindy was pretty hot.

Of course, the problems in the relationship weren't all Joan's fault. I had my own issues. I was drinking too much and starting to backslide into bouts of depression from time to time. I'm sure there were times she found it exhausting to be around me.

I started thinking a lot about Eve. I was bored living with Joan and began wondering if all that drama had really been so bad.

I'm sure part of it stemmed from watching the sitcom "Cheers". Shelly Long's character Diane reminded me so much of Eve. She was smart, attractive, pretentious, annoying and almost never boring. As they say, the grass is always greener and nothing makes your old relationship seem great faster than your current shitty one.

Joan and I finally sat down one day and had a long discussion. We agreed things weren't working out between us. I said I'd find another place to live. She was very civil and said there wasn't any great rush.

Chapter 70: Working Man

I met a friendly guy at work named Trevor. He was a couple years younger than me. His main interests seemed to be reciting lines from Monty Python episodes and drinking as much cheap beer as possible. His current living arrangement was about to end so we decided to get an apartment together.

We found one across the street from a place called Greenlake. It's always been my favorite part of Seattle. It's a natural lake located in north Seattle that formed roughly 50,000 years ago. It's about three miles in circumference and ringed by grass and a variety of trees.

We both really wanted to live in that neighborhood so we settled for a place that only had one bedroom. I agreed to pay two thirds of the rent if I could have the bedroom and Trevor slept on an old couch we picked up at a garage sale.

Around this time, Pacific Northwest Bell was going through the final phase of divesting from AT&T. I had chosen to stay with PNB and Joan went to work for AT&T's new phone equipment division. We both still worked in the same building but at least now we were on different floors.

My company would soon change it's name to US West. We provided local phone service in fourteen western states.

The breakup of AT&T also meant our customers could choose their long distance company. We spent a lot of our time and energy trying to help people understand the new regulations.

For the first few months, the vast majority of them expressed the opinion they wished the government had just left things alone. I got the impression it was one of those situations where people were eager for change to happen but only if it didn't feel like there was any change happening.

Change was rapidly taking place inside our business as well. We started using computers. They were slow and sometimes aggravating but it was still way more efficient than the paper files we used previously.

A lot of the older employees worried they wouldn't be able to handle the new technology and did their best to avoid using it. But eventually we were all sitting in front of a computer screen pulling up accounts and handling customer calls from larger and larger geographic areas. It was amazing how much more efficient we became over the next few years.

When I first started with the company you constantly had to update a paper file you kept on your desk that held information about services that were available, addresses and order writing rules. If a customer called about a pending service order you had to get up from your desk, walk over to a big filing cabinet and look for a piece of paper that had information about their request. Maybe you'd find something and maybe you wouldn't.

Now you could type their phone number or work order number into the computer at your desk and instantly provide them with the answers they needed.

It was a stressful job but there were funny moments here and there. One Monday morning I was talking to an Asian man who had a heavy accent. I kept having to repeat questions because I couldn't understand his answers. He finally started laughing and said, "Whatsamatta, Jim, you potty too much this weekend?"

Another incident involved my name. My friend Ellen gave me the nickname Jim-Bob because I grew up in the country and she liked the "Waltons" t.v. program. A new employee in the office overheard her call me that and later transferred a customer to me, introducing the call by saying "Sir, I have Jim-Bob on the line for you now."

One of the worst co-workers I ever had to deal with was a guy named Spooner. He was good at sales but he stunk and was always dying his hair blue or bright red or black. And he wore t-shirts that had slogans like “My parents went baby seal clubbing and all I got was this lousy t-shirt”. The shirt had a picture of a bloody baby seal on it.

Ellen left the company but we stayed friends. She and her husband lived by Greenlake and sometimes I would go hang out with them. When Joan and I were still living together I would often complain to Ellen about what was going on and ask for her advice. Later they moved to Portland but we still keep in touch.

Chapter 71: Gold Dust Woman

Joan and I continued to sleep together from time to time. It seemed like we got along much better now that there were no expectations about the relationship moving forward in any sense. We were friends with benefits.

My fondest memory of her is from the night ABC presented “The Morning After”. We had started watching the movie at her place but after a while we got in the mood and started fooling around.

I remember having Joan on top of me, lunging up and down as the missiles left their silos and we were swept away into our own kind of sweet annihilation. I don’t even remember her laughing when she came.

I felt a little guilty we were enjoying hot sex while the country was getting nuked. But it did make the movie a bit less depressing.

Joan eventually met someone and told me we needed to end our sleepovers. I told her I completely understood and agreed but over the next few weeks I was shocked how bad it hurt to be completely cut off from her.

Sure, I had wanted to break up with her for quite a while but I never thought about the possibility she might meet someone new before I did.

My ego screamed "What a heartless bitch! How can she do this after all the good times we shared?". My feelings were totally irrational and unfair but we had been together for a year and a half so I guess it's natural I would feel some jealousy and pain.

The guy she got involved with really liked doing cocaine. I heard through the grapevine she was partying pretty hard every weekend with him and his friends.

I went over to see her one night and she looked pretty bad. She was getting too thin and she had dark circles under her eyes. She said she'd been up the past forty eight hours straight.

I missed being with her. My mind was starting to play that trick where you can only remember the good things about the person you were anxious to get away from for so long.

I was also starting to get a little worried about what this new relationship might be doing to her health.

It was a weird time. Coke had always seemed pretty exotic, a drug for rock stars and Hollywood people and the denizens who frequented places like Studio 54.

But now you'd walk into a party at a co-worker's house and see regular, middle-class folks bent over a mirror on a coffee table, snorting up powder that consisted of cocaine, baby laxative and God knows what else.

The coke culture was so different than the pot culture. When you smoked pot, most people sat back and relaxed and took things in stride. You might nurse a beer or maybe eat something or just listen to some tunes. Everybody was your friend and it was all good.

When you went to a party where people were snorting coke, it seemed like there was all this nervous, paranoid energy floating around in the room and lots of secret meetings in bathrooms and everybody was chain smoking and talking really fast and constantly leaving and then coming back and then leaving again.

You couldn't do coke and then sit around and listen to a Pink Floyd album. There's no way you could sit still that long. I actually think coke was the cause of a lot of bad music that came out in the 80's. Nobody could stay in one room long enough to make good music.

I will admit, my curiosity got the best of me and I did coke a few times. Fortunately, it was too expensive for my meager phone company salary.

The only time I really got into it was New Year's Eve 1985. I was with some friends who seemed to have an unlimited supply. We stayed up all night engaged in a seemingly endless cycle of doing coke, drinking champagne, smoking cigarettes, doing more coke, drinking more champagne, smoking more cigarettes, doing more coke…

I even drunk dialed Joan and left a really annoying message. "Hi Joanie, it's me, Jimmy. I'm kinda drunk and pretty high but I just wanted to say I hope 1985 will be a great year for you. You're such a great person. You know, we really had a lot of fun together… I probably should have appreciated those good times more when they were happening. You know, if you ever need a friend you can always call me or come see me, I will always be there for you…".

I'm sure she thought it was pretty pathetic.

I was so sick the next few days. I was incredibly hung over, my lungs felt like they'd been slow roasted on a spit and I was horribly depressed. Cocaine is one of those drugs that makes you feel like you can fly and then buries you alive.

I finally let go of Joan. It was hard when I'd see her in the building where we worked but time gradually healed my wounds.

Chapter 72: Free Money

I went through a brief "yuppie" period after Joan and I split up for good. I didn't have a yuppie income but I still managed to get caught up in the mindset.

I started wearing ties and dress shirts to work and my politics swung to the right for a while. I was quoting George Will to my dad. I even bought a used Fiat because it kind of looked like a BMW. I was a yuppie on the cheap.

Work and making money seemed to become the national religion for a while. CEOs were suddenly viewed as cool guys, especially if they were risk takers. People started working longer hours every week, trying to prove they were the employee who truly had the passion and drive. People in management started giving motivational speeches that were suppose to somehow convince us what we did for the company was the ultimate measure of our worth.

You weren't encouraged to give a 100 percent effort because in this new world of business that simply wasn't enough anymore. You were told the new standard was a minimum of 110 percent. I was never sure exactly how all this effort was actually measured... seems like you would need a treadmill or something.

Of course, there were some businesses where employing this new message was a bit tricky. Most of the people who worked at US West were in a union so the company had to settle for telling folks to give 110 percent but make sure you take all your breaks and lunches and overtime pay.

So, in actuality I would say they were doing well to even get a 95 percent effort out of us. In fact, I knew several people who probably wouldn't give more than a 60 percent effort to put out a fire in their own house.

Another subject we heard a lot about was "quality". It wasn't enough just to buy a pair of shoes. They had to be a certain brand and they would justify the price by claiming they planned on owning that amazing pair of shoes for the rest of their life.

It seemed like stuff you might hear a lot in New England, especially in the old money WASP Muffy and Biff neighborhoods. These are shoes with character and breeding, shoes that were descended from shoes that came over on the Mayflower!

It even started to affect what people bought at the grocery store. You couldn't just buy grapes, they had to be imported from Chile. You couldn't just buy meat, you had to buy Kobe steaks from Japan. Nothing was worth having in your house unless it had been shipped across five time zones.

A woman I knew invited me to a Christmas dinner party where all the dishes were based on recipes from Bon Appetit magazine. I didn't want to be rude so I spent the whole evening pretending to care what kind of olive oil we were dipping our handcrafted designer bread in and where the damn fancy lettuce came from.

The whole time I was thinking how much more fun it would be just going out and having a cheeseburger with regular people who didn't feel the need to constantly analyze whatever it was they were about to cram in their mouths.

Of course, it was marketing based on making you feel like what you bought proved you were better than most other people. It had always been done but now in the hyper-capitalist Reagan era the dial had been turned way up.

The economy was heating up and people were eager to talk about work and money, money, money. Women were wearing power suits with shoulder pads, guys were wearing suspenders and when you told someone how much you made, you always said "k" instead of thousands. You didn't get to know people, you "networked" with them.

It wasn't just me. The whole culture of Seattle was changing... not too long before I arrived it was basically an oversized blue-collar town that depended on Boeing jobs or ones connected to timber or shipping.

Now all of a sudden, Microsoft and a multitude of other information age companies were in the spotlight. And local outfits like Nordstrom's were starting to expand their operations nationwide. The once sleepy city was now wired on caffeine and awash in a sea of venture capital and stock options.

There were a couple reasons my politics leaned right for a while. Like a lot of people, I was put off by how wimpy the Democrats in Congress seemed to be at that time. While the Republicans were busy playing doomsday poker with the Soviets, many of the Dems seemed more concerned about pronouncing the names of Central American socialists correctly.

And on a personal level, I was still a little bitter about the attitudes displayed by some of the professors I'd had in Eugene. It never happened to me but I'd seen them bully students who dared to question the prevailing liberal orthodoxy that held sway on campus. That really didn't seem right in an environment that's supposed to promote and support the free exchange of ideas.

I was also making an attempt to get into management at US West. When I started with the company, I'd told myself if I wasn't a manager after four years I would quit and do something else. I'm sure a lot of other people made a similar vow at some point at their careers with the company.

Trevor moved back to California so I had the apartment to myself. I decided to try the dating ads in the local alternative newspaper. I figured if I wrote a truly witty ad I was bound to meet some nice, interesting, sexy females.

I got ten responses. I decided I wanted to meet five of the women who'd written back to me.

The other five were a pretty colorful group that included one one who'd just been released from prison and another that spent the majority of her letter talking about her cat, Mister Sparkles.

I found that meeting people this way was really hard work.

The first woman I met seemed stiff and unpleasant and gave off a vibe that said she was generally resentful I'd been born a male.

She sat across from me in a restaurant and asked, "So, what kind of stuff are you into?"

I told her I liked sports, especially football and basketball. I also liked to read and go to movies and listen to music.

"What kind of music? Hard rock?"

"Sure, sometimes. Especially in the car".

"Well, I hate hard rock", she said. "They might as well just call it rape theme music. Those musicians are just Nazis with long hair".

The date with the second woman went even worse. She immediately started mocking me because I was from a small town and sometimes read science fiction.

I don't recall either of them smiling even once during our dates. I'm not even sure why they answered my ad… maybe they just liked to check in once in a while and re-validate their belief all men were unworthy.

The third date was productive in the sense that the woman happened to be a sex addict. Unfortunately, she was also kind of nuts. We had a brief (mostly naked) relationship.

The fourth one never showed up where we were supposed to meet and the fifth one never saw me because I spied her through the window of the restaurant and decided not to go through with the date. I suddenly understood why she neglected to include a picture with her letter.

Chapter 73: My Best Friend's Girl

Dave moved to Seattle in September of 1984. He'd been working for a regional library system in Wenatchee for a couple years.

His job had been to drive around to the different small towns in the area and supply them with new books or help the librarians with any other issues they might have. He'd enjoyed it but was now itching to get on with the next stage of his education, a Master's Degree at the University of Washington.

It was a lot more fun living with Dave than Trevor. After all, he was one of my best friends and we had a lot of common interests.

Trevor was a nice guy but he always seemed to be sweating profusely and because he drank so much beer he always smelled like he worked at a brewery.

That made him a less than desirable wingman when we'd go out and try to meet women. Of course, it's not like Dave and I had great success picking up ladies in bars either.

This was better than college. We actually had some money now and we were enjoying life. We went to a lot of movies, hung out at Greenlake, ogled girls and drank a lot of martinis. We continued to live in my same apartment and he set up a bedroom of sorts in the dining room area.

Dave had been briefly engaged to a girl during his last year in college. She was someone he'd known in high school. She ended up breaking off the engagement and he took it pretty hard. He ended up spending a lot of time alone in his room playing solitaire, trying to figure out what went wrong. One weekend he got high on mushrooms and punched a car.

Right before he left Wenatchee, he had become romantically involved with a co-worker named Sandra. She was a few years older than him and tended to be on the moody side.

She came over to stay with us for a few days. Dave was somehow able to score three tickets for the Bruce Springsteen concert happening in Tacoma. He told me what was up but we kept Sandra in the dark and told her we were taking her to a great seafood restaurant we'd heard about. We broke the news to her as we were driving down I-5 and approaching the Tacoma Dome.

Her mouth dropped open in shock when we told her we were actually going to a concert and told her to look at the giant neon sign that advertised who was playing that night.

This was the "Born in the USA" tour. The show lasted over three hours and it felt like a concert, political rally and church revival meeting all rolled into one. We were clapping and dancing and sweating and by the end of it I think the audience was more exhausted than the band. It was a magical night.

Sandra went back to Wenatchee a few days later. She and Dave stayed friends but he really wanted to be with someone who wasn't always looking for a reason to be unhappy.

He got a part-time job at the University of Washington bookstore. He met a younger woman there named Renae and they started dating. They were very attracted to each other but she was a Mormon and when things started to get serious she insisted he convert to her faith.

Dave gave it his best shot. He went through an "Introduction to Mormonism" class but it just didn't take. Dave (like many of us) felt disconnected from religion in general and one that featured Jesus hanging out with the Indians before Columbus arrived was really a stretch.

Right around the time Dave and Renae finally called it quits, he met a woman named Miranda. They met on a bus one day. He told her he worked at the U of W bookstore and a couple days later she showed up there to ask him out.

I couldn't believe he met somebody else that fast. I was feeling pretty down about my romantic status and sat home alone a lot brooding (usually with a bottle of red wine sitting next to the chair).

Ranae and Miranda were very different physically. Ranae was blonde, slender and very cute in a wholesome way. Miranda had dark hair, sexy curves and always dressed very fashionably.

She'd grown up poor in Seattle but had used her charm and good looks to create a new sophisticated persona. The first time I met her I told Dave she seemed very classy and rich. I could tell he was falling hard for her.

Unfortunately, her survival instincts would eventually start to override her feelings for Dave. He began to feel uneasy around her.

He noticed she was starting to tell little lies and his money mysteriously disappeared every so often. She always claimed she was innocent or misunderstood or that he was just being mean to her.

It began to become apparent that part of her couldn't stand the happy monotony of a trusting, giving relationship. I also thought she might be feeling conflicted because maybe deep down she really wanted to be with a rich guy.

She had an interesting dual nature. Sometimes she seemed like Princess Miranda, the woman who wore tasteful scarves and enunciated her words and you would swear to God she belonged in an expensive apartment overlooking Central Park.

Other times she was Seattle Miranda, the hot girl who always had a hustle going and would invariably revert back to hanging out with the sleazy kids she knew in high school, laughing at the normal suckers behind our backs.

She had spent some time in Italy before meeting Dave. She decided to go back there and invited Dave to come along. He was so excited… he was going to Europe with a gorgeous woman he was crazy about. He started learning Italian so he'd be somewhat prepared to live over there.

But then she changed her mind and said she was going without him. He was never exactly sure if she had another man waiting for her or if she just felt like he was going to somehow cramp her style. He was heartbroken for a while. This time, however, he didn't eat mushrooms and punch a car.

He would meet his wife Paula at the bookstore in 1988. She was attractive, smart, honest and not a Mormon.

They had a lot in common and their personalities fit well together. They got married in 1992 and I was Dave's best man. They had a daughter named Sophie in 1999.

Miranda came back to town not long after Dave and Paula first started dating. She made an attempt to start things back up with Dave but he turned her down. He was happy being with Paula and didn't feel like going through another round of Miranda's brand of craziness.

During the mid-80's, John Erickson was living a couple hours west of Seattle in a coastal town called Port Angeles. He would come over and spend weekends with Dave and I sometimes.

Dave had to work on Saturdays so John and I spent the day together, spending countless happy hours combing through Seattle's many record stores, discussing different bands and sharing musical trivia.

John placed an ad in the same alternative newspaper I had previously used and had much better luck. He met a very nice woman named Kit. She'd moved out here from the Chicago area.

John and Kit got married in July of 1985. It was the same day they held the Live Aid concerts. They were married in a park that looked out over Puget Sound and then the reception was held at a club located near downtown Seattle.

There was an open bar and Dave and I were only too happy to take advantage of it. Our old buddy Marty had come up from Portland and the three of us sat there for hours enjoying shots of Crown Royal. Kit's dad was paying for the booze and kept glaring at us every time we ordered another round.

We knew John wasn't all that crazy about his new father-in-law so we didn't exactly feel guilty about driving up his liquor bill.

Chapter 74: Red Rain

I have a confession to make.

I love coffee and I love alcohol, especially wine.

The coffee I drink in the morning gives me energy and confidence and the courage to face the world. I probably drink too much of it.

The alcohol I drink (mostly) at night helps me write and go inside myself where I can explore and remember and dream while my eyes are open.

When I lived by myself I got pretty hooked on red wine. For me, the buzz from red wine is different than white wine. White wine is usually a fun buzz and helps me loosen up.

Red wine is dangerous for me. It would make me feel like Icarus, able to fly off my apartment balcony and go wherever I wanted, unstoppable and invincible.But then I would reach a point where the red rain would weigh down my wings and I would come spiraling down in a torrent of anger or depression.

The next morning I would get up, drink my coffee and start the whole cycle over again.

Chapter 75: Life Wasted

During the 80's the Middle East became our new stomping grounds and Saddam Hussein went from being a disreputable U.S. ally to an international petroleum thief and potential terrorist leader.

We would spend the majority of two decades watching him play cat and mouse with two presidents named Bush and another named Bill Clinton.

I remember sitting in a motel room down the street from Disneyland on August 2, 1990. I was with my wife and young son. I turned on the television just to see what channels were available and there were breaking news reports on all the network channels. Iraq had invaded Kuwait.

Over the next few months, the population of the world got acquainted with the rap sheet of Saddam Hussein and his thuggish Sunni military. He (especially in America) was no longer viewed as just another tinpot Middle Eastern dictator. All of a sudden, he was the veritable Anti-Christ of oil.

Of course, not all that long ago we'd been selling him weapons so he could fight the Iranians. But that's not something the Bush administration liked to talk about much.

It was amazing. Somehow our Vietnam wounds and cynicism had faded away during the 80's. Now we were being called to form an alliance of nations that would smash Saddam and save the Kuwaiti people and their blessed oil wells.

I have to admit, I got caught up in the war frenzy just like most other people. I would sit down in our basement hour after hour, watching the war preparations unfold on our big-screen TV, taking in the endless analysis of George H.W. Bush's cat-and-mouse game with the Iraqi government.

There was a tepid anti-war movement in the country but it couldn't seem to get much traction. A few rock stars like Tom Petty and Lenny Kravitz tried to speak out but the majority of the public didn't feel like listening to what they had to say. Most of the country had gone Rambo during the Reagan years.

Maybe there was something in our collective American consciousness that was saying we wanted a good alley fight after spending an exhausting almost fifty years playing nuclear chicken with the Soviets.

The night the war started, I was at an AC/DC concert in Tacoma. There had been news reports all day that the U.S. and its allies were on the verge of confronting the Iraqi military.

There was an announcement made during an intermission that we were officially at war. During the band's next song, Angus Young turned around and pulled down his schoolboy pants. He was wearing underwear that looked like the American flag. The audience went crazy.

My wife and I both had the next day off work. We sat and watched as the SCUD missiles were fired into Tel Aviv. It was truly amazing watching this live spectacle on a large-screen television, almost like engaging in a crude form of virtual reality. We were so relieved there weren't any casualties.

The war didn't last long. We were all shocked when Bush senior and his advisors decided not to capture Saddam and take over Iraq. It made the war seem like a joke with a multi-million dollar buildup and no punch line.

Apparently it also felt that way to a large number of influential Republican politicians and policymakers, including Dick Cheney and Donald Rumsfeld. Twelve years later they would help George Bush's oldest son take our military back to Iraq.

On the morning of September 11th, 2001, I got up at the normal time and was watching the news when they broke away to show smoke billowing out of one of the Twin Towers in Manhattan.

My wife came downstairs to get coffee and I said, “Hey, come here and look at this”.

Seconds later, the second plane hit. My wife burst into tears and I held her. We both wondered what the hell was going on.

I was working at the phone company in Seattle in the Federal Government group. The Department of Justice was one of my accounts. I was horrified by the events of that morning but also a bit excited… I figured I’d be busy on the phone all day expediting orders for my various government contacts.

I did get a call from the FBI in Nebraska but that was about it. I guess they had everybody out investigating if we were going to be hit again in other ways.

We had all the television sets turned on at work and spent most of the day watching the continuing news coverage.

It was such a strange, paranoid time. Rumors were flying and it was hard not to get caught up in the hysteria. For the first few days I felt really uncomfortable every time I saw a plane in the sky.

The anthrax scare was even worse. It got to the point where people were scared to even open their mail.

These events were like jet fuel for the right-wingers on the radio. They harped day and night about how Arab-Americans weren’t condemning the attacks furiously enough and they continually demonized Bill Clinton for not doing more to kill or capture Osama bin Laden back in the late 90's.

Limbaugh, Hannity, Coulter and all the rest threw verbal gasoline on the fears of scared Americans. They amplified the threat and roared about the clash of civilizations. They wanted us to believe there was a terrorist hiding outside every house, apartment building and business in the United States.

It wasn't long before this President Bush started pushing for an invasion of Iraq. The atmosphere in the country was still ripe with fear... all the administration and the media attack dogs had to do was talk about mushroom clouds and theoretical meetings between Al-Qaeda agents and the Iraq government.

I supported sending troops to Afghanistan but the whole Iraq thing just didn't feel right. I could tell we were being played.

There were large demonstrations held all over the world protesting Bush and Cheney's plans. My wife and I participated in one with roughly 25,000 other people in downtown Seattle. It was really exciting and we naively thought maybe we were making a difference.

The administration paid no attention to the protests. They knew they had to invade Iraq while the majority of the U.S. population was still angry, fearful and confused. We went to war in March of 2003.

I don't know if George W. Bush's administration had anything to do with the attacks on September 11th. But I have to believe there's a strong possibility they did. They came into office wanting to get rid of Saddam Hussein and just like clockwork they were handed a situation that made most Americans scared and ready to pound pretty much any country in the Middle East except Israel.

That's a pretty huge coincidence.

Chapter 76: She Loves the Jerk

On Halloween in 1984 I dressed like a nerd. When I got to work, one of the clerks in the office looked at me and said “I thought you were going to wear a costume this year”.

Her name was Rosemary Mills. She was tall, brunette and very good-looking. This particular day she had on a cowl-neck sweater and was sporting a hairdo that made her look like she should be playing bass on stage next to Prince.

We started talking to each other every day. She loved giving me a hard time. For some reason, she thought I was very straight-laced and she should be the one to loosen me up.

She’d grown up in Seattle and hadn’t spent much time out in the country. She liked teasing me about the name Sunnyrock, asking me if I grew up on a lizard ranch. I teased her back, asking what day Summer would occur on in Seattle this year.

At first I thought she might be a lesbian. Not because she looked like a lesbian or activated my gaydar in any way but because I'd always see her hanging out with gay men who worked in the office. I guess I was still kind of naïve… I wasn't aware of the "fag hag" concept.

I soon discovered she was much more than just a single woman who happened to have a couple gay male friends. She was Bette Midler without the singing ability. She seemed to have dozens of gay friends both inside and outside the company.

I liked her immediately. She seemed to have a lot of confidence and I found that very attractive. She also had a great sense of humor and an ability to laugh at herself.

She told me she had a little boy named Brendan. The father wasn't in the picture and that's the way Rosemary wanted things. She was very proud and didn't want to depend on anybody else for anything.

She asked me to go see a play called "Angry Housewives" with her. We went out for Italian food in Pioneer Square and then went to the show.

Even though we had a nice time, I was feeling hesitant about getting further involved with her. I was still somewhat paranoid about the single mother thing. I wanted to date someone who was purely interested in me and not just looking for an adult male to complete their nuclear family.

I had recently gone out with another woman and I used that as an excuse for not continuing to see Rosemary. She was pretty understanding but still kind of aggravated. She asked me what color the woman's hair was and I said blonde. From then on she always sarcastically referred to this other woman as "Helga".

Things didn't really progress with "Helga". But Rosemary kept flirting with me at work over the next few weeks and our mutual friends kept encouraging me to give the relationship a chance.

I finally decided to give it another shot. I'd spent enough time around her that I was starting to think maybe she really didn't have any hidden "daddy" agenda. I asked her out and when I went to pick her up she introduced me to her son and her best friend, Mike.

We went out for Mexican food and then back to my apartment. Dave had gone down to Oregon for the weekend.

This was the first time we'd truly been alone. We quickly discovered how strong our sexual attraction to each other was. I had never felt this kind of passion with a woman before.

Sometimes we'd rent a movie to watch but we could never get past the first third or so. We were just too anxious to make love.

But even with this amazing passion I was still kind of hung up on the single mother thing and having a hard time defining the way I felt about her. I wasn't quite ready to make a serious commitment.

I met another woman at work named Darlene. She had long dark hair and beautiful green eyes. She was training in her spare time to be a firefighter.

Unfortunately, she was kind of an airhead and it was tough carrying on any kind of satisfying conversation. But I was bowled over by the way she looked.

I foolishly thought that if I spent enough time with her we would eventually make some kind of connection and I would enjoy her company as much as I did Rosemary's. I was like all those women who think they can turn a gay guy straight or a bad guy into a good guy. I thought I could find locate and unleash Darlene's intellect and personality.

This new development really irritated Rosemary. "You've got to be kidding me", she said angrily. "I thought we had this great connection but for some reason you keep complicating things. First Helga and now this...what are you trying to do, date every woman you meet?".

I was seeing both of them for a few weeks. It was so cool... for once I felt like a player! I'd come a long way since that snowy Friday night years ago when I wept because I thought nobody would ever want to be with me.

Of course, I was conveniently overlooking the fact that my fun was being had at the expense of two other people's feelings and trust.

Eventually, Darlene found out I was seeing Rosemary behind her back. She tearfully said she couldn't see me anymore. I know she wasn't in love with me, just hurt and embarrassed I'd cheated on her.

Chapter 77: Somebody To Love

I hadn't spent much time around gay people before I started working at the phone company. Or maybe I should say people I knew for sure were gay.

I knew a couple Latino brothers back in high school who acted very gay, Vaughn the bong swallower in Corvallis and of course my ex-brother-in-law, Rick.

Some of the gay people working in our office were from the Seattle area but several of them had moved here from eastern Washington or from other states.

I quickly learned (just like with straight folks) some were funny, some were obnoxious, some were altruistic, some were selfish, some were lazy and some were compulsively ambitious. In other words, they were just people and the one thing they had in common was a desire to sleep with members of their own sex.

One of the first people I met at the company was Kenny Loomis. He was a wonderfully generous, considerate guy who loved nothing more than listening to or telling a good story.

As a matter of fact, it would often take him a couple of hours to eat a meal because every time he would get the fork close to his mouth he would start laughing and end up setting it back down on his plate. Rosemary and I were both friends with Kenny.

Chip Walker was another friend of ours. He and Rosemary had met when they were working as operators. He had an amazing high-pitched laugh that had gotten him kicked out of movie theatres on several occasions.

Jack Eisner was interesting. When I first started with the company he was an intense first-level supervisor who would monitor our customer calls and if he heard something he didn't like he would come storming over to your desk and demand you put the customer on hold. Then he would provide you with the correct information and go out of his way to make you feel about six inches tall.

If there was ever an all-gay army somewhere, I'm sure Jack would have made a first-rate drill sergeant. Sometimes I got the impression he had been mistreated earlier in his life and was now making the rest of us pay for it.

Over the next few years, the AIDS epidemic radically changed his demeanor. He'd lost a lot of friends and apparently this changed his perspective on what was really important in life. He began volunteering with a group called Seattle Shanti and changed his name to Jackson Street. He became caring, humble and politically correct almost to a fault.

I was never sure why he changed his name. He was a skinny little white guy and now he was calling himself something you'd name a character if you were writing the script for a 70's blaxploitation movie.

Keith Tillman was a married "straight" man who was obviously having trouble totally committing to the heterosexual team. He was married to a woman named Melanie. She was another straight woman who seemed to have a lot of gay male friends. Sometimes I would go have drinks with them.

His pores always seemed overly scrubbed, his jeans were always a bit too tight and it seemed like he was always checking out any good looking guy that happened to walk by. When I was around him my gaydar was going off like a fire alarm.

Rosemary's best friend Mike, had been diagnosed with HIV in 1988. It was devastating news for all of us. We'd lost so many friends during the past few years it was hard to be optimistic about his chances.

They'd been friends since the late 70's. Back in those days they would go out to gay nightclubs and dance the night away. It didn't matter if they were supposed to go to work the next day. They often got by on just a couple hours of sleep.

Mike's dad never knew he was gay. He died of a heart attack a couple years before Mike passed away. He always figured Rosemary was Mike's girlfriend.

We were hoping a cure would be discovered soon. Mike started being a lot more conscientious about his health but you could tell the disease was beginning to take a toll. He had always been thin but now he was starting to look really frail.

Rosemary made every effort to help him. I could tell the situation was absolutely breaking her heart. I tried to console her the best I could but it wasn't easy. There's not much you can say when you know the story isn't going to have a happy ending.

He was involved in a clinical study regarding a new series of treatments. Unfortunately, it turned out he was in the group being given the placebo drugs.

He was getting weaker and weaker over time and finally had to quit his job. He lived with his partner Alan.

During May of 1992 he went blind and dementia started to set in. Rosemary was there the day he passed away. She held him and helped him leave this world and hopefully go on to a better place.

We talked about her loss many times over the coming years. It reminded me somewhat of Jeff Argent's tragically premature death. They were two young men with so much potential who got cheated out of experiencing so much of what life has to offer.

Chapter 78: Seasons of Wither

By this time, Janet was living back in Sunnyrock. The years hadn't been kind to her.

She stayed in the Seattle area for a year after I moved out of our apartment but never really seemed very happy. She and her daughter Angela moved to southern California and tried to make a go of it.

Unfortunately, she hooked up with an abusive loser named Darrin. They moved to Sunnyrock (I assume to sponge off my dad) and before long, Angela had two sisters, Amy and Sarah.

Janet and Darrin fought a lot and she applied for a lot of restraining orders. She would generally make him stay away a couple days and then let him come home after they'd both cooled down.

One time I went to visit her and she said “Let me tell you, Jim, Darrin is crazy. No matter what I do he won’t leave me alone. I call the cops, I get restraining orders, I beg and plead but he still comes around. That’s why I’m so glad you’re here today... for once I can enjoy some peace and quiet”.

Then I went to use her bathroom and saw him asleep in her bed.

It was so strange seeing her in this downward spiral. Our shared childhood was calm and middle-class and we always talked a lot about how great our lives would be when we grew up. Neither of us knew exactly what we’d end up doing or where we’d end up living but we had hope and dream of being happy.

Now she was one of those women who kept having baby after baby after baby and chain smoked and drank endless cans of sugary soda and didn’t eat and looked like she was aging twice as fast as everybody else our age. She even started losing her teeth.

It always felt strange when I’d happen to talk to somebody we grew up with and they’d happen to ask how Janet was doing these days. They were always shocked when I told them what a rough time she was having.

She seemed desperate and cunning and very, very anxious. I never really felt like I was getting the truth when I asked her a question.

The worst part was how she treated Angela. More often than not, when the poor kid would ask her a question Janet would explode and berate her for a minute or more. "You're just like your father, always wanting something, always on to the next thing, you never appreciate what you have. I try so hard to make a nice home for us and it's never enough, never good enough for you. You're a spoiled little brat, you know that?".

Angela was used to it. I was always amazed how she never seemed particularly bothered by her mother's outbursts. I guess it was just a survival trait she developed.

I always wondered if this anger was generated by Janet's smoldering resentment of the way her ex-husband Rick had left her in Eugene. Maybe when Janet was yelling at Angela she was really yelling at him.

Janet was also starting to show signs of mental illness. She told Nona that our old friend Ronnie Felson wanted to murder her. Another time she told our folks she was Christ and she'd returned to save humanity from sin.

Things grew very tense between Dad and Janet over the years. He kept giving her money so she could make a fresh start but nothing ever really seemed to improve.

He let her and the kids live rent-free in the house across the river and she damaged almost every room. At one point she even stole checks from him and cashed them for thousands of dollars.

And Darrin was always a thorn in my father's side. Dad ordered him to stay off our property during one of the many periods when Janet had filed for a restraining order. Darrin came over anyway, Janet called my dad and my dad drove over there and kicked Darrin's ass. Apparently the 30 year age difference didn't make all that much of a difference.

I felt so bad for Dad. I could tell he was feeling really tortured about his daughter... sometimes he acknowledged she was mentally ill and desperately needed help and other times he acted like she was just plain bad.

A few years later, Darrin died when he fell off a roof. Janet later hooked up with a guy named Jake and had two more children. They moved to Colorado for a while but things quickly turned sour after one of the little girls accused him of molesting her. Janet took Jake's side in the dispute and ended up having all the kids taken away from her and placed in foster homes.

She eventually ended up back in Sunnyrock. Angela also came back after she turned eighteen. She was somehow able to forgive her mother for the betrayal back in Colorado. I was always amazed she did.

Janet was finally diagnosed as having schizophrenia and severe thyroid problems. She went on medication, then off again, then on again and then off again and was in and out of mental health facilities several times over the years.

It got to the point where Dad and Nona wouldn't even speak to Janet. However, he did leave her in the will. I control all the funds and send her money every month. I also bought Angela and her family a house in Brisco. The other kids don't want anything to do with their mother.

Janet lives in a group home in Brisco now and seems to have found some kind of peace. She's on pretty heavy medication and seems to understand that's the price she must pay in order to keep it together and avoid having to go back to the institution. She and I are getting along pretty good these days.

It seems like going home to visit has become more and more painful. I still enjoy the sunshine but my hometown almost seemed like a skeleton of what it was when I was growing up. There are fewer and fewer real businesses and more and more shabby little antique stores.

It's like time is a vulture and it's picked the meat off my hometown. There doesn't seem to be a lot left other than bones.

People decided at some point they'd rather just drive to Brisco or Boise to do their shopping. I guess I can't blame them, they wanted more selection and better prices just like anybody else.

And maybe I feel some guilt. This town and the surrounding area had given me a good childhood but I left as soon as I got old enough. Those feelings probably don't make a lot of sense but it's still hard to avoid having them.

Sometimes somebody financed by the government makes an effort to energize the town with an artistic statement. One time when I went to Sunnyrock I was greeted by the sight of large murals adorning the sides of empty buildings downtown. They featured pictures of pioneers and friendly native Americans.

Those murals always made me feel weird. It was like somebody had bought a new suit for a guy hooked up to life support.

Chapter 79: Fool (If You Think It's Over)

I got a call from Eve in August of 1985. She was now living in San Diego, working for a big corporation. She'd moved out west after getting her Master's Degree in Wisconsin.

I was shocked when I received the call. I had figured my abrupt proposal cancellation back in Wisconsin would have permanently poisoned her feelings about me.

It was kind of spooky. I wondered if somehow she'd received a mental message I'd been thinking about her when things started going badly with Joan.

After all, this was the woman who always thought we were destined to be together. Maybe Kenny Loggins had come on the radio and told her I was available again.

She sounded happy. “I love living down here”, she said. “The climate is really good for my lungs. Haven’t come close to getting bronchitis or pneumonia or anything. And the heat feels so good after living in Wisconsin. You wouldn’t believe the winters back there”.

She invited me down for a visit. I decided to take her up on her offer… I wasn’t going out with Darlene the firefighter anymore and things weren’t completely settled between Rosemary and myself. Well, at least they weren’t as far as I was concerned. And I’d always wanted to see San Diego.

It was great to see her again. Her health had declined a bit more but she was tanned and seemed really enthusiastic about her job. She couldn’t tell me a lot about what she did because it concerned military contracts and weapons systems.

While I was there, she still had to go to work but we spent as much time as possible together. I took her car during the day and explored the city and nearby beaches.

Mark McShane called me while I was in San Diego. His brother Bret had died from lung cancer. He was still living in Orange County and asked me to come up for the funeral.

I reluctantly turned him down. I felt bad but I only had so much time to spend with Eve.

That ended up being one of the biggest regrets of my life. Mark eventually forgave me but I always felt really bad about it. I’d known Bart for twelve years and I was wrong to pass on going to his funeral so I could have a little more time for romance.

When the week ended I told Eve I wanted to stay in touch and see how things developed.

When I got back to Seattle, I told Rosemary that Eve and I were back together. She was really hurt… she thought my trip to San Diego was going to be platonic or at the very most just a nostalgic fling.

At this point, Dave had moved out and found his own place. I was living alone again.

I kept in touch with Eve over the next couple months but gradually I started losing my struggle to stay away from Rosemary. Our attraction to each other was just too strong.

My love life was getting ridiculously complicated. I was now cheating on Eve with the woman who I'd cheated on when I went to visit Eve. It was getting to the point where I was starting to wonder why any woman would want anything to do with me.

It was sort of ironic… it seemed like the worse I behaved, the better I did with women. But I knew I was going to have to settle down and make a decision soon. If I kept on fooling around the way I had the past few months, someone might be tempted to shoot me or poison me or perform surgery on me during the middle of the night with a steak knife.

I was also getting to know Rosemary's son, Brendan. He didn't like me too much at first because he didn't want to share his mom with anybody. Or at least with a boyfriend kind of guy.

After the first time I babysat him, he told Rosemary I'd been really mean to him. But she just laughed because she knew he was just jealous.

Rosemary's best friend Mike also didn't care for me too much at first and I certainly couldn't say I blamed him. I had put her through a lot the past few months.

Eve decided to come to Seattle for a visit around Christmas time.

Her health seemed to have declined more even since our time together in San Diego. She kept commenting on how cold Seattle felt to her... which was ironic considering only a couple years earlier she'd been living in Wisconsin (where it's so cold the highways crack when they start to thaw out in March).

One night we went out to dinner with another couple. Earlier in the day I had mentioned to some friends at work that we were going to a place called the Greenlake Grill. That was a mistake, especially considering how fast gossip travels in offices.

We were having a nice time. I had invited Eric and Courtney Martin to join us. Courtney was a good friend of mine from work who was going to night school to get her Master's in Psychology. She and Eve had some interests in common and I figured they might hit it off.

About halfway through the meal, I happened to look up and saw Rosemary and her friend Christy Bates staring at us through one of the restaurant's windows. I felt like I was going to have a heart attack.

All of a sudden, Rosemary realized I was looking back at her. She and Christy panicked and ran off down the sidewalk. They totally looked like Lucy and Ethel when they would get caught spying on Ricky Ricardo and one of his celebrity pals.

I didn't say anything to my dinner partners. Somehow I managed to hold it together and then I told Liz Eve that evening when we were alone. Surprisingly, she thought it was pretty funny.

I wasn't mad at Rosemary for spying on me. I found it flattering that she would risk her dignity to see what the competition looked like. She always referred to Eve as "Evil".

Eve seemed different this time. We'd been reacquainted long enough now that she was starting to let her guard down a little.

She'd gotten a lot more serious about money. On one hand, she was seriously irritated that I was making more "k" than her and on the other she wasn't too happy about the fact I was perfectly content to work in a customer service job.

"Oh well," she said. "My dad was kind of a slow starter too. He was kind of just slogging along until my mom fixed him".

I wasn't sure what that meant but it sort of sounded like something they'd do in a female-controlled version of Stepford. I felt a chill run up and down my spine.

She also commented that I'd put on some weight since college. This was something I was pretty touchy about. I really, really wanted to point out to her that this pretty much always happened to healthy people as they aged but I held my tongue.

As her visit drew to a close, we talked more and more about what we should do.

She felt like we should get married. She said, "I don't know how much longer I have to live but I really want to spend that time with you. I'm on a waiting list at Stanford for a heart and lung transplant but I doubt they're going to call me in time. I'd rather just forget about it and be happy during what time I have left".

When she left, we still hadn't made a decision. I felt bad because I knew how frustrated she was with me. I thought about it a couple weeks and then called her and proposed. We decided to get married in San Diego in late April.

I immediately started struggling with the decision I'd made. I lay in bed every night, debating the pros and cons of marrying her. I asked lots of my work friends for advice but even that didn't seem to help me all that much.

The bottom line was I didn't feel the same way about her I had back in Eugene. We'd both changed during that time apart.

And I got the feeling a lot of what she felt for me stemmed from a desperate desire to marry somebody, anybody before it was too late.

Which really bothered me because it wasn't all that different than what I'd experienced with the two single mothers down in Corvallis. I wanted to settle down with somebody who specifically loved me and wasn't just trying to fill a hole in their life.

On a practical level, I didn't feel like I could both work and do a decent job of taking care of her. It seemed like at this stage of her life she might be better off living with her wealthy family.

I struggled with it and struggled with it and struggled with it and finally came to the conclusion nobody should enter into a marriage if they felt as unsure and unhappy as I was feeling. I called her up and called it off, once again breaking her heart.

I did get a call from her six months later. She said she just called to say hello and to tell me she had received a heart and lung transplant.

I assumed from her tone that what she was really saying was "You're a stupid ass and if you'd married me everything would have turned out just fine. But you chickened out and I'm gonna live a long, full life and I wouldn't take you back in a million years". That was the last time we ever spoke.

I don't know if she ever really got the operation. I hope she did and I hope she lives to be ninety years old.

I had another brief relationship right after Eve and I broke up. I should have just laid low for a while but I guess in a selfish way I was feeling good about escaping what I thought would end up being a really bad situation.

Sharon was another co-worker (though from a different floor in our building). She had grown up in Seattle but then moved to Hawaii after high school. While she was there, she got pregnant and married.

Things didn't go well when they split up. She and her daughter moved back to Seattle but she never really got over living in Hawaii. She was saving up so they could move back there.

Spending time with Sharon proved very frustrating. She acted like she was interested in me romantically but when I would make a move she always seemed surprised. One weekend she invited me to go to Vancouver, Canada with her and a couple of friends. We stayed in a hotel but she insisted we sleep in separate beds.

And I was being a bit of a baby. I'd had some pretty good luck with women recently and I felt like I was enough of a catch that I shouldn't have to patiently earn Sharon's sexual affections. I mean after all, I was Jim Hawthorne, the guy who was so sought after women spied on him at the Greenlake Grill!

When I got back from that trip I finally took a few days and really thought about everything I'd been through during the past year. I'd spent time with four different women.

Darlene had been attractive but thick as a brick, Eve had been like a sad ghost and Sharon was as self-centered as I was.

Rosemary was the one woman I always enjoyed spending time with. She was sexy, smart and good-hearted. And she always took me back, no matter how big of an idiot I'd been.

I realized it's rare to find someone who loves you that much. It's not something that should be taken lightly.

I called her and said I was done running around and ready to make a commitment.

Chapter 80: Beautiful Boy (Darling Boy)

Brendan got married in 2007. His wife is a lovely girl named Lindsey and she moved out here from Kansas. He always says it's amazing how similar she and I are personality-wise.

They had a little boy named Kelton in 2008. He's a wonderfully happy little guy who loves to yell out "ha, ha". And he's fascinated with any kind of remote control.

I hope he has a good life. The future seems scary but that's nothing new. Every generation has worried the future will be worse than the present but that's because we always seem to see the bad stuff on the horizon before we understand the wonders that are unfolding all around us.

Maybe humanity will perish in a storm of nuclear fire. Or maybe we'll discover a way to generate endless amounts of energy and everyone will live for centuries. It's impossible to say at this point.

Good luck, Kelton. I love you and your mom and your dad and will do everything I can to help you during the years I have left on the planet.

Chapter 81: Let's Get Married

We decided to get married in September of 1987. I moved in with Rosemary and Brendan at the beginning of the summer so we could save some money prior to the wedding.

Brendan and I had developed a good relationship by this time and he was excited about having both a mom and a dad. Rosemary decided she'd better have a talk with him now that we were officially becoming a family.

She explained that she had made him with another man she knew before me. That information really shook him up… I guess he'd always thought his birth was strictly an arrangement between his mother and the stork.

So this was an especially good time for me to move in and become his full-time dad. We felt like it kind of filled an emotional hole in his life.

Dave had recently made a new friend at the bookstore named Harry Goodman. He had moved up a couple years earlier from southern California. He was gay, had a caustic wit and loved going to the movies even more than Dave and I did.

Harry had always found California uncomfortably warm. Seattle's more temperate climate suited him much better.

He was a hard worker but didn't hesitate to bend the rules when he felt the need. One day when he was working at the bookstore he left for his fifteen minute afternoon break, walked across the street to a movie theatre and took in a two hour matinee.

The thing I liked most about Harry was his irreverence. When he was working for a tugboat company, he accidentally sent out an e-mail that mocked several of the company's executives. When he was called in to discuss the matter, he sat down, looked at the angry managers and simply said, "Ouch, tough room".

Harry, Rosemary and I have grown very close over the years. We get together for dinner at least a couple Saturday nights a month and have taken several vacations together. They also watch reality TV together sometimes...yet another thing I detest but like Rap music it doesn't appear it will be going away any time soon.

I made up a list of songs Rosemary and I liked and Harry and Dave were nice enough to put together some mix tapes for the reception.

I was a little shaken when my dad arrived for the wedding. He looked pretty frail.

He'd been in a bad accident back in March of that same year. He was riding a horse on our north ranch and it tripped on a gopher hole. The horse fell on Dad's left leg, breaking it in three places.

The horse ran off. Dad had to crawl three miles to his pickup. When he got there, he somehow managed to boost himself up off the ground and into the cab of the truck.

He had to drive with the door open so he could keep his leg straight. When he got to town he pulled into a gas station and told the attendant "I need three things... bring me a Seven-Up, call my wife and get me an ambulance".

It took a long time for his leg to heal. Dad was definitely a tough guy but it was easy to see this experience had taken a lot out of him.

We had the wedding at an Episcopal church Rosemary's mom and dad attended. It was in a wealthy neighborhood located across Lake Washington from Seattle.

As I sat there waiting for the ceremony to begin I reflected back on the long, strange trip I had taken to get to this point in my life. And I also wondered what the future held for us. I was excited about sharing my life with Rosemary and Brendan.

It was a beautiful church and a really nice ceremony. Rosemary looked gorgeous and got through it with champagne and a Valium. I had a few shots of Jack Daniel's before the ceremony and any jitters I had seemed to drift away.

Dave was my Best Man. Mark McShane, Ellen's husband Jim and Rosemary's best friend Mike Hamm were the other groomsmen. Brendan was the ring bearer. He looked extraordinarily cute in his little tuxedo.

Almost exactly twenty years later we'd be watching him marry a wonderful girl named Lindsey who had come out here from Kansas.

Rosemary's brother Dick volunteered to videotape the ceremony. It didn't turn out that great… for some reason he kept filming his own wife and kids instead of what was happening up front.

The reception was held in a side room at the church. I had brought my stereo in and hooked it up. Dave and Harry had spent several hours working on some nice mix tapes people could dance to.

About six songs into the first tape, "Addicted to Love" by Robert Palmer started playing. Rosemary's mother got up and sprinted across the room. She wasn't sure how to turn the stereo off so she yanked the electric plug out of the wall. I've always loved giving her a bad time about that.

I guess she figured the tune was too sexy to be heard inside a church building. I thought that opinion was a bit ironic considering we would be leaving for our honeymoon the next day… you know, that period of time most people spend having a whole bunch of sex.

Chapter 82: A Dream Goes On Forever

We stayed at the Four Seasons hotel in downtown Seattle on our wedding night. I had a dream I was back in Sunnyrock on that cold December night in 1974. I was watching myself weep as the snow came down around me.

But then I saw another figure, hidden away in the shadows. It was Rosemary and she was also watching the young Jim suffer. I could tell by the look on her face she desperately wanted to help me, to let me know I wasn't alone in the world. But she couldn't do anything yet… there was a path I had to follow and struggles I had to endure before we could begin our happy life together.

Epilogue: Every Picture Tells a Story

When I told friends and relatives I was writing a book, most of them asked what kind. When I said a memoir, I was usually greeted with a look of puzzlement.

I could tell they were thinking "Whoa, this guy really has some ego. He's just a regular person like me. I doubt anything has happened to him that merits a memoir."

Well, I'll have to let readers like you be the judge of that. If you've hung in there this far into the book, then hopefully I've entertained you in some way.

What inspired me to write a memoir was my sincere belief that everybody's life is interesting in some way. Every human mind is filled with memories and pictures and dreams and desires stored away during the time we've been conscious here.

The past five decades have been an amazing era of change, confusion and exploration for most people. This book is just my little slice of that awesome human drama.

What’s your story?

Epilogue 2: Friends

I'd like to thank my wife Rosemary for her support and creative input, my friend Dave for encouraging me to write all these years and my friend Terry for helping me navigate the murky waters of the publishing business. This book wouldn't have happened without you guys.

Made in the USA
Charleston, SC
03 October 2010